JOE

'The future is always better than the past.'

Joe Dolan

'That fella has a very unusual voice; he could be black or white or from anywhere in the world.'

Larry Gogan, RTÉ DJ, on hearing a recording of Joe for the very first time

'Joe never changed. He was always the same guy. Even though I was a nobody – and I was a nobody – Joe would always have time for you. ... And I grew very close to him .... He was never competitive in the sense that he had to be bigger than everybody else. Joe was convinced that he could be big, but that didn't mean that everyone else was small ....

'He was no saint and he could be volatile and he could fall out with anybody at any time, but Joe was one of the most compassionate guys I have ever met.'

Fr Brian D'Arcy

'Joe was a team player who understood it was everyone pulling together that made the show work. And he would always insist on everyone staying in the same hotel, even though I used to think that if Joe stayed in a different hotel the rest of the lads might get to sleep sometime.'

Ben Dolan, Joe's brother

'In those days (early Drifters) Joe always thought that Ben and I were plotting against him. Ben and I were into country music whereas Joe was a rock 'n' roll person ... We were drinking one night and Joe said, "If you ever bring a George Jones' song to me again you can shove it where the sun don't shine."'

Seamus Casey, manager

'The women were stone mad about Joe. They would scream their heads off through the entire show. I remember in ballrooms like The Arcadia in Cork you literally couldn't hear the band over the sound of the screams. I'm not kidding you, it was like The Beatles.'

Tommy Swarbrigg, The Drifters

'Every time you met Joe Dolan, it was like drinking champagne for the very first time. And that was how I felt about him.'

Sam Smyth, Today FM broadcaster and *Irish Independent* journalist

'I spent the whole night picking Joe up off the floor because he was being pulled off the stage and that's the way it was for that first year … Joe being pulled off the stage and us picking him up. We were his musicians and his security.'

Frankie McDonald, Joe's trumpet player

'An awful lot of people, including myself, never fully grasped how big Joe was and that's really because he never flaunted it. He had no airs or graces despite his celebrity. Joe was just one of the guys and he liked it that way.'

Ronan Collins, RTÉ

'Growing up in Mullingar, Joe was a kind of a hero to all of us, since he was the guy with the biggest car, the lifestyle we all aspired to, lots of money and plenty of women hanging off him … I caddied for Joe frequently and everybody wanted to caddy for Joe because he was great craic and he was also a great tipper.'

Michael O'Leary, Ryanair

'On New Year's Eve they used to have a Champagne Ball in the Greville Arms and I'd be there with Joe and Joe Healy and their whole coterie down there, all party animals. You were a wimp if you went to bed before daylight. These guys were all like extras from a Tarantino movie. You took your life in your hands going down there.'

Phil Coulter

'When we met I liked him from the start. Dickie Rock said to me that the reason myself and Joe always got on so well was because we were both culchies. But I always admired Joe.'

Brendan Bowyer

'When he spotted a neighbour or some local acquaintance on the security cameras, Joe popped up like a jack-in-the-box, to engage in a bit of banter, catch up on the goings-on in their lives and to tell them his latest jokes.'

Thomas Murphy, proprietor Thomas's of Foxrock

'I always thought Joe was a lovely fella, who was very funny. Joe would always be smiling, laughing, having a bit of craic and enjoying himself. He had a great sense of his own place in showbusiness and he knew exactly what he was about.'

Gay Byrne

'We loved it whenever Joe arrived home in the morning from a performance at a dance hall in Ireland, just in time to give us a lift to school in his fancy car. And my mother loved it as well because she could get a lie-on in bed.'

Adrian Dolan, Joe's nephew, godson, band member and producer

'I remember Joe looked so young and he had his hair in an Elvis style. And that big smile of his, I remember the smile. I was literally star-struck that day just looking at the guy.'

Sean O'Dowd, Ding-A-Ling, on first meeting Joe in the sixties

'There was no auld bullsh*t with Joe. He wasn't walking around afraid to take off his mask in case people found out what was underneath. Joe wore his heart on his sleeve and I loved him for that.'

Finbar Furey

'Joe was great company and a great singer. He was one of those guys who had a voice. I was always pleased to meet people with a voice, because some of the British pop acts didn't all have proper singing voices, and he did.'

Tom Jones

'He started crying as he stood over me ... and then I woke up. Joe was now in such a state of shock that he had to get a brandy to steady his nerves. The two of us sat on high stools drinking brandy till noon that day, with Joe still in his underpants.'

James Cafferty, Joe's promoter, on the morning the singer thought his friend had died

'Joe was the first pop star in my eyes. He was the one who had the women throwing their knickers at him – not my mother, mind you – but all the young ones up at the front. I guess I took a lot from him, from what I saw of Joe on stage, not that I ever had knickers thrown at me.'

Ronan Keating, Boyzone

'[Joe's voice] really was uplifting; no matter what problems you had, you were in a nicer place when you heard that voice.'

Maxi, RTÉ's 'Risin' Time'.

'Joe was born to be on a stage, you could see that from the way he was completely comfortable up there. And he loved it, judging by the way he performed.'

Daniel O'Donnell

'Joe connected emotionally with the audience. They always walked out of his show thinking they just had the best night. And I love the fact that everyone from nuns to hip young things loved him.'

Brenda Donohue, RTÉ broadcaster

'Joe was the Irish Elvis; he could sing and, besides the boring jokes, he was actually a bit of a mate. And Joe's fans were great to me; the good thing about his fans is that most of them are hard of hearing.'

Dustin The Turkey

'Every time I met Joe it was big laughs and smiles and hugs. He was a disarming sort of a character who you loved to meet. And the wives all loved Joe; they all gravitated towards him. My wife, Helen, cried like a child the day he died.'

Paddy Cole

'People say the longer it goes the easier it gets, but the first year you thought he was just gone away and you were expecting him to come back. And it's not any easier.'

Kathleen Oakes, Joe's niece and goddaughter

**Eddie Rowley
with Joe Dolan.**

Eddie Rowley is showbusiness editor of the *Sunday World*, Ireland's biggest selling newspaper. He has previously written best-selling personal biographies and inside-takes on Boyzone (*In Person; Living The Dream* and *Our World*); Ronan Keating (*Life Is A Rollercoaster*); *Westlife On Tour: Inside the World's Biggest Boy Band*; Daniel O'Donnell (*Follow Your Dream; My Story; My Pictures & Places*); Julia O'Donnell, *The Mother's Story*; and *A Woman's Voice*.

Our

Joe

JOE DOLAN
BY THE PEOPLE WHO KNEW HIM BEST

Withdrawn from Stock

EDDIE ROWLEY

THE O'BRIEN PRESS
DUBLIN

First published 2010
by The O'Brien Press Ltd.,
12 Terenure Road East,
Dublin 6,
Ireland.
Tel: +353 1 4923333
Fax: +353 1 4922777
E-mail: books@obrien.ie Website: www.obrien.ie

ISBN 978-1-84717-219-8

British Library Cataloguing-in-Publication Data
A catalogue record for this title is available from the British Library

1 2 3 4 5 6 7 8
10 11 12 13 14

Editing, typesetting and design: The O'Brien Press Ltd
Printed and bound by Scandbook AB, Sweden
The paper used in this book is produced using pulp from managed forests.

PICTURE CREDITS

The author and publisher have endeavoured to establish the origins of all the images used. If any involuntary infringement of copyright has occurred, sincere apologies are offered and the owners are requested to contact the publishers.

The author would like to thank the Dolan family, EMI Music Ireland and *Sunday World* archive (photographers Val Sheehan, Brian McEvoy, Kim Haughton) for permission to include images on cover, inside cover and in picture sections. Other images courtesy of: Sean Magee, picture section 1, p1 (bottom); Charlie Collins, picture section 1, p8 (top); Mark Doyle, picture section 2, p5; Press Association p8 (bottom); Photocall Ireland, picture section 2, p2 (top); Thomas Murphy, picture section 2, p7 (bottom).

ACKNOWLEDGEMENTS

It is a privilege to get the opportunity to write this book and it would not have happened without the support and co-operation of Joe's family, particularly his brother Ben, who has been so generous to me with his time over the last two years. I enjoyed many a day in Mullingar with Ben while researching all the great stories and family history. Like Joe, Ben is one of life's gentlemen who lives and breathes showbusiness and is a great storyteller.

Sincere thanks also to Adrian and Ray Dolan, who are still flying the flag in their Oh Me Oh My band, featuring the songs of their uncle Joe. Also to Joe's brother Paddy, and his daughter Kathleen, for their great memories.

Seamus Casey, Joe's manager, also took the time to reminisce with me about the wonderful singer he managed for forty-seven years. Gentleman Seamus proves that you do not have to be ruthless to achieve success in life. I would also like to thank Seamus's son, Ronan, who produced his own great record of Joe's singing career. I found it invaluable for checking facts while penning this book. Thanks Ronan for all your support and for the fun we have had. There's no business like showbusiness.

Thanks to Tommy Swarbrigg, Jimmy Horan, Des 'The Doc' Doherty, Joey Gilheaney and Sid Aughey, otherwise known as The Drifters. A big thank you to Frankie McDonald for his contribution.

My thanks to Val Sheehan, Fr Brian D'Arcy, Sam Smyth, Larry Gogan, Brendan Bowyer, Jimmy Magee, Phil Coulter, Finbar Furey, Paddy Cole, Ronan Collins, Johnny Carroll, Sean O'Dowd, John Mulholland and Pat Jennings.

Thanks also to Taoiseach Brian Cowen, Ryanair's Michael O'Leary and former 'Late Late Show' host Gay Byrne of the Road Safety Authority, who took time out of their busy schedules to give me their own little nuggets of personal associations with Joe.

I was also fortunate to get the opportunity to talk with superstars Tom Jones and Robbie Williams, both of whom have fond memories of Joe. Thanks also to Daniel O'Donnell, Ronan Keating, Maxi, Brenda Donohue, Darren Smith and Dustin.

One of the people who kept me in close contact with Joe through the decades was my cousin Thomas Murphy. Joe and Thomas were great men to party, but they also raised a lot of money for charity. Thanks Thomas, you're one of the best.

Joe's promoter James Cafferty recalled an eventful life with Joe, as did Joey Purcell and Denis Mee.

My thanks to Jas Mulligan, George Hunter, Syl Fox, Kevin Farrell, Eoin McHugh, Hilary Jones (RTÉ), John Delamere, Rose Kelly-Smith, Reggie Duffy, Mags Keating, Brigid Cummins, Desi Egan, 'The Fish', Gordon Maher, Joe Cooney, Alan Corcoran, Marc Roberts, Don Collins, Bernie Swan, Joe Ward and Amanda Carroll of Meteor.

Special thanks to Willie Kavanagh, David Gogan and all the staff at EMI Records in Ireland for supplying me with some great photographs from their Joe years, particularly the cover shot of this book.

In writing *Our Joe*, I was lucky to have the support and encouragement of talented people like Des Ekin, himself a celebrated author of *The Stolen Village* and a columnist with the *Sunday World*. Colm MacGinty, the editor of the *Sunday World* and a proud Westmeath man, gave me access to the paper's photo archive for the book and encouraged me all the way through the writing process. I'd also like to thank Gerry Lennon, the paper's managing director, who also expressed his support and best wishes from the start.

DEDICATION

To my wife Patricia and our girls, Kate and Laura

CONTENTS

MY FRIEND, JOE

Everyone who knew or encountered Joe has a story to tell. And I'm no different. Joe Dolan was the first celebrity I ever interviewed. That interview, conducted in the seventies, while I was still a nervous, greenhorn student, would give me a leg up the ladder in journalism and life. It helped me to land a job as a trainee reporter with the *Midland Topic* newspaper in Joe's hometown of Mullingar.

Like all teenagers, at the time I was mad about performers and bands, influenced by their fashion and fascinated by their lifestyles. I was also passionate about writing and hell-bent on pursuing a career in newspapers. Growing up on the border of Meath and Westmeath, I had pop stars virtually on my doorstep. The Swarbriggs were based in Mullingar. And the midland town was also home to Ireland's biggest pop star … Joe Dolan. He became a pop star to me the moment I heard him singing 'Sweet Little Rock 'n' Roller' on Radio Luxembourg.

Powered by youthful naïvety and enthusiasm and armed with a pen and notebook, I set out one day to track down the great Joe for my big interview. This was a major expedition as it involved hitching a lift along lonely country roads on a fourteen-mile journey from my rural home. And I never thought for a moment that he wouldn't be in when I eventually knocked on the door of Joe's office in the town.

The man who answered wasn't the smiling, moon-faced Joe of the seventies, but the genial and ultra-friendly Seamus Casey. Seamus, who had turned his back on the sedate lifestyle of a country schoolmaster for the bright lights and razzmatazz of showbusiness as Joe's band manager, was probably bemused by the timid teenager seeking an interview, despite not being employed by any publication. The genial manager should have sent me off with my tail between my legs that day, but, as I would discover time and again through the decades, Seamus Casey is a gentleman. He arranged for me to call by another day and promised that he would have Joe waiting to chat with me at a specific time.

I was a bag of nerves meeting the great Joe Dolan on my second visit to his Mullingar headquarters. But the moment I stepped into his office, Joe was cracking jokes and had me laughing. The image of the big celebrity instantly melted from my mind and I found myself talking to a great character who put me at my ease. I came away with a wealth of stories from Joe's life and times that afternoon, but I didn't realise then that I had also ignited a friendship which would last four decades, right up to his passing on St Stephen's Day, 2007.

A local newspaper proprietor and editor called Dick Hogan was impressed enough with the Joe article to later give me a job as a trainee reporter on his paper, then known as the *Midland Topic*. I was now on my way to a career in newspapers, thanks to Dick Hogan … and Joe. Shortly after getting a job on the paper, I was hitching a lift home one evening when a big Merc went flying past me like a jet, before suddenly breaking and creating a cloud of dust as it came to a screeching halt. As I went running towards the car, with the smell of burning rubber in the air, I realised that the driver was Joe Dolan. 'How'ya, Eddie, hop in,' Joe said with that big smile which charmed millions of fans.

On the short journey to the County Meath village of Clonard – short at the speed Joe was driving – there was no talk of hit records, sold-out shows or big TV appearances. Instead, Joe was more interested in how I was getting on at the paper. Even at that early stage of knowing him I realised there were two Joes: the incredible singer and stage performer, and, away from the spotlight, the unassuming man who just loved people and their company. When we arrived at my stop, Paddy's pub of Clonard, Joe decided he'd drop in for a quick drink. And I grew a couple of feet taller that evening as I swanned through the door of Paddy's with the great Joe Dolan by my side. Joe stayed for less than an hour, but in that short period he lifted the atmosphere in the bar and there was the sound of raucous laughter as he traded jokes with the locals.

It was also through Joe that I got my first sample of the big time in show-business when the *Topic* assigned me to cover one of his record-breaking ten sold-out nights at the Chariott Inn in Dublin's Ranelagh. It was the venue where all the top international stars performed in Ireland back in the mid to late seventies. That Saturday night show had all the razzmatazz of a Las Vegas extravaganza.

Before the performance, I also got my first taste of the backstage experience when Seamus Casey ushered me to Joe's dressing room for a brief interview with the star. I could get used to this, I thought. Joe was in great form that night, buzzing with excitement in the build up to the show that was about to unfold. He said he particularly loved performing a concert where he could fully 'connect' with his audience. He found shows like that the most satisfying, rather than dances where people weren't totally focused on the band, so the singer was just performing rather than engaging with the crowd. He simply loved an interaction with people. When Joe hit the stage that night, I doubted if his own hero, Elvis Presley, had ever experienced such an outpouring of emotion from an audience. The following week I had my first big front-page story in the *Topic* about Joe Dolan taking Dublin by storm. Now I had finally hit the big time as a journalist … thanks, again, to Joe.

Of course, apart from my professional interest in Joe as a singing star, I was also a fan. So imagine my excitement in the late seventies when Seamus Casey rang me at the *Topic* one day and asked if I would be interested in writing a short biography and press release covering the latest events in Joe's showbiz career for the Irish and international media. This involved interviewing Joe about his new recordings, tours and future plans for a news update that would be published in all kinds of newspapers and magazines. It was a huge honour for me to be given the opportunity to play that very minor role in Joe's career at the time. For that brief period, I was on Joe's team. It doesn't get much better for any fan.

In my personal life, I also enjoyed many great nights of entertainment with friends at Joe's shows in Westmeath venues like the Greville Arms Hotel in Mullingar and The Beehive near Delvin. No words can adequately describe the atmosphere and excitement that Joe generated at those home events from the mid-seventies to the early eighties. They were probably his best-ever performances and you could see that he was bursting with joy singing in front of his own people.

As life moved on, I slowly climbed the ladder in journalism to become the showbusiness editor of the *Sunday World*. Joe was among the first to congratulate me when I got the job, as he was a fan of the paper. I was now working with many of his own friends. His close buddy, Brian D'Arcy, was, and still is, a columnist; another long-time pal, the journalist and broadcaster Sam Smyth, was also a showbusiness and investigative reporter with the '*World*' at the time; and photographer Val Sheehan, the man who captured Driftermania in Joe's early days and shot the cover picture for Joe and The Drifters showband's first album, *The Answer To Everything*, was the paper's fashion photographer.

Having good contacts is the key to success in journalism, and I arrived at the *Sunday World* with great connections like Joe Dolan. Whenever I rang Joe for an interview during the good times and in his final couple of years when his health began to deteriorate, he never failed to oblige. I knew that Joe's door was always open to me. Today, I truly appreciate the easy access I had to one of Ireland's greatest-ever entertainers. It has given me a unique insight into the man, his life and his incredible talent as an entertainer.

Back in the late seventies I took my then teenage cousin Thomas Murphy from Dublin to see Joe playing at a dance in Mullingar's Horizon ballroom. Thomas was instantly taken with Joe's star quality and, of course, he was already aware of the big-time celebrity. Everybody in Ireland knew who Joe Dolan was. Thomas was also highly impressed to discover that Joe knew who I was after the star acknowledged me from the stage during the dance that night. In the strange twists and turns of life, Thomas Murphy would go on to establish his own food and wine shop in Dublin's Foxrock, where Joe settled down in the early eighties. From that moment on, Thomas became one of Joe's closest friends in life. After my own move to Dublin, I found myself enjoying Joe's company at family occasions and social events organised by my cousin, Thomas, through the decades.

Joe and I never talked about showbusiness or the media on days and nights socialising at family functions or evenings out as friends. We simply traded jokes. It was all about fun and having a laugh over a few drinks, more often than not a few drinks too many! At private occasions, I saw how he managed to remain an ordinary Joe away from the stage, despite his iconic status in this country. There was nothing showbizzy about him when he was in company. He was just as happy to sit back and let the other fella tell the yarn or crack the joke. Joe never threw shapes or demanded to be the centre of attention. And that's why people loved him and accepted him as an ordinary person who just happened to have an extraordinary talent as a singer.

I remained in close contact with Joe right to the end. In the years before his passing, we traded jokes by text on a weekly basis. While I was personally in touch with Joe throughout his illness, it wasn't until the final couple of weeks that I realised my friend might not survive it. Whether he was in denial or just painting a positive picture for family and friends, Joe never indicated to me, or indeed to any of his close family and associates, that he was knocking on death's door. I knew it was coming on St Stephen's Day, 2007, but when Thomas Murphy phoned me from the hospital with the sad news, it felt like a death in the family. I suspect it was the same in most homes throughout the country. The thought of an Ireland and an entertainment scene without Joe Dolan was just so hard to accept.

It was also difficult to believe that my life with Joe had come full circle. I had taken my baby steps into the world of journalism by doing my first celebrity interview with Mullingar's favourite son after he had obviously decided to give a kid a break on that autumn day in the seventies. But I never thought then that I would one day be reporting on his funeral for the *Sunday World*. And what a funeral it was. Simply magnificent. Just like the man himself.

Over the years I have written books with some of Ireland's most successful stars, including Daniel O'Donnell, Boyzone, Ronan Keating, Westlife and the singers on one of Ireland's biggest-selling albums, *A Woman's Heart*.

Now I am privileged to produce a book on my friend, Joe Dolan, or 'Our Joe' as the fans call him. Although tinged with sadness, it has been a labour of love. Joe's story is a remarkable one, a classic rags-to-riches tale of a poor country boy who became a pop superstar in the sixties and seventies and who had an enduring appeal over an incredible five decades.

Joe's early life and career in this book and that of his family is recreated mainly through the recollections of his heart-broken brother, Ben, who gave generously of his time as he relived his childhood and adult life with Joe, and their glory days on the stage together. During one of the many interviews Ben recorded for this book, he took me on a drive in his sleek Mercedes around the neighbourhood of Grange, in the countryside on the outskirts of Mullingar, where he and Joe grew up.

We stopped outside the modest cottage where the Dolan children were reared by parents, Paddy and Ellen, and the myriad of memories from his childhood came flooding back to Ben. This was the cottage where the Dolan brothers' love of music was nurtured by their mother. Ben pointed out a modern housing estate across the road. It was once a field owned by local farmer Johnny Weldon and there the Dolan boys helped out with the sowing and picking of potatoes and other crops as they grew up.

Then we drove down a country road until we reached the spot where the family spent summers working in the bog, cutting turf for the winter fuel. There were fields where rabbits were shot and the local Lough Ennell where the Dolan boys and their friends swam and went fishing. Times were harsh, but as Ben recalls, there were fun times too and Joe was always in the middle of them.

Another time we stopped off at the County Hall in Mullingar (now the Arts Centre) where we met up with the eldest Dolan brother, Paddy, who shared his own memories of growing up with Joe. In the sixties, Paddy ran the cloakroom at dances in the County Hall (taking care of thousands of coats was big business in those days). Paddy recalled with obvious pride how his young brother, Joe, went on to be the biggest star to perform in the venue.

Over gallons of tea at Mullingar House, the pub which Joe co-owned with Ben, their lifetime manager Seamus Casey, now in his seventies, strolled through times past as Joe's lifetime manager. He recalled the fun, paranoia, foibles and talent of the man he loved.

While working together in Dublin and on assignments around the country, photographer Val Sheehan of the *Sunday World* took me on many a journey through the days when he was on the frontline of Driftermania, capturing the wild scenes that greeted Joe and the band in ballrooms around the country during the sixties. Val worked closely with Joe as The Drifters' photographer in those early days and he gave me a fascinating insight into how fame turned the heart-throb's life upside down in those days.

Joe's nephews, Adrian and Ray Dolan, grew up with their uncle who lived between their home and his Mullingar apartment in the sixties and seventies. Later, in the eighties, they would join Joe's backing band and perform with him until his final show. Adrian and Ray shared their personal memories of Uncle Joe, shining a light on the life of the man inside his family.

My long-time friend Larry Gogan, the legendary and much-loved RTÉ radio personality, met Joe at the very start of his career, following the release of The Drifters' first single, 'The Answer To Everything'. In a studio of RTÉ 2fm Radio, where today Larry is still one of the most popular DJs in the country, the broadcaster revealed how they became friends, his wife Florrie's fascination with the singer and Joe's kindness in his darkest hour.

The singer Finbar Furey was just a teenager when he first met Joe in Mullingar, while competing in the All-Ireland Championships, playing the uileann pipes. They both had mutual friends in the Westmeath town and there was an instant rapport between the pair. At his home, Finbar told me about his days carousing with Joe 'on the tear' in the Dublin mountains.

Showband star Brendan Bowyer was a big influence on Joe in the early days and the two showband legends became buddies out of the spotlight. Still performing all over Ireland, Brendan sat in his dressing room at The Helix in Dublin, sharing memories of his pal Joe, including their highjinks in Las Vegas.

Journalist and radio presenter Sam Smyth started his working life as a ballroom promoter in his teens. He was a huge fan of Joe Dolan and, like many, felt honoured to be a personal friend of the entertainer. Sam took time out from his work reporting on the politics of the day from inside Dail Éireann to chat in the olde-worlde Buswells Hotel about the Joe he knew and loved. He revealed his many nights socialising with Joe in the singer's hometown of Mullingar where he was introduced to the B-Specials.

Two of Ireland's favourite female radio broadcasters, Maxi and Brenda

Donohue of RTÉ, were among the millions of women who fell under Joe's spell and they opened their hearts about the remarkable man they knew and loved.

While researching the book, I was amazed to discover the network of people from all walks of life who were connected in one way or another to Joe, everyone from Tom Jones to Gay Byrne, Robbie Williams to Phil Coulter and Ryanair's Michael O'Leary to a former Mayor of Galway. He even struck up a friendship with a turkey! Their stories, and the stories of ordinary folk whose lives he touched paint a picture of a man who came from a humble background, worked hard, played hard, was generous to a fault with his time and money and lit up the world.

CHAPTER 1

TO RUSSIA WITH LOVE

In the winter of 1978 Joe Dolan is on a remarkable, sell-out tour of the USSR, with his brother, Ben, and the rest of the band. As his chauffeur-driven limousine cruises through the bleak, bone-chilling streets of Moscow, heading for their concert venue, a little old lady suddenly appears out of the night. She waves down the car, the glare from the headlights revealing a shock of white hair peeking out from underneath her hat and framing her rugged face. Dressed from head to toe in black heavy clothing, the old woman cuts an eerie figure in the darkness.

'Stop! Stop and see what she wants,' Joe urges his two startled female Russian interpreters.

The driver rolls down the window and the lady in black starts calling for Joe by his first name. Joe shoots a quizzical look at Ben, who shakes his head; he doesn't know what's going on either. The old lady says something in Russian to the driver.

'She says your mother is looking after you,' the interpreter translates.

'Jesus Christ,' Joe whispers, completely bewildered, and not a little scared. 'What would that auld wan know about Mammy.'

*　*　*

Although Joe has been a sensation in the ballrooms of Ireland and Britain for the last couple of decades and has notched up Number-One hits and performed on 'Top of the Pops', Ben has never seen his younger brother more excited at any other stage in his gold-plated career.

For Joe, nothing so far has matched this adventure across the USSR, where more than 150,000 local people are queueing up to see him perform on his first tour, in this strange winter wonderland thousands of miles from home.

'Mullingar to Moscow, Jaysus, can you believe it!' Joe remarks to Ben, as they while away the time over a game of cards in the comfortable surroundings of a luxury hotel bedroom before the night's show.

Their conversation wanders back to their childhood years and they reminisce about singing at traditional Irish music sessions in their modest cottage nestling in the countryside on the outskirts of Mullingar town.

Ellen, the matriarch of the Dolan clan, reared her family on a diet of music. She played the fiddle and the accordion, had a sweet, lilting voice and used music as a form of escapism from the daily grind of life in the grim environment of poverty-stricken Ireland in the 1940s and '50s. The apple doesn't fall far from the tree, and Joe and Ben inherited their mother's love of music. It was Ellen who first spotted that there was something special about her youngest child, Joe, as she watched him perform in the kitchen of their little house. Then a widow, she had used her pension money to buy the young buck an impressive piano and send him to a local woman for music lessons.

From the frosted window of his hotel room, Joe peers out at the snow-covered rooftops of the Moscow skyline, as he reflects on his mother's encouragement and the personal sacrifices she made to grow his talent. In his wildest dreams he had never imagined that being blessed with the gift of a distinctive voice and having a music-loving mother to nurture his singing would lead to him becoming a superstar in Russia.

But here he is, on a whistle-stop journey around the biggest country in Europe, doing a punishing twenty-three major concerts in as many days. It doesn't get much bigger than that in the career of any international artist.

Joe turns to Ben. 'I wish Mammy was around to see all of this today,' he says wistfully. 'God knows what she'd make of it.'

CHAPTER 2

THE MILK MAID

In her early life, Joe's mother was a familiar sight on the streets of Mullingar and around the by-roads of the surrounding districts. Ellen Brennan, then in her late teens, was also as reliable as the Angelus bells for her time-keeping.

The milk maid meandered up and down the highways and byways of Westmeath every day on her horse and cart. On board was her cargo of fresh milk in large containers, ready to be dished out to customers who came from all quarters with their jugs and other utensils of various shapes and sizes.

'Our mother was the original milk maid in Mullingar,' Ben reflects today as he delves into his family's history with me. 'She used to tell us how for years she'd come up the town with the pony and cart selling her milk to the locals.'

A pint of milk was the general order from her clients. Ellen would scoop up the milk in her pint jug. Then she'd dip it in the milk can again. 'There's a drop for the cat,' she'd say.

'Everyone got a drop for the cat, even if they didn't have one,' Ben laughs.

Ellen was from a thriving dairy-farming family of ten who lived in a thatched cottage in an area known as Walshestown. One of the daily calls on her milk round was to the Dolan farm at nearby Portloman, not far from Mullingar, and on the shoreline of one of the area's famous lakes, Lough Owel. The Dolans were a relatively prosperous family of nine, and one of the handsome sons, Paddy, had caught Ellen's eye. From her vantage point on the cart, Ellen would eagerly scan around the farmyard at the Dolan homestead, searching for him when she arrived with her supply of milk.

It was Ellen who would strike up banter with the more reserved farmer's son; but soon Paddy was smitten with the attractive young milk maid and his pulse would race a little faster whenever he heard the sound of her horse and cart coming into the yard. Their friendship blossomed into a full-blown romance, eventually leading to marriage with the blessings of their respective families.

Paddy was the eldest of the Dolan siblings, but although it was traditional for the first-born son to fall in for the farm, he and Ellen opted to make their own way in life. Paddy got a job as a barman in a Mullingar pub and the couple set up home on the town's Austin Friars Street. Bicycles were the era's most popular mode of transport. Paddy spotted an opening in the market and set up a sales and repair shop in the town. The location in Austin Friars Street was ideal as St Loman's Hospital was on that side of Mullingar and most of the staff travelled to and from their workplace on push bikes. This provided Paddy with a steady trade.

It was an idyllic time in the lives of Ellen and her husband and their happiness was complete when they were blessed with the gift of children. The youngsters transformed their quiet house into a hive of activity as boisterous and mischievous toddlers vied for Ellen and Paddy's care and attention and gave their parents endless hours of fun and entertainment. However, the joy of parenthood was shattered when one of their brood, Michael, aged four, became seriously ill with pneumonia, and, despite medical care and the prayers of the close-knit community who had cocooned them in a blanket of support, he died. Ellen and Paddy were inconsolable over the loss of their beloved son.

It was also a time of economic hardship, and making ends meet now became a constant, worrying struggle for the young couple. As the years passed, Paddy's bicycle trade began to falter, due mainly to the fact that he allowed his customers' credit to mount up. 'There wasn't much money around at the time, so when people fell behind in their debts, they had little hope of catching up,' Ben explains.

Sometimes clients would arrange to meet Paddy in a local pub to settle their debts, knowing that they'd be treated to several rounds of drinks; this invariably cancelled out any profit he'd hoped to make out of their transactions.

Paddy's generosity of spirit and his love of people were admirable human traits, but they spelt disaster for his business life. Stressed and depressed as he struggled to make a living for his family, the bicycle shop owner was eventually forced to accept an offer on his property. When all his financial affairs were settled, the family was left with nothing. The couple and their young children moved in with Ellen's sisters, who were still living out on their childhood farm in Walshestown. They had offered to accommodate the hard-up family until they got back on their feet.

In the meantime, Paddy applied to Westmeath County Council for housing for the family. A former neighbour in Austin Friars Street provided him with a shed to carry on his bicycle trade and this continued to bring in a meagre income. When the letter eventually arrived from Westmeath County Council it was like a gift from heaven to Ellen. She read it over and over. The family had been approved for one of the modern semi-detached cottages then under construction in a new development at Grange, a mile-and-a-half outside Mullingar town. It didn't have water on tap or an indoor toilet, but it was a palace to Ellen. The cottage was her first brand new home and it was set in a perfect location, straddling both the town and the country.

To cap the new turn in the family fortunes, Paddy was offered part-time employment as a council maintenance worker, thanks to the fact that he owned a horse and cart. His new job was to draw materials for work being carried out on the local roads of Westmeath, and it would pay more than his haphazard bicycle trade.

'The fact that we had a horse and cart was the mainstay of the family as there were no lorries, so the council was looking for fellas to draw the material for road maintenance. My mother and father had come from … I wouldn't say an easy life, but a handy life growing up, so they would have been relieved to be back on their feet at that time,' Ben says.

Paddy and Ellen and their happy gang of seven children – Dympna, James, Paddy, Ita, Imelda, Ben and Vincent – were a year settled in their compact, three-bed homestead at Grange, when the couple's final child came into the world on 16 October 1939. Little did his parents and siblings know then, as they gathered around the cradle upon his homecoming from the town's new hospital, the magic that baby Joe would go on to create during his time in the world.

CHAPTER 3

KITTY

S tanding outside the Dolan family pub, Mullingar House, Ben points to an imposing building at the end of another street across the road. The town's impressive cathedral has been a part of the Dolans' lives since childhood and would ultimately be the setting for Joe's final moment in the spotlight at the end of his days.

Ben remembers how on Sundays, after the family climbed on board their transport for the jaunt to Mass, the same argument would flare up. Joe and his brothers pestered their father for control of the reins as they set off from Grange in their pony and trap. 'We all took turns,' Ben says.

Young Joe always wanted to take the reins. 'Ah, I don't think so,' Paddy would tell him. 'There's too many people along the road to watch out for and you might do them harm.' Seeing little Joe's disappointment, his soft-hearted father would always change his mind and give in.

'That boy has you wrapped around his little finger,' Ellen would laugh as young Joe's face lit up like an excited child experiencing the magic of Santa Claus on Christmas morning.

'Giddy-up, Kitty!' Joe would shout, giving the pony a gentle slap.

'Slow down! Slow down!' his father ordered.

Joe wasn't a big fan of Mass. Driving the pony and trap gave him a thrill and it compensated for the boring ceremony in the cathedral that seemed to drag on for an eternity. Along the route from Grange to town, Joe's heart would skip a beat as he approached a scattering of neighbours sauntering to Mass on the country road.

'Careful now you don't knock somebody down,' Paddy always warned, moving in closer to his young son.

'If there was room in the trap, we'd stop to give a neighbour or two a lift,' Ben recalls.

A local kid, Jimmy Horan, remembers how Joe's father, Paddy, often gave him a jaunt to Mass in the pony and trap with the family. 'Paddy was a lovely man, a gentle man,' Jimmy recalls. Young Horan would grow up to become a musician, backing Joe in The Drifters.

'Woah!' Joe shouted at Kitty, pulling fast on the reins to pick up a pedestrian whenever he was in charge of the pony.

'You're a great gossoon,' his neighbours would say as they climbed on board.

'Giddy-up, Kitty,' Joe roared, as their journey continued.

Paddy was always warning his young sons against speeding with the pony and trap whenever they were going out on their own. One day, Ben, Vincent and Joe were flying along in the countryside and as they reached a junction they pulled fast on the reins. 'In the heat of the summer the tar had boiled up on the road,' Ben recalls today. 'The pony went down on her knees and broke the shaft out of the trap. The job we then had trying to come up with a story for what had happened, without telling the truth.' He laughs at the memory.

When Kitty wasn't working, the pony was allowed to roam free and graze on the grass growing by the side of the road. Joe would be sent to fetch her in the morning, but the animal had usually disappeared out of sight. His first task then was to find which direction Kitty had wandered off along the roadway. This was easy enough, as Kitty left little heaps of clues along the road and Joe simply followed her trail of droppings. Sometimes Kitty was allowed to feed off the grass in a field across the road from the Dolan home. The owner was a good-natured local farmer by the name of Johnny Weldon and it was there that Joe and his older brothers got a taste of farming life.

Johnny was the father of six beautiful daughters, so he was delighted to have the obliging Dolan boys living nearby to lend a hand when there was hard, manual labour required on the land. In return for their help when he was planting his crop, Johnny would give the Dolans a couple of drills to sow their own potatoes. At the time, families could apply to the local county council for their seed potatoes and get them free of charge.

'What are yez at? Spread them out more!' Johnny would bark authoritatively as Ben, Joe and the gang dropped the seed potatoes in the lines of drills the weather-beaten farmer had manually ploughed with his horse. The farmer also drew manure from his yard with the horse and cart, and the boys helped him to spread it along the drills with forks. When the potatoes were ready to be dug out, Johnny would enlist their help again for the back-breaking task of picking the spuds. The brothers would sweep the fields on their hands and knees as they collected the potatoes by hand in buckets and baskets.

'It seemed like hard labour to us at the time,' Ben recalls today. 'But when you're a kid, even being asked to fetch a bucket of water feels like hard labour. Johnny was very good to us and I often think now that we did more harm than good working in his fields because we weren't skilled labourers.'

The hard-working landowner was very fond of the Dolan brothers and would sing their praises to Paddy and Ellen. 'You're rearing great young fellas there,' he'd say whenever he called in for a chat and a cup of tea. 'I'd be lost without them.' Joe and his siblings were also aware that Johnny was good for a few bob, in return for various chores on the farm, including the morning and evening routine of milking the cows. 'Have you a job, Johnny?' they'd occasionally ask, if they thought there was the chance of earning some cash. 'Yeah, thin the turnips.'

'What do we have to do?' Joe asked the first time. 'Take out the small ones and leave the others a foot apart along the drill,' Johnny explained. Then he added, 'It's sixpence a drill, boys.'

Joe's initial enthusiasm soon wore off after a couple of hours crawling up the rows of drills on his hands and knees in the muck. 'Is there any end to this feckin' field,' he muttered to Ben.

After settling in Grange with Ellen and his children, Paddy Dolan had also fallen back on his farming skills to put food on the table. He grew vegetables in their sprawling back garden and leased a couple of acres from a local landowner, to sow oats.

During the harvest, Joe would sit on a fence around the field, watching his father and his brother, Paddy, cutting the ripened crop of oats with a scythe.

'Can I have a go with that yoke?' Joe'd plead, itching to work the scythe.

'It's too dangerous, wait till you get bigger,' his father would reply.

Joe would sulk, but later he'd join his brothers in the task of gathering the crop and wrapping it in bundles before stacking them in the field to dry out. The harvested oats were drawn home in the pony and cart, steered by young Joe. A manually-operated threshing mill was then borrowed from a Mr Geoghegan who lived in the locality. One of the Dolan boys worked the small foot-operated contraption, while another would feed the oats into it.

'Then we had a device called a winnowing machine, which was hand turned and you'd throw the oats into it. It would blow the chaff out and the oats would fall into a bag,' Ben explains.

Afterwards, the oats was taken to Gallagher's mill outside the town to be crushed.

Every night before going to bed, Ellen steeped the oats in water to make gruel, a form of porridge, for the family breakfast. In the morning it was solid, then milk or buttermilk was added to the mix before it was ready to be eaten. If it was rock hard and unsuitable for porridge, the gruel would be cut into chunks and fried on a pan.

Joe had a fond memory of this breakfast treat. 'It tasted absolutely delicious,' he said.

The shine on Kitty the pony's coat was also attributed to the benefits of a diet that consisted mainly of oats. When the cereal was being crushed, a bag or two was always set aside for the pony's feed throughout the year. Kitty thrived on a daily diet of boiled turnips mixed with a handful of oats that Joe would religiously feed her.

'We kept a pony for as long as I can remember,' Ben says today. 'Kitty is the one that Joe always remembered and I'm sure he was sad when she eventually died of old age. I do remember that later in life Joe would often mention Kitty at the shows. He'd tell audiences, "I used to ride Kitty when I was a young fella." It always got a laugh.'

* * *

The harsh life took its toll on Joe's father. Watching through the kitchen window as her husband unhooked the horse and cart in the yard, Ellen confided in a friend that she was worried about his health. She could see Paddy struggling with the daily routine of work. Where once he had strutted off to his job with the council, he now seemed to shuffle along like an old man with the woes of the world on his shoulders. He was short of breath and didn't have the energy for chores that required a lot of physical strength. Paddy would regularly doze off in the chair by the fire.

'Are you sure there's nothing that ails you, Paddy?' Ellen often asked.

'Ah, there's not a bother on me, apart from the usual auld pains,' he'd insist.

As Ben remembers, his father suffered from rheumatic pains for years. 'He was very fond of shooting and fishing when he was young and everyone said the pains were from the wetting he got. Clothes wouldn't have been that good at the time,' he says. 'I remember him taking a cure which consisted of cider and DeWitt pills, so-called because it was the name of the doctor from Navan who supplied them.'

Paddy wasn't the sort of man who complained about his aches and pains, or any other ailments that came to torture him. Colds and flu and the cuts and bruises of hard manual labour were all borne in a dignified manner by the quiet man.

Reflecting on his father's battle with ill-health Ben says, 'It got to the stage where the pain was so bad that he couldn't physically work. There were still a lot of us in the house to rear, so I'm sure that played on his mind and it must have been a terrible time for him. It must have been worrying for my mother as well, but she was kind of proud and she'd never look for help. She always kept the fair side out.'

When Paddy did not turn up for his council job with the horse and cart, his ganger came knocking on the door of the Dolan home.

'Is the boss in?' he asked, when Ben answered the knock.

'I'll get Mammy for you.'

Ellen explained that Paddy was sick and would not be able to return to work for some time. The council overseer was sympathetic. He was also conscious of the fact that there was a shortage of horse and carts for council work at the time.

'Are any of the lads old enough to take over his job with the horse?' he asked.

Lurking in the background was her eldest son, Paddy, his beaming smile betraying his delight at the opportunity that was now being presented to him. Paddy couldn't be more thrilled at getting the chance to leave his schooldays behind and move on out into the adult world. 'I thought all my birthdays had come together. I was going to work,' he recalls.

The following morning young Paddy was up at six, to go searching for the horse along the road. Later, he yoked up the horse to the cart and set off to work. As he left town, Paddy stopped to pick up two more council employees waiting for him at the bridge over the Royal Canal. Then he was off with the men to work on the roads around the village of Killucan, arriving on the job at eight. At the age of sixteen, Paddy Junior was now the family's main breadwinner.

Ben says, 'From then on, it was Paddy who reared the lot of us. It was his wages that kept us above water.'

Then he laughs, 'I remember one time Paddy was writing a record of his work time for the council. It read: "I worked on Monday and Tuesday with the horse and cart. And I worked on Wednesday with meself."'

* * *

In the 1940s came the Second World War, which was a fearful time in the Dolan home. James, the eldest, had flown the nest and joined the airforce in England. His sister, Dympna, had followed to become a nurse in Coventry, where she would experience, at first hand, the terrible casualities of warfare during the bombing of that city. Ellen and Paddy lived with the constant worry that James and Dympna were in real danger during this time of conflict, and they were always remembered in the nightly prayers.

During the war, and for a period afterwards, food was rationed in the country's shops. Butter and sugar, in particular, became much sought-after luxuries. Ellen Dolan would make the trip into Lipton's grocery shop in Mullingar with her ration coupons in her handbag and young Joe by her side. In the store, a two-foot-square slab of fresh butter was produced from behind the counter. From this, the shopkeeper cut and weighed out two-and-a-quarter pounds, which was Ellen's allocation for her family under the rationing scheme. The shop attendant moulded the butter into shape, slapping it between two wooden paddles.

'Give that a good whacking and make sure you squeeze all the water out of it,' Ellen insisted. 'It's butter I want, not water.'

The rationing of sugar created a war of a different kind among the Dolan siblings. Every one of them lived for the daily treat of bread and butter with a coating of sugar. This was regarded as a feast fit for a king. To ensure that every family member received their fair share, Ellen had devised her own scheme of sugar rationing among her offspring. Each one had his or her own jar, into which she divided the sugar in equal measures. It was then the responsibility of every individual child and teenager in the house to use their sugar sparingly until the next ration was due at the grocery store in town.

It had seemed like a fair and ingenious method of avoiding conflict in the home. But the best-laid plans often backfire, particularly when there are mischievous children involved. Ellen had not legislated for the deviousness of her little clan. Under the cover of darkness, shadowy figures regularly moved swiftly in the night, topping up their dwindling sugar supply by raiding the jars of their sleeping brothers. This inevitably led to rows at breakfast time.

'Mammy, my sugar is all gone,' Joe wailed.

'What am I going to do with the lot of you?' Ellen would sigh, shaking her head, exasperated as the bickering erupted.

Running wild as young children in the midlands during that era, Joe and Ben had little idea of the carnage that was happening out in the dark world, apart from one incident.

Ben recalls: 'I do remember there was a lot of talk in the house about a Kiernan man from Patrick Street in the town who was lost. He was a fighter pilot and we heard that he had been shot down. It made a big impact in our house because we knew the family.'

The end of the war was greeted with a huge sense of relief in the Dolan family. Their prayers had been answered. James and Dympna had survived unscathed.

CHAPTER 4

IT'S THE FERRET!

As he sits by a turf fire one cold winter's evening, Ben recalls the Dolan family's annual pilgrimage to the bog.

When each season swept in, it created a different form of labour for the brothers. In the cycle of the year, the boys dreaded the time arriving when they would be roped in with the gang as they geared up to cut and save the turf for winter fuel.

'I hate the feckin' bog,' Joe remarked to Ben one time.

'Who doesn't?' his brother shrugged as they set off for a day toiling on the peatland with their father and other family members. Ben reminded Joe of how he himself had to strip off his smart clothes and join the crew in the bog on the day he made his confirmation, and how he was later sent home in agony when a gust of wind blew turf mould into his eyes.

'You cried for two days,' Joe laughed.

The Dolans usually set about this annual task in June during the school holidays and the work would go on over the summer. A day on the bog for the family began shortly after eight in the morning. They would hear the shrill starting horn sounding for the workers down at Flanagan's saw mill in Mullingar as they set off with the pony and cart. It seemed to the boys that time stood still in the bog. Throughout the long, tedious day they would ask their father at regular intervals, 'What time is it now, Daddy?' Paddy would retrieve a pocket watch from his waistcoat and announce the time. A look of disappointment swept across young faces. 'Is that all it is?' someone would mutter.

The turf was cut by hand with a slane and thrown up from the trench to be caught by a fellow worker. It was then piled on to a bog barrow and carted away, to be laid out on the ground to dry. Later in the day, during a break from the cutting and catching, a fire was lit and water fetched from a well down the road, to make the tea. Matches were broken and thrown on to the water as it was believed that this prevented the smoke from getting into the kettle. Then everyone would tuck into their sandwiches. This was the best part of the day for the Dolan brothers. 'You'd be thinking all day about the tea and sandwiches,' Ben laughs today. 'It was just simple sandwiches, but a gourmet meal wouldn't have tasted better. It was also a break from the tedious work. When you're a kid there's no joy or satisfaction in that kind of work.' After this welcome sojourn, their tasks would continue till dusk, by which time they were dead on their feet.

Later, the family would return to the bog, to foot the turf; this involved standing it in small pyramids of four to six sods, to dry out over a period of weeks. Once it was fully dry, the peat was brought home in the pony and cart. Joe and his brothers then had the laborious, back-breaking task of stacking the mountain of turf sods in a shed where they were stored for the fire. A well-built stack helped to dry out any remaining moisture in the sods of peat; this gave it a longer life as it burned, so it was important to construct the stack with care.

When the job was finished, Joe would sometimes wince with the excruciating pain from shreds of turf that had pierced the flesh and were torturing him with slow, burning stings underneath his fingernails. But he would never complain. Deep cuts, scratches and bruises were accepted like badges of honour in his rural lifestyle.

* * *

Shooting the cute little rabbits that basked in the evening summer sunshine in neighbour Johnny Reilly's field never cost Joe a thought either; this was all part of the cut and thrust of country life. And, apart from the delicious rabbit stew his mother would later cook up in a big pot, it was great sport for the boys in the family.

Cartridges were hard to come by in the aftermath of the war, but even when they were available their father could not afford to buy them. Instead, Paddy made his own ammunition. The ingredients came from a variety of sources: a railway worker supplied Paddy with fog signals which provided caps for the cartridges. These were gadgets that were pinned to the railway tracks whenever there was dense fog. They would explode with a loud bang when the wheels of the train crossed over them, thus alerting the train driver to slow down as he was close to the town's station. The powder was supplied by another of Paddy's friends who was stationed at the local army barracks.

He would make the shot by melting lead and spilling it on to an old pan which had holes in it like a sieve. This created the tiny lead balls. Paddy had also devised a little machine to roll the cartridge. The cartridge was then shoved down the barrel of the gun with an old muzzle loader. With cartridges so scarce, every shot fired had to be accurate.

The home-made cartridge exploded in a cloud of smoke, so Joe or his brothers could never be sure that they had hit their target until they went to the spot where the rabbit had been enjoying a relaxing summer's evening just minutes earlier.

'Jaysus, missed the little bugger,' Joe shouted. 'No, I got him!'

There were dramatic moments while hunting rabbits, as Ben recalls one evening when we are travelling along the road by Reilly's field.

'Often when we'd go shooting we'd have to flush out the rabbit from a burrow,' Ben explains. 'This was done with the help of a ferret. We'd send the ferret into the burrow and then a purse net was placed at the opening. When the rabbit came running out he'd get caught in the net. After a while that became too simple, so we put the ferret in and then tried to shoot the rabbit as it came out. Every now and then someone would shout, "It's the ferret!" One evening Joe fired and then his face dropped. "What's up?" I asked. "I shot the bloody ferret," he said.'

*   *   *

Although they were the hardest of times, Ellen created an atmosphere of gaiety in the home with her regular music sessions. From the moment they could crawl, her children were encouraged to sing the traditional songs she would teach them as they gathered around the fire in the evening. And they would warble the old songs they had learned at school. Ellen played the fiddle and the accordion and had a voice as sweet as a bird in a dawn chorus. She was never happier than when her house was full of people gathered together for *craic agus ceoil* and a sing-song that would last for hours.

'Whenever we had visitors my mother would get us up to sing for them. We were always mortified at that age, but she'd sit there listening as proud as punch,' Ben recalls.

When the mood came upon her, Ellen would plot out an evening of entertainment with the precision of an army general sending his troops into battle. She would despatch Joe, Ben and Vincent, to keep a look-out for one of her star performers, a cousin by the name of Frank Gavigan. He was renowned as the finest traditional musician in the area.

'We all loved Frank,' Ben says. 'He had a quiet personality, but a great sense of humour. And he was very laid back; he even spoke slowly; there was no rush on him.'

Frank worked in the post office in Mullingar, over eight miles away from his home in Rathconrath. Come hail, rain, snow or sunshine, he made the daily trek to and from his workplace on a pushbike, passing the Dolan house along the journey.

'Go out and watch for Frank,' Ellen would command.

The boys maintained their vigil perched on a fence, waiting patiently for the outline of Frank to appear on the horizon, as he wheeled along home on his bicycle after a long, tedious day on the job.

'Mammy has your tea ready for you,' Joe would shout as Frank reached the Dolan house.

Frank always gave the young brothers a knowing smile as he pulled on the brakes and alighted from the bike. No matter how exhausted he felt at the end of the day, the prospect of a music session never failed to lift his spirits.

'Ah, good man, Frank, you'll have the tea with us,' Ellen would greet the affable musician as he arrived into the kitchen.

Ben recalls that tea was a modest affair. 'It would be a rasher and egg or just an egg. Or maybe an egg with another egg. But Frank always appreciated it. "You can't bate a rasher and egg," he'd say. Frank was family.'

After the meal, Ellen would retrieve her accordion from a back bedroom. 'You'll play us an auld tune, Frank,' she would say.

'I will surely.'

'Play us "Peter Street".'

As the evening progressed, Ellen would join in on the fiddle.

'Now, Ellen, will you give us "Father O'Flynn".'

Neighbours would drop in and sing impromptu while others danced around the kitchen. 'Play us another one, Frank!' they'd encourage the musician. And the children in the house, including Ben and Joe, stepped into the limelight to do their party pieces. Ben recalls how they would sing songs like 'By Killarney', 'Believe Me, If All Those Endearing

Charms' and 'The Spinning Wheel'.

Shortly before midnight, Frank would announce that he was off home to his bed. Then the postal worker slipped out into the night air, threw his leg over the crossbar of the bike and set off on the rest of his journey to his house in Balgarrett at Rathconrath, all seven miles of it. As Frank built up speed on his bicycle, to get home to his bed before a morning call for work, he did not have an inkling of the influence his musicianship was having on the youngster who had closed the door behind him. And neither did young Joe.

Sadly, Frank Gavigan died in 2006. Three years later, Westmeath honoured the traditional musician when Labhrás Ó Murchú, head of Comhaltas Ceoltóirí Éireann, unveiled a memorial bearing Frank's name at Rathconrath.

*   *   *

Joe had a wicked tongue and was a powder keg of childish divilment. His foul language regularly got him into trouble with his mother.

'Joe Dolan, don't ever let me hear you talkin' like that again,' she'd admonish him whenever she'd catch her youngest child swearing like a trooper. Joe was always embarrassed when his mother overheard him firing off a barrage of curses and swear words at his siblings or among his friends. 'I reared you better than that,' Ellen would add.

Even the owner of the local bar-cum-grocery shop was amused by the colour of Joe's language, finding it highly entertaining. 'Wait till you hear this fella cursin',' he would nod to whoever was in the shop as he spotted Joe arriving to pick up messages for his mother. The grocer would then engage Joe in a line of questioning that never failed to draw the type of responses he had hoped to elicit from the youngster. Customers were doubled over with laughter in the shop at Joe's rapid fire string of expletives that would give a Reverend Mother a heart attack.

Later in life, Joe was always very conscious of his language as a public figure. He got out of the habit of swearing for fear of using an expletive during a live interview. 'Oh, I'd never use bad language on stage because it sounds dreadful and often there are children at the shows,' he told me. Although he would let the odd swear word slip in private, Joe mostly used the term 'buckin'' in place of the word that rhymes with it.

His childhood pranks were not always appreciated by the adults who had been at the receiving end. Mrs Begley was standing at her door in Patrick Street as Joe's brother, Paddy, made his way home from work through the town on the horse-drawn cart one evening.

'How'ya Mrs Begley,' Paddy nodded warily as he approached, noticing that the local woman had a face like thunder on her.

'Come here to me, Paddy Dolan, till I have a word with ya about that brother of yours,' she fumed.

'What brother?'

'That little pup, Joe.'

'What's he done?'

'He was bangin' on my door goin' home from school today.'

'Bangin' on your door?'

'It's not the first time I caught him at it.'

'Oh, sorry about that …'

'He's a pure nuisance.'

'I'll have a word with him …'

'You'd better put manners on the pup or I will the next time I catch him.'

'Right so, Mrs Begley.'

Joe was defiant when Paddy confronted his little brother later that night. He denied even being in the vicinity of Patrick Street when the crime was committed that afternoon or on any other occasion. Paddy was not convinced and warned young Joe that a terrible fate lay in store if Mrs Begley ever got her hands on him. Joe laughed.

A week later, locals were amused to see Mrs Begley, in her apron and scarf, chasing a youngster down the street while brandishing an old sweeping brush. 'Come back here, Joe Dolan, ye little pup!' she roared. 'Bejaysus I won't,' he shouted as he disappeared around a corner like a greyhound.

As he made his way home from work along the dusty street that same evening, Paddy spotted an angry-looking Mrs Begley in the distance, maintaining a vigil at her front door.

'C'mere to me, Paddy Dolan ...'

'Oh, Jaysus ...'

*　*　*

As soon as he was old enough, Joe became the family's main messenger boy. Ellen would send him to town on minor errands. 'I want you to get me a few messages,' she would say, giving him a small list of groceries. The list had become necessary after Joe had made a couple of disastrous trips, returning home without the household items she had sent him to fetch.

'Joe was the world's worst at remembering what our mother would have sent him into town to buy,' Ben recalls.

He tells how one day Ellen handed Joe a half-crown, to purchase a pound of butter in town. Joe popped the precious coin into his pocket and set off on the mile-and-a-half walk into Mullingar. On the outskirts of town, he ran into a group of school friends playing with a home-made go-kart, and he joined in the fun. As he raced down hills and crashed into ditches on the contraption, the hours slipped away.

Later, as he strolled up and down the streets, occasionally stopping to drool over a luxury item in a shop window, Joe shoved a hand into his pocket and found the half-crown nesting at the bottom of it. Joe was in an excited state when he eventually arrived home to Ellen.

'Where have you been?' she asked crossly, glancing up at the clock on the mantlepiece.

'There's after being a miracle in town,' Joe blurted out, his eyes bulging.

'What kind of a miracle?'

'When I put me hand in me pocket I found a half-crown.'

'And where's the half-crown now?'

'I bought chocolate and comics and, look, there's the rest of it,' he said, holding out a handful of coppers.

'And where's me butter?'

Joe's jaw dropped as he suddenly remembered.

'Oh, the b-b-butter ...'

* * *

Later in life, Ben would remind his own children of their good fortune by telling them stories from his poor background. 'I often told them of the day the visitors were coming and how my mother coped with the little we had,' he says.

Ellen had been in a fluster all day. Two of her female friends from town were coming around in the evening and would be having a meal with the family. She had dusted off her best cups, saucers and plates and set them aside for her guests. The 'good' cutlery had been retrieved from the back of a drawer and polished until it sparkled when rays of sunlight caught it through the kitchen window. The girls in the house had been put to work scrubbing and cleaning floors and walls.

In the evening a beef stew was slowly simmering on the range, its delicious aroma wafting around the house. Ellen was fretting that there was not enough meat in the pot to feed all the adults and children in the house. 'Now boys,' she suddenly announced, 'I want you to listen to me.' Ellen warned Joe, Ben and Vincent that they were to be on their best behaviour when the visitors arrived, especially when they were eating at the table. 'I'm sorry now, but there's only enough meat for the adults tonight, so you're not to ask for any.'

'No meat!'

'No, Joe, and don't be asking for it tonight.'

As the two ladies, dressed to the nines, sat down to their meal, Ellen cheerily took the lid off the stew before dishing it out to her guests and the children who were sitting stiffly at the table.

'Do you want meat, Ben?'

'No thanks, Mammy.'

'Vincent?'

'No, Mammy.'

'Do you want meat, Joe?'

'No.'

After the dinner a pot of tea was brewed on the hot range and Ellen took a small apple tart out of the oven. Joe's eyes started dancing in his head.

'Can I have some of that tart?' he asked Ellen.

'No, Joe, you can't have tart when you wouldn't eat the meat,' she quietly reprimanded him, adding, 'And that goes for the rest of you boys.'

* * *

Through the years, Joe's father, Paddy, battled to return to employment amid the breakdown of his health and, for a time, he joined his son, Paddy, doing jobs for the council. Gradually, though, work became unbearable for him. Ellen could see her husband physically wasting away before her eyes. Her worst fear came to pass in the summer of 1950 when Paddy, then aged sixty, suffered a stroke and died three weeks later in hospital.

On the day of his father's funeral, eleven-year-old Joe stood silently by Ellen's side in the country graveyard at Walshestown, with tears running down his face as he watched the men lower his father's casket into the cold, dark hole in the ground. However, his tears that day in the graveyard were for Ellen. Joe was upset as he witnessed his mother's heart-rending distress over the loss of the husband she had adored.

CHAPTER 5

WALTONS' PIANO

As a kid, Joe lived in a fantasy world with his imagination inspired by the comics he devoured. 'Joe was a serious kid for reading comics,' Ben recalls. 'A woman called Maggie Murray ran a shop just across from where we have our pub today. She stocked sweets, but part of her trade was selling new and second-hand comics. She was a very tall woman and I remember that her shop had a low ceiling, which made her seem even taller. Maggie didn't know anybody's name and she called any male who'd come into the shop, "John". Joe was a regular customer. "Yes, John!" she would address him. Joe laughed. He would buy the second-hand comics and then return them the following week. Maggie would then give him a trade-in against the next batch of comics he bought. There was a little bit of money changing hands all the time.'

One day, their mother, Ellen, was standing at the gate of her home, chatting to neighbours when Joe went racing past, riding Kitty bareback at the speed of light. 'That fella is as wild as a buck goat,' she sighed. As Ben tells it, in his imagination Joe had just robbed the local bank and was fleeing the Mullingar sheriff and his posse. Ellen was always worried about Joe, fearful that some harm would come to her youngest child amid his boyhood activities. 'Boys,' she would say, 'You never know what divilment they get up when they're out of your sight'

However, Ellen was also delighted to see that Joe shared her passion for music and singing. She noticed how the wiry schoolboy had become popular among the neighbours who enjoyed the *céilís* she hosted in her home. He was frequently requested to do a solo spot.

Joe would puff out his chest as he stood centre stage in the kitchen, entertaining the gathering with a couple of old Irish songs, including 'The Spinning Wheel'.

'That young fella has a great voice, Ellen, you should encourage him to keep up the singing,' Frank Gavigan told Joe's mother.

When Joe arrived home from school one evening, Ellen called him into the kitchen where she had been busy preparing vegetables for the family meal.

'Joe, I want you to learn music,' she told her son. 'I want you to learn how to play the piano.' Sitting down at the table, Ellen explained that she had been talking to Molly Carroll, a local woman who gave piano lessons in her home. 'I asked Molly if she'd take you after school for lessons and she has agreed.'

The blood drained from Joe's face. 'Piano lessons after school sounded like a prison sentence to me,' Joe recalled. 'I had nothing to do with choirs either at the time because you had to go and practise with them after school. I thought that was unfair. I thought it wasn't right to have to hang around after school when you could have been doing other things.'

After school was a time for letting off steam with his friends, playing hurling and football and going on all kinds of exciting adventures. How could he tell his peers that he would not be able to play with them because he had to go to piano lessons. He would never live it down.

'Joe,' Ellen insisted, after his vehement protests, 'it's only an hour out of your day in the afternoon and you'll be made up for life.'

Joe remembered how he shuffled off to Molly's two-storey, red-brick house on Patrick Street like a condemned man on his way to the hangman's noose that first afternoon.

'How did you get on?' Ellen asked when he arrived home.

'Grand,' he muttered. To his surprise, Joe became excited at the prospect of mastering the piano and learning to read the music notes. Despite her sharp, schoolmistress appearance, Molly was warm, patient and encouraging. She filled Joe with dreams of playing in great halls and theatres around the world, to audiences who would jump to their feet to applaud him.

'Some day you'll be playing in Carnegie Hall,' Molly said.

'Where is that?' Joe asked.

'In New York,' Molly smiled.

'New York! How would I get there?'

'Well, Joe, practise, practise, practise,' Molly told him.

Over the next couple of months Joe's initial enthusiasm for the piano began to wane. 'Sure I thought I'd pick up the piano in no time and then I'd be free to do my own thing,' he recalled. Instead, Joe was struggling with the tuition and he was losing interest. His pent-up energy was pulling him in other directions. Oblivious to this, Ellen was delighted with what she perceived to be Joe's dedication to his piano classes. She was also looking forward to seeing his reaction when the delivery van arrived. Unbeknownst to Joe, Ellen had been saving money from her widow's pension, to purchase a piano for him. It had been her own long-time dream.

The delivery van from Waltons music store in Dublin caused huge excitement, and not just in the Dolan household. Children and adults swiped back net curtains and peeked out of windows and doorways, to watch the drama unfold as the magnificent musical instrument was carefully hauled out of the vehicle by two burly delivery men in white coats. Joe lurked in the background as a crowd gathered while the men from Waltons struggled to manoeuvre their cargo through the cottage door, with beads of sweat running down their faces. When their mission had been accomplished and after being revived by a couple of mugs of tea, the two men set off again on their return journey to the 'Big Smoke' as Ellen sat on a chair admiring the expensive mahogany piano that occupied an enormous space in the tiny room. She could hardly believe it.

'Joe,' she called, 'Come in here and play us a tune.'

'No, Mammy,' he shouted, disappearing out of sight.

Ben recalls that over the next couple of days, Ellen was disappointed to notice Joe's lack of interest in the magnificent instrument. Every day she herself would sit at the piano and attempt to tinkle a tune from the music books she'd also ordered from Waltons. A couple of weeks later, as she strolled through the town, Ellen encountered Molly Carroll. In the course of their conversation, she told Molly about her new prized possession. 'Tell me,' Ellen then asked, 'how is our Joe getting on with the lessons?'

'Well, it's a shame he gave them up because he was doing great,' Molly informed her.

'Gave them up?'

'Oh Ellen, sure it's two months since I last saw Joe.'

'Well, wait till I get home ...'

Joe admitted that he felt ashamed when Ellen confronted him. 'I didn't care about the bloody lessons at the time, but deep down I knew it meant a lot to my mother,' he recalled. 'I used to swear a hole through a pot that I was at Molly's in the afternoons, so I felt terrible when I got caught out. I promised my mother then that I'd go back to Molly and I kept it up after that.'

*   *   *

The spine-chilling sound coming from the bedroom was like a banshee crying in the night. It had tortured the family in the house, driving them demented for several weeks. Ben was teaching himself to play the fiddle. Ben's passion for music had become an obsession, one which would ultimately set his brother Joe on the road to stardom. The first instrument Ben tried to master was his mother's fiddle. Ellen was full of encouragement, helping him to learn an old Irish favourite called 'An Chúilfhionn' [The Coolin]. Its slow air suited the learner, but it soon grated on the nerves of his family as Ben strangled the tune over and over.

'It'll sound better in time,' Ellen assured anyone who complained about the screeching of the strings as Ben wrestled with the bow in the kitchen. 'I couldn't master the fiddle at all and it got on my nerves eventually,' Ben remembers. 'One night I got so frustrated that I said, "That's it, I'm giving up." I think everyone was delighted.'

When Ben left school at the age of sixteen, he immediately started working as an apprentice carpenter. Ben was a gifted craftsman, a talent he had inherited from his father. He loved the work; chiselling, planing, fitting and shaping sash windows, doors, joints and various pieces of furniture and fittings. The ease with which he tackled all the tasks and challenges that he confronted in his work set him apart as a hugely talented tradesman.

Sensible and focused, Ben, who did not drink or smoke, put his heart and soul into music in his spare time. After failing to mate with the fiddle, he moved on to the accordion. He had become really excited about playing the squeeze box after watching the celebrated accordion wizard Jackie Hearst from Newry, County Down, giving a thrilling performance at a show in Mullingar. Jackie was a great showman, throwing all kinds of shapes as his fingers danced across the keys of the large instrument he was hugging. 'I had this dream of playing the tango, which was my favourite dance at the time,' Ben recalls. He could see himself standing in the spotlight of a fabulous ballroom, dazzling the colourful dancers with the magic he created on the glittering accordion. His high expectations ultimately turned to dust. 'I tried hard, but I just couldn't get comfortable with the accordion at all,' he remembers. 'Eventually, I just knew in my heart that it wasn't the instrument for me.' His love affair with the accordion was over, but the dream of being a musician lived on.

'Music is an addiction for which there is no cure,' Frank Gavigan told him.

* * *

Ben then remembers falling in love with the saxophone, as he stood mesmerised in a dance hall in Mullingar, watching local star Dinny Hughes wowing the crowd on the instrument. 'Dinny was the biggest attraction in the area as the front man in his own hit band,' he recalls. 'His musicianship was in a class of its own and I was hooked.'

When Ben informed Joe that he was taking up the sax, his young brother shrugged. 'Jaysus, anything is better than that bloody fiddle,' he quipped.

Ben reckoned the saxophone was going to cost him a small fortune, so for months, like a squirrel gathering nuts, he scrimped and saved and secreted away his spare cash. He didn't spend a penny more than the money he handed his mother every week out of his wages. Every now and then, Ben would take out the collection of coins from under his bed where he had stored them in a glass jar; then he'd empty his horde on to the kitchen table and count the pile with great expectations. Every week brought disappointment, until one day his little bank account added up to a whopping £35, the price he'd been told the instrument of his desire was going to set him back.

'Where are you going to buy a saxophone?' Joe asked, as he watched his brother counting the money.

'Dinny Hughes will get me one,' Ben told him.

With so much money at stake, and mindful of his own lack of knowledge about the saxophone, Ben had decided not to attempt to choose the brass instrument himself; he was terrified of being conned out of his hard earned cash by some unscrupulous seller. Filled with a mixture of apprehension and excitement, Ben made his way to Dinny's home. The band leader was friendly, quiet-spoken and encouraging. He invited the young Dolan teenager into his parlour and went to put the kettle on. Sitting in the corner of the room, displayed on a stand like a priceless object of art, was Dinny's own saxophone. Over a cup of tea, Dinny agreed with Ben that the saxophone was a beautiful instrument with a lovely tone. Mastering it would require patience and lots of practice, Dinny warned in response to Ben's probing. Finally, Dinny Hughes agreed to source a saxophone for the young wannabe musician and Ben handed over his bundle of cash.

Ben can remember being like a cat on a hot tin roof as the days turned into weeks and there was no sign of the arrival of Dinny and the new saxophone. Every evening upon his return from work he would ask: 'Did Dinny come today?'

'No, Ben. Dinny didn't come today.'

Ellen was dubious about the arrangement Ben had entered into with Dinny.

'I stopped mentioning it, but then one evening my mother said, "Dinny never bought you that saxophone." I said, "Ah, don't be worrying, Mammy, Dinny will get it for me alright,"' Ben remembers.

It also transpired that Ellen wasn't so sure about Ben's new musical direction. 'Would you not be better sticking with the fiddle and the accordion,' she suggested. Ben shrugged.

Several more weeks passed, and now Ben himself was worried about the fate of his cash as there was still no sign of Dinny coming up with the sax.

'Dinny Hughes still hasn't bought you that saxophone,' Ellen reminded him, as if he needed reminding.

Ben grunted.

'Sure Dinny's no fool,' his mother added. 'He knows that if you learn how to play the sax, you'll be doing him out of business.'

Ben was silent. 'I began to think, Jaysus, maybe she's right,' he recalls. 'And then one evening I answered a knock on the door of our house, to find Dinny standing outside with a huge smile on his face and cradling a saxophone.'

'He said, "You were probably getting worried that I had run off with your money, Ben?" I insisted, "Oh God, no, not at all." Dinny then said he had to go Waltons to get the sax for me.'

When Joe arrived home, he found Ben in the kitchen, red-faced from trying to blow a tune out of the sax. 'You'll burst before you ever play that yoke!' Joe teased.

In the weeks that followed, Ben said he became more and more disillusioned as he tried and failed to play anything that resembled a familiar song.

'Go up to Dinny, maybe he'll give you some lessons,' Ellen suggested helpfully, noticing his frustration and disappointment.

Ben took her advice. 'I can't get any note out of this,' he told Dinny.

Dinny Hughes was sympathetic and arranged for Ben to come back for some lessons. Over a period of weeks, Dinny gave the budding musician some basic tuition on the instrument. 'Now, there are three important things you need to remember if you're going to play the sax,' Dinny added.

'What are they?' Ben asked, sitting on the edge of the couch, eager to learn from the master.

Ben says Dinny then gave him a familiar answer, one Joe had already heard over and over, 'Practise, practise, practise.'

Ben nodded and smiled.

'I'm serious, Ben. Don't expect to pick up the sax and be able to play it overnight. It's going to take a lot of practise … and patience.'

'Fair enough.'

*   *   *

Joe dreaded going home in the evenings. Ben had been driving him mad for weeks trying to play the sax. It seemed to Joe that he was welded to the instrument. Whenever Ben was about the house, everybody dived for cover when the infernal instrument came down off the peg behind the kitchen door. Ben had hung it by its strap on the back of the door, and whenever he dropped in for a bite to eat between jobs, he immediately retrieved it to practise. At night, he'd blow it for hours on end.

'It's like a feckin' fog horn,' Joe cried in despair.

At first, Ellen was reluctant to criticise Ben's persistence in trying his best to become an accomplished player. 'Music is one of the great joys of life,' she'd say. But eventually his mother ran him out of the kitchen when even the family dog started making his objections known in a loud and raucous manner. Widgeon, the Cocker Spaniel, would howl in agony whenever Ben blew a tune.

'Would you go up to the bedroom and play that thing and don't be annoyin' the dog!' Ellen eventually ordered her son in a fit of exasperation.

But, ultimately, the maddening advice Molly Carroll and Dinny Hughes had instilled in Joe and Ben to 'practise, practise, practise' saw them blossom into fine young musicians. Apart from mastering the piano, Joe now displayed remarkable musical skill on the fiddle and the accordion.

Frank Gavigan would tell Ellen: 'That young fella Joe is a natural-born player. Mark my words, he's going to be an All-Ireland Champion one day.'

*　　*　　*

Joe's eldest brother, Paddy, had got a job working in the County Hall, where big bands like Maurice Mulcahy and Mick Delahunty were being hired for dances. He was running the cloakroom and sometimes he would get Ben to fill in for him. Although he didn't know it at the time, this would be Ben's university for the music business as it gave him the opportunity to see the best bands in the country playing on stage. Joe was too young to go to the dances and he was envious of the great experiences Ben was now enjoying.

The Clipper Carlton were the new craze – the first of the showbands – and when Joe heard that they were playing at the County Hall, he just had to see them.

'I knew my mother wouldn't let me go, so I had to find a way of sneaking away to the dance that night,' Joe recalled many years ago. 'I didn't have the price of the dance, so two hours before it started I nipped into the County Hall, went to the toilet and sat there as quiet as a mouse until all the dance-goers arrived. Then I left the dance and got a 'pass out', which would allow me to get back in. That part worked well and I now had a free ticket.'

Joe then raced home, where the next stage of the plan was to pretend to his mother that he was going to bed. Then he would slip out the bedroom window. However, before Joe had a chance to make his getaway, Ellen caught him washing himself with a basin of water.

'Where are you going?' she demanded, sensing that he was up to no good.

Joe knew that the game was up. 'To the County Hall,' he whispered.

'You are, in your hat. Get up to that bedroom!'

Joe was devastated. 'I lay turning and twisting in the bed that night thinking about the great showband that Ben was enjoying … and the hours I had put in sitting on a bloody toilet for nothing,' he laughed.

* * *

Years later, his brother, Paddy, entertained Joe with stories from the cloakroom at the County Hall.

'One night after a Farmers' Dance, Paddy discovered that a man's grey crombie coat had been left behind,' Joe recalled. 'It was still in the locker room a year later when the Farmers' Dance came around again.'

Sometime during that night, a half-drunk, chubby-faced farmer went to the cloakroom looking for a coat he had left behind him the previous year.

'What kind of a coat was it?' Paddy asked.

'A grey crombie coat.'

'There's one there in the locker for the last year.'

'Well, bar there's £58 in the pocket, it's not mine,' the farmer said. He added that the money had been the proceeds from a sale of cattle.

Paddy checked the pocket and there was no money in it.

'There's a hole in the lining; it'll be down there,' the farmer told him.

'Sure enough, the wad of cash was in the lining, with an elastic band around it,' Joe said. 'Then I asked Paddy, "Did he give you a few bob?" He shook his head and said, "The ignoramus took the coat and the money and never even said thanks."'

*   *   *

A coat featured in another of Paddy's yarns that Joe loved to tell: 'One night a fella, well known to Paddy, was leaving the dance with a girl on his arm when he pointed out a man's coat to Paddy in the cloakroom. He didn't have his ticket, so Paddy took him at his word. Half-an-hour later another young lad came looking for his coat and produced a ticket. It was for the same coat. "What did you do?" I asked Paddy. He said he got up on his bicycle and cycled to the house of the young wan the fella had left the dance with. "I knew he'd be taking her home," Paddy explained. When he reached the house, Paddy had a quick scout around and found the couple courting on a patch of grass at the back of her family home, with the coat underneath them. Paddy then marched up and pulled the coat from under the amorous pair on the ground. "Ye bloody hoor," he said to yer man. "Ah," sez the coat thief, "Sure, Jaysus, Paddy, I couldn't put her lyin' on the damp grass!"

* * *

As Joe began to outgrow his schooldays, Ben recalls Joe coming home one evening from the local technical school and hanging his satchel on the back of a chair in the kitchen.

'I won't be needing this for much longer,' Joe announced. A bright and popular student in the school, Joe enjoyed his days in the tech. The teachers liked him, and he loved the company of a close-knit group of friends, with whom he had formed a close bond through the years. But now his schooldays were coming to an end.

'Have you given any thought to what you're going to do?' Ellen asked. 'I haven't a clue, Mammy,' Joe admitted.

In truth, Joe was dreaming of a life on the stage, playing in a band. But the teenager could not tell his mother. She would never accept him wasting his education like that. He knew she had high hopes of him getting 'a big job'. She was constantly telling him that he had brains to burn.

Ben remembers how concerned his mother was at the time, 'Joe was still very young, but she didn't want him coming out of school and hanging around. I said, "Maybe, I could get him a job as an apprentice carpenter?" My mother didn't think Joe had the hands for that type of thing. I joked that they were only there to finish off his arms. She was afraid that he would drift in life and waste his education. "Ah, something will turn up, wait and see," I said.'

CHAPTER 6

THE LOCAL PAPER

Ben remembers Joe being in a pensive mood as he stood by the window of the family home in Grange on his first day of work. It was an autumn morning and Joe was watching the leaves blowing in the wind under a clear, blue sky as Ellen stirred the porridge bubbling in a pot on the hot stove.

'Don't be late now on your first morning,' Ben told him, as he pulled out a chair and sat down to his early morning breakfast. Ben could see that Joe was anxious about the day that lay ahead. He remembered how he too had been nervous setting off to work on his first day starting out as an apprentice carpenter.

'Come over to the table, Joe, and eat your porridge,' Ellen said as she scooped his ration into a bowl. Joe tossed sugar over it, poured in some milk and dug in his spoon before taking a mouthful. He shovelled in another mouthful, then pushed the bowl away. 'Eat up, Joe, you'll be starving later in the morning,' his mother urged.

'Joe's stomach was in a knot with nerves and it had killed his appetite,' Ben tells me. 'I pulled over Joe's bowl and emptied the remainder of the porridge into my own dish. Then I quickly devoured it before setting off to work myself. "See you tonight," I said to Joe. He just nodded. As I was leaving, our mother assured Joe that he'd get on fine at the *Westmeath Examiner*. "You'd better get goin', Joe, in case your pushbike gets a puncture on the way into town," I said as I was going out the door. "You don't want to be late on your first day."'

By a stroke of good fortune, Ellen had secured a job for Joe in the printing works of the local *Westmeath Examiner* newspaper. With Joe now out of school and having proved himself to be a bright student, Ellen insisted that he shouldn't settle for any old job. Not that there was a lot of choice on offer, with the times that were in it. Ellen realised that he would be lucky to find any sort of employment in that bleak period that was sending thousands of young people fleeing to the boat for England, but she still clung on to high expectations for his career. In the months leading up to Joe's end of term at the tech, Ellen did novenas, praying that young Joe would get a good start in life as he went out into the adult world. She prayed to every saint in the book who might accede to her plea, including Saint Jude, the patron saint of lost causes. 'One of them will answer me,' Ellen would say. Joe wasn't impressed when he heard about St Jude.

Ben talks of how Joe's first job came about. While shopping in Mullingar town in the late summer, his mother met Mr Cox, the manager of the *Westmeath Examiner*, on Dominick Street and they stopped to chat. The pair were acquainted as Ellen knew his family. In the course of their small talk, Ellen mentioned that young Joe had just left school and she was worried that he couldn't find a decent job. He was full of brains and she didn't want him to waste them. 'If you come across anything suitable maybe you'd keep him in mind,' she added. As luck would have it, Mr Cox had an opening in the printing works for a young trainee compositor.

'I'm willing to give Joe a try-out if he's interested,' the kind, easygoing man told Ellen. Joe could start as a general employee, cleaning up the printing works and carrying out other odd jobs. 'If Joe fits in and shows promise and interest in the work we could eventually train him up as a compositor,' Mr Cox said.

Ellen floated home on a euphoric cloud that breezy afternoon. The *Westmeath Examiner* position had gold status. Ben explains: 'It was one of the best jobs in town and one that was virtually impossible to secure as it was considered to be a closed shop to outsiders. It was a job that had been handed down from father to son. Generations of families had passed through the printing works of the *Examiner*.' Now Joe Dolan would join the roll call.

Joe laughed that he was like a nervous bride at the chapel door on his first morning as he slipped into the *Examiner* printing works and inhaled the odour of ink, oil and grease that filled the air. Inside, men were busy working on the machine as they prepared for the week's printing jobs that included tickets and posters for local events, as well as the newspaper itself. As he watched the hive of activity, Joe noticed Mr Cox strolling in his direction with a sweeping brush in his hand. 'Right, Joe, the lads will show you what to do. I want you to keep this place spick and span,' the smiling man said, handing over the brush.

The following Thursday morning, as Ben cycled to a job in town, he spotted his young brother struggling along the street hauling a bundle of newspapers under each arm. Joe was delivering the weekly *Examiner*, filled with tales from the courts, rows in the council and the prices fetched at the local livestock mart that week. It was Joe's job to supply the latest editions to all the outlets in town. Joe hadn't a notion on that crisp autumn morning as trudged from shop to shop with news hot off the press that he would soon be making the headlines himself.

* * *

Standing nervously in the wings with his hands plunged into his sharp, black drainpipe trousers, Joe remembered debating in his mind why he had decided to enter the talent contest. The nerves were a torture. He could hear the roar of the crowd, their clapping and hollering, as one by one the other acts slipped out from behind the curtain and sauntered apprehensively to the centre of the stage, before launching into their performance. As he waited for his turn to come around, Joe checked his crisp, white shirt in a mirror and was mortified to see the nervous sweat patches forming in the arm pits. He shifted from foot to foot, filled with fear and excitement over the fate that awaited him as he mentally prepared for his own moment in the spotlight.

Paddy recalls that he could hardly believe what he was witnessing. Perched on an uncomfortable seat in the middle of the audience, Joe's older brother barely recognised the young teenager who burst on to the stage. Wide-eyed and with a beaming smile, Joe was a bundle of exploding energy as he made his entrance. Paddy had never before seen Joe perform in this fashion, strutting across the stage while he pumped life into the song, 'Ma, She's Making Eyes At Me'. In mid-performance, Joe caught Paddy's eye and gave him a wink, clearly indicating how much he was loving the moment.

It seemed that the whole town of Mullingar had turned out for the exciting event, billed as the 'Roy Croft *Radio Éireann* Beginners Please Road Show'. The winner of the talent contest would ultimately be decided by a clapometer. Joe's close pal Jazzer Mulligan had rallied all their friends to make sure that the applause for him would be thunderous. When the dust finally settled on the contest, Joe stood beaming in the middle of the stage. Even without the enthusiastic support of his family and friends, the spontaneous burst of applause from the entire audience at the end of his performance clearly indicated that he was the favourite to scoop the top prize.

A stunning teenage girl in a beautiful dress, with an angelic voice to match her engaging personality, had emerged as the runner-up to Joe.

Thelma Byrne stood self-consciously, blushing on the stage, after step-ping back into the limelight, to collect her prize. Waiting his turn nearby, Joe was in an excited state as he watched Thelma receive seven and sixpence.

Next, Joe stepped forward, to accept the winner's award. Surely he would receive double or treble the amount Thelma had picked up for second place? Roy Croft heaped praise on Joe for his outstanding perform-ance. Joe, he said, had a unique voice and a remarkable stage presence. Croft predicted that the Mullingar teenager would have a glittering future in store as a singer, if he choose to go down that route in his life. 'I think you'll agree that we have heard someone very special here tonight,' Roy told the audience, to tumultuous applause. Joe didn't hear a word. His thoughts were on the lump of cash he was about to pocket. And, in his mind, he had already spent the money. Joe left the building with the applause still ringing in his ears.

'Well, to hell with that!' he sighed with a look of fury on his face.

'What's up with ya? Sure, Jaysus you were great,' his brother Paddy said, giving him a slap on the back.

'Yeah, and what will this buy me?' Joe fumed, swinging the silver cup he'd received as the winner's prize.

* * *

All eyes were on the handsome young musician in the tight trousers and red, open-necked shirt, who was swinging his hips, eyes closed as he strung spine-tingling sounds out of a stylish electric guitar. The bar was packed with men and women in their late teens and twenties enjoying the modern music created by this self-indulgent entertainer who appeared to be in some kind of a trance. Joe leaned against a wall in a corner of the Galway City pub, watching the charismatic musician in action. He was excited by both the sound of the guitar and the style of the performance. It was a moment of immense inspiration for Joe who had casually dropped into the pub while on his first holiday from his job with the *Westmeath Examiner*. He knew instantly that he wanted to be the guy with the guitar.

Ben remembers Joe arriving home and announcing. 'I'm buying an electric guitar.'

His brother was impressed. 'How much have you saved?' Ben asked.

'Saved! Sure, Jaysus, I haven't a penny; I spent the lot in Galway.'

'It'll be a while then before you can afford the guitar,' Ben remarked.

'Ah Jaysus, no, sure I can't wait; I'm goin' to Dublin next Saturday to look for one.'

Ben was speechless. Knowing that Joe was reckless with money, his blood ran cold at the thought of his young brother borrowing beyond his means and ending up in financial difficulties. 'Can't the guitar wait until you have the few bob for it?' Ben said eventually. Joe raised an eyebrow, indicating that he was not going to be dissuaded from realising his dream. Ellen was also very concerned when she heard about Joe's plans. 'Never buy a thing till you have the money,' she insisted, adding: 'And chances are when you have the money you won't want it anymore.'

Ben had sleepless nights, worrying over Joe's leap into financial debt. Realising that Joe was stubbornly storming ahead with his purchase, he gave his brother an old acoustic guitar, to use as a trade-in against the newfangled electric version. 'I had an old guitar that I'd bought off a fella who had fallen on it and burst it when he was blind drunk coming home from England on the boat,' Ben recalls. The well-used instrument had been badly damaged, but Ben had skilfully restored it, bringing it back to its original glory. 'They might give you a good deal for this guitar when you're buying a new one off them,' Ben said. 'Jaysus, thanks!' Joe was delighted.

The following Saturday night Joe arrived in from Dublin with a broad smile, hauling his new guitar and an amplifier. Ben went into shock. 'How much did all that cost?' he spluttered.

'Ah, just short of seventy pounds for the lot.'

'Seventy pounds! Jaysus, Joe …'

'Ah, sure, it's no problem. The fella in the McCullough Piggot music shop was happy enough to do a hire purchase deal with me.'

'And what did he give you for my guitar?'

'A pound is all I got for it, but it was enough to get me and this little baby home.'

'A pound! Ah God, Joe.'

*　*　*

At this stage in their musical career Ben describes how he approached a local dance band in the Westmeath village of Ballynacargy and secured a place in the line-up of the group as a saxophone player. With his dark, matinée idol good looks and impressive, swaggering performances on the brass instrument, he made an instant impact. The showman helped to swell the crowds and soon Ben was in demand as a musician for hire. He began juggling his time between two bands, Tommy Farrell's and Henry Murtagh's, moonlighting at dances by night while holding down his day job as a carpenter.

Joe was envious of Ben's exciting new lifestyle and he yearned to be part of the action. Now serving his time as a compositor, after settling into the routine of life in the *Examiner* printing works, Joe passed his days daydreaming. In his imagination, he was centre stage, singing and throwing sexy shapes on his guitar as the crowd danced wildly to his performance.

Ellen kept him focused on his apprenticeship, reminding him time and again that he would have security for life, if he minded his job. Joe quietly agreed for the sake of harmony, but his fantasies insisted on pulling him into a world that revolved around the night, dance halls and bands.

Then came a key moment in Joe and Ben's lives. Ben remembers clearly arriving home from work early one evening in a fluster. 'Where's

Joe?' he asked his mother.

'He said something about going up to Morrisons to play cards. What's wrong?' Ellen responded.

Ben quickly explained that the two bands had asked him to play at separate dances that very same night. He had persuaded Henry Murtagh's group to take Joe in his place. Ellen wasn't happy. She didn't want a band interfering with his apprenticeship.

'He'll be grand,' Ben assured his mother as he bolted out the door to the home of their neighbours, the Morrison family. Joe squealed with delight when he heard the news. 'You'll need a black suit,' Ben added. 'Can I borrow a black suit, lads?' Ben explained to Joe that he wouldn't be getting a fee for the night's work. 'I'm not getting paid myself, but there'll be a good feed,' he added. 'Sure, I'd nearly pay them to let me do it,' Joe laughed.

Ellen wasn't enamoured with the turn of events. Ben and Joe had moved away from the *céilí* music of her era, which they now regarded as old fashioned. The electric guitar wasn't her favourite instrument and the boys were now playing a modern style which she didn't appreciate at all. 'I don't know what the world is coming to when the two of ye can play with a band,' Ellen remarked as Joe and Ben left the house that evening, accompanied by the electric guitar and the saxophone.

It was four o'clock in the morning when Joe returned from the dance. Ellen was in the kitchen at her wit's end with worry that he had met some terrible fate. She had been expecting him home around midnight. 'Where have you been till now, I nearly got the guards?' Ellen said sharply. 'Ah, sure I had to stay for the feed after the dance,' Joe explained.

Ben had been home hours earlier, but had got out of bed to hear his brother's story. Joe spewed out his night's experiences breathlessly like an excited child. He had surprised himself at how easily he'd fitted in, playing guitar in perfect time with the other band members. He'd even sung a few songs, which seemed to go down well. The hall had been packed with dancers and several had come up to him afterwards to chat.

Ben yawned.

'They paid me two pounds for the night,' Joe added.

Ben sat bolt upright and then nearly fell off the chair in shock.

'Two pounds!' he spluttered.

'What did they pay you, Ben?' Ellen asked.

'Oh … the same.'

Ben couldn't admit to his mother and young brother that all he got for his night's work was 'a feed'.

'They want me back, Ben,' Joe added.

Joe didn't sleep that night, but a couple of hours later he was on his bike and cycling to work at the *Examiner,* full of vigour. 'My mind wasn't on the job that day,' Joe laughed as years later he recalled how excited he was having played in a band that first time. 'I relived every moment of the dance for days afterwards. I don't think I was ever happier at any moment in my life before then. There was nothing to beat that buzz I got on stage. I loved it, and I wanted more.'

Happiness is fleeting, however. The journey of life was about to take Joe through a period of great personal loss and heartache.

CHAPTER 7

DARK DAYS AND
THE DRIFTERS

The moment he came through the door and caught Ben's dark expression, Joe knew that the news wasn't good. His heart suddenly pounded against his chest with the fright. 'My mother had been diagnosed with breast cancer,' Joe recalled in an interview.

It had all happened so fast. Ellen, always vibrant and engaged with life, had discovered a lump. She hadn't initially mentioned this to her sons, but when the GP referred Ellen to the hospital for tests, the boys were worried. Even though Ellen did not talk about it, they could see that their mother was stressed over this unexpected turn in her life. Then came the shocking revelation that she had a malignant tumour.

'My mother was then treated for the cancer at St Luke's Hospital in Dublin and she battled it for two years without complaining,' Joe said.

Ben also remembers that Ellen tried to maintain life as normal in the house throughout her illness. 'Oh, she didn't want to be a burden or make a fuss at all,' he reflects. 'At night she'd say, "Go on out, I'll be alright." With my mother it was always the best side out.'

Towards the end, however, Ellen went into the care of her son, Paddy, and his wife, Caroline, in their Mullingar home at Ginnell Terrace. Joe and Ben were then forced to take their first tentative steps into an odd, new life as young bachelor brothers sharing the same house.

In the weeks that followed, Joe and Ben gradually slipped into a new routine. When Joe arrived home in the evenings from his job at the *Examiner*, he would light the fire. Then, as soon as the range was hot, he put on a pot of potatoes to boil, and retrieved the pan, to fry up the evening meal. Unbeknownst to Joe, Ben had contrived to arrive in from work later than his young brother. Ben had an aversion to housework and cooking. 'I was being a bit sneaky because I knew that by the time I got back, Joe would have the fire lit and the pan on, and he'd be cooking whatever we were going to eat.' After a couple of weeks, Ben smiled as he noticed how his cunning plan had paid off. Joe had now settled into this evening routine without questioning his brother's time-keeping. Ben was still enjoying his home comforts, but now they were being provided by Joe.

The occasional performance with Henry Murtagh's dance band took Joe's mind off the worries he harboured over the state of his mother's health. 'Joe would say, "I can't explain it, but I'm in another world when I'm playing with the band." As soon as he strapped on the guitar and the band cranked up, Joe forgot about everything else that was going on in his life,' Ben recalls.

Ellen had been happy to hear that Joe's apprenticeship as a compositor at the *Examiner* was going well. She was relieved to see him settling into such a fine trade. It was a comfort to her knowing that her youngest son had been given such a great opportunity and there had been good news about his future. Joe now had a new boss, Kevin Cadogan, who indicated that there would be a full-time position for him when he completed his time as a trainee. Kevin had taken a shine to the good-humoured, quick-witted young employee. Joe was a popular figure among his fellow workers and his work rate was top class. He had dreams of a future in the band business, but, for now, he was determined to complete his apprenticeship. Joe knew how much it meant to his mother. Ellen would be so happy ... and proud.

In the middle of a big production day at the *Examiner* on a cold winter's afternoon in January, 1959, Joe felt a tap on his shoulder. 'It's your mother, Joe.'

In that moment, nineteen-year-old Joe's life changed forever. Ellen's death tore at his heart and the tears came in waves. 'Joe was really cut up,' Ben recalls. He had never experienced such emotional distress in his young life. Of course there had been heartache when his father, Paddy, passed on. But Joe was much younger then, and Ellen – the woman their whole world revolved around – was still in his life. It was such a comfort to have his mother by his side at that time. Now she was gone, leaving a myriad of great memories that only compounded the pain he felt as they flashed through his mind. In a heartbeat, the joy had gone out of his life. 'I would have given anything to have had her back,' Joe said in later life.

'The funeral went by in a blur for Joe and all of us,' Ben says. Neighbours and friends came to pay their respects and to offer their support. 'Sorry for your trouble, Joe.' He heard those words over and over from people who came up to shake his hand in sympathy. Several of Ellen's friends reminded Joe that his mother had been spared further pain. Joe graciously acknowledged their expressions of comfort as he stood, broken, in the frosty air on a winter's day in the country graveyard at Walshestown. As he stared at the plot where his mother had been laid to rest alongside her beloved husband, Paddy, no words could lift him out of his deep despair.

*　　*　　*

The busy routine of his work at the *Examiner* was a welcome distraction in Joe's life in the weeks that followed. It filled his days and helped him to cope with the early stages of his bereavement. Lifting the latch on the door to his family home in the evening, however, brought the darkness back. Everywhere he turned, Joe could see Ellen. There were so many reminders of her in the house; so many of her favourite things were all around, including the majestic piano that had been her pride and joy. So many happy memories of great music sessions in the home with family and friends, and Ellen at the core of it all.

After a time, the pain did ease for Joe and he rebounded. He was never the type to wallow in his misery. 'I was never depressive, even in my lowest days,' Joe said later in life. 'In fact, I'm unbelievably optimistic. I always think there's something good around the corner.'

*　*　*

In September, 1959, Ben caught the eye of a pretty young woman at a dance in the Westmeath village of Moate. They made a very handsome couple as they waltzed and jived together throughout the evening, with a great display of style and panache. As they chatted, the conversation turned to the band. Ben's dancing partner had been impressed by the musicians on stage. Realising that the attractive woman was a fan of music, Ben heard himself telling her that he had his own band. Her eyes lit up with excitement.

'She asked me if we would play at a dance in Castletown Geoghegan the following January,' Ben recalls. 'Even though we had no band, I agreed and settled on a fee of a tenner.'

He had been contemplating starting a group with Joe for some time. After gaining experience with Henry Murtagh, Ben felt he now had the confidence and know-how to lead his own band of musicians. The timing for his grand adventure had never seemed right, but now his attempt to impress a pretty woman had finally forced his hand. 'I came home and told Joe and he was all for it. So we then set about getting some local musicians together for our own band.'

* * *

Parish priest Father McGathey looked like he had just spotted the devil casting his evil spell in the centre of the dusty hall when Joe, Ben and the boys played that first night. The man of the cloth was aghast as he noticed how young women were flashing their knickers. Their skirts were flying up in the air while they jived with wild abandon to the rock 'n' roll sounds of the sharply-dressed Dolan brothers and their motley crew of musicians from Mullingar. The dour, old-style priest appeared horrified by the modern music that Joe and the boys were pumping out from their vantage point on the stage. Judging by the expression of disgust on his face, Father McGathey considered it Satan's music. Neither did he welcome the small, rakish army of young male 'townies' who had pursued the band to the ICA dance in the Castletown Geoghegan parish hall. Father McGathey was on the verge of heart failure as he patrolled the hall, keeping an eye on the young men from Mullingar who were hotly pursuing the pretty girls from his parish on that frosty January night in 1960.

'The crowd loved us and sure we thought we were great,' Joe recalled. 'Ben said, "I don't think Father McGathy was too impressed." I just laughed and said the poor auld divil would be grand. Sure what harm was anyone doin'? It was just a bit of harmless craic. That night as I put on my overcoat and left the hall, I knew I'd give anything to be able to play in a band every night of the week.'

Their brother, Paddy, then booked Joe and Ben to play a dance in Mullingar parochial hall on the following St Patrick's Night. 'It was a six-hour gig,' Jimmy Horan recalls. 'It was then that I joined Joe and Ben's band playing the bass guitar, which was a brand new instrument to Ireland at the time. I had been playing rhythm guitar with a group called Skiffle and Aces in Mullingar. When I got my bass there was only one more in the country and Tom Dunphy of The Royal Showband was the proud owner. I had seen Jet Harris of the British band The Shadows playing the bass and I ordered one from Piggotts. There were no tutors, so I had to learn it myself. Halfway through the dance that Paddy's night, the lead broke on Joe's guitar. At that time there was no spare stuff, so I gave Joe my lead and I continued swinging my guitar around for the rest of the night, even though it wasn't plugged in and there was no sound out of it. But sure no one noticed at that time, they were too busy watching Joe. Even though we were only starting out, Joe was brilliant from the word go.'

The night was a huge success and led to shows in the Greville Arms Hotel and in St Loman's Hospital before they moved out to neighbouring counties. One of their big gigs at the time was as a support band in the Ierne Ballroom, Dublin. Jimmy Horan has vivid memories of arriving home at cock crow and then having to go to his day job as the assistant manager in Liptons grocery store. 'I remember playing Friday nights, coming in at six in the morning and then having to go to work till nine that night in Liptons. It was a six-day week then. During work days Joe would call down to me from the *Examiner* and then we'd walk home together for the dinner at one. Then we'd walk back to work and it would be all band talk the whole way. We lived the dream.'

* * *

Ben set about saving up his spare earnings towards the purchase of a van for their dance band as soon as they started getting inundated with dates to play at dances. Their popularity was now spreading far and wide and it gave Ben the confidence to make their first major investment. But, instead of opening a deposit account at the local bank in Mullingar, week by week the carpenter hid his savings in the body of their mother's piano at home in Grange. As the months slipped by, Ben's secret stash of cash edged towards £200, the price he reckoned the vehicle would cost.

'A couple of weeks passed and I hadn't checked on the money. Then, one night I decided to count it out, before I went looking for the mini-bus,' Ben reveals. 'I put my hand down and took out the bundle of paper and I couldn't believe my eyes. It was just like confetti.'

Ben's mind exploded with a mixture of fear, confusion and rage as he stood riveted to the spot. In a moment of brief relief, Ben thought that maybe it was Joe blackguarding him.

'Joe, are you actin' the maggot?' he shouted to his brother.

'What do you mean?'

'C'mon, what did you do with the money, Joe?' Ben pleaded again and again, almost in tears from the fright.

'I never touched the money.' Joe was adamant.

Ben remembers the sinking feeling he experienced as the source of the disaster dawned on him. 'I realised it was a feckin' mouse that had chewed its way through my savings. Oh, I was sick,' he says.

Seeing his brother's genuine distress, Joe resisted an almighty urge to burst out laughing. 'Maybe if you go to the bank with the money they might replace it,' Joe said helpfully.

'Ah for Jaysus sake, sure they'd never do that,' Ben sighed.

'Worth a try.'

When Ben explained the bizarre incident to the bank manager, he was sympathetic. The bank boss explained that the money could be replaced, but that the process would probably take up to a year. Ben arrived home deflated. 'I'll have to start saving again,' he sighed. Joe nodded and then a broad smile lit up his face as he produced a trap bearing a lifeless rodent. 'Caught the little fecker,' he laughed. A year later the money was replaced by the bank.

*　*　*

Ben remembers how his shiny mini-bus was sparkling in the morning sunshine as Joe went out to inspect the band's new mode of transport. Just a few days before, he had travelled up to Palmerstown on the outskirts of Dublin to view the second-hand vehicle, after it had been advertised for sale. Ben had observed that the bodywork and interior were in mint condition. He liked the shape and style of the spacious motor, and he was particularly impressed by the spot lamps. In addition to being their new mode of transport to dances around Westmeath and the neighbouring counties, it was the right image for the band, he thought. Ben agreed a price and the seller delivered it to the Dolan home a few nights later. It was the following morning when Joe saw the new band wagon for the first time, parked outside their front door.

'Where are the spot lamps you were talking about?' Joe later asked Ben, who was preparing for work.

'What do you mean?'

'There are no spot lamps on that bus.'

Ben says he stormed out the door to investigate, only to discover that the light fittings had been removed. 'Well, the bastard ...'

Ben then embarked on a forensic check of the mini-bus, to determine that everything else was in order, before he contacted the car dealer to lodge his complaints. When he returned to the house, Joe noticed his brother's sudden mood change. 'What are you so happy about?'

'Look at this ...'

Ben had found a banjo and sheet music for all the modern songs of the day in a case stored under one of the seats. Later, he contacted the seller, to complain about the removal of the spot lamps, but he simply insisted that they were never part of the agreement. Ben was furious.

'When I told Joe, he said, "Did you tell him about the banjo?" I said I did, but the guy didn't seem to be bothered about it,' Ben recalls. 'Joe seemed delighted with himself. "I had a look at the songs and they're great. There's that Cliff (Richard) and The Shadows hit, 'Travellin' Light', and there's a load of Elvis stuff. Your man who sold you the mini-bus has done us a big favour. We've got a whole set of songs here for our band." I realised that he was right, so Joe put the smile back on my face.'

*   *   *

The success of the band soon spelt trouble for Joe down at the *Examiner*. Still in his apprenticeship, the late nights playing at dances had been affecting his time-keeping. Joe had received several verbal warnings from his exasperated boss Kevin Cadogan after regularly missing the clocking-on time at the local paper and sometimes not turning up at all while sleeping through the day after a long night on the roads of Ireland.

One evening when Ben arrived in from his job, a despondent Joe broke the news ... he had been sacked. 'Ah for feck sake, Joe, I told you this would happen.' Ben was furious with his brother for throwing away the golden opportunity he had been given at the *Examiner*. 'I was determined to see Joe qualify as a compositor, so that he could have security in his life,' Ben explains. 'The band, after all, was just a bit of fun that might fizzle out overnight. I told Joe that I'd go and have a word with Kevin to see if he'd take him back.'

Joe agreed to allow Ben pitch his case to Kevin Cadogan. Ben says his brother genuinely felt guilty about not finishing the apprenticeship their mother had secured for him. Joe knew in his heart that Ellen would have been bitterly disappointed in him. 'It was the only reason he had been crestfallen when Kevin gave him his marching orders that day,' Ben says. Joe mentioned the sacrifices his mother had made for him and the dreams she had for his future. If Ben managed to persuade Kevin to take him back, he resolved to be diligent and reliable so that he could fulfil his mother's ambition for him by becoming a qualified compositor.

Joe remembered Ben looking relieved when he returned from the *Examiner* offices that day. 'Kevin said he'll give you another chance but this is the last one, Joe. I gave him my word that you'll be there on time from now on and that you'll mind your job,' Ben told him.

Joe's eyes danced in his head. 'Jaysus, that's great!'

'I was talking to Paddy and Caroline as well … they're going to take you in, Joe, and get you out to work in the morning,' Ben added.

Joe went to live with Paddy and Caroline and their family of seven children, sharing a room with two of the boys. And Ben arrived in every evening for his tea after work, having lost his cook. Caroline was like a second mother to Joe, and her offspring loved his sense of fun. They had already grown close to their uncle Joe over the years when he was their regular babysitter. Joe mesmerised and enthralled the children with the weird and wonderful fairytales he created on the spot for them at bedtime. The kids pulled the blankets up around their faces, listening wide-eyed with fear as Joe took them on a scary journey through his increasingly terrifying ghost stories. 'He used to tell them terrible yarns; I remember the tale of the man with "the big, long whiskers" was one of their favourites,' Paddy says. Joe's niece and goddaughter, Kathleen, also known as 'Goggeen' in the family and so-called because it was how her brothers and sisters pronounced her name when they were younger, remembers how she and her six siblings would be trembling as their uncle brought his ghoulish characters to life. 'Joe used to put the fear of God into us,' she says, smiling fondly. 'He would have us sitting down around him and we'd ask, "What happened last night, Joe? What did you see coming up the stairs?" And he'd tell us, "I saw a mad ghost …" and the story would go on from there. Sure, we wouldn't be able to sleep afterwards.'

Shortly after going to live at Paddy's home, Joe arrived in during the early hours of the morning and long after the family had retired to bed. As he crept up the stairs, Joe heard the tinkling of an old piano in the sitting room. Assuming that someone in the family was still up, he went to have a brief word. When he popped his head around the corner, Joe was surprised to discover that there was no one in the room. Baffled and now doubting his ears, he quietly slipped back up the stairs. As he reached the landing, the piano started playing again.

'I remember Joe coming into our room and calling me, "Paddy! Paddy!"
I jumped up in the bed with the fright as I didn't know what was after happening,' Paddy tells the story.

'There's somebody downstairs in the house,' Joe whispered.

Paddy pulled on his pants and grabbed the handle of a brush on the landing. 'I went down real easy with a big pole in my hand and Joe behind me,'
Paddy says. As he burst into the sitting room wielding his weapon, Paddy
was confronted by the intruder. A kitten was stepping along the keys of the
piano. Paddy collapsed into a chair laughing. Joe didn't know where to
look he was so embarrassed. The kids thought the story of the kitten who
terrified Uncle Joe was hilarious when they heard about it the following
day. 'That finished Joe telling ghost stories,' Paddy laughs.

Like an excited child, in the sixties Joe would insist on opening the presents from Santa on Christmas Eve when he arrived into Paddy and Caroline's house after the children had gone to bed. 'Joe couldn't wait until
Christmas Day to see what we had got from Santy,' Kathleen laughs. 'It was
years later that Mammy told us about Joe calling and getting Daddy to
open up all the toys so that he could see what Santy was bringing us. He was
a big child, really. The next day he'd come for his Christmas dinner and
there'd be a look of surprise on his face when we showed him the presents
we'd got. Later, when I had children of my own and they were all small, Joe
would come around and he'd be in the middle of them like a mad thing
playing with guns and bows and arrows. When we were young we didn't
realise how big Joe was. He wasn't a star to us. He was just Uncle Joe
coming into the house.'

* * *

As the year 1962 got underway, Joe set a train of events in motion that
would change the course of his life forever. Somehow, despite the demands
of a hectic schedule with The Drifters, he managed to complete his

apprenticeship at the *Westmeath Examiner*. It was a moment to stop and reflect on the opportunity his mother, Ellen, had given him. Getting his apprenticeship was Joe's way of honouring Ellen. But in the years since her passing, Joe's life has been transformed as he toured the country with the band. He was hooked on the wild reactions of the dancers who flocked to their shows from Dublin to Donegal. It gave him a confidence and a belief in the life he was about to choose. He looked to the future … and it wasn't in the printing works of the *Examiner*. And he was sure that the decision he was about to take would have the blessing of his mother.

Joe collected his wages for his first week as a qualified compositor on the Westmeath weekly newspaper and promptly quit his job. 'It's not that I don't appreciate the chance I got here, but there are other things I want to do with my life,' he told his boss.

Ben was furious. 'What the f**k have you done, Joe!' Ben, still working as a carpenter by day, was aghast that Joe had thrown away his safety net for the risky business of life as a singer. 'What if our band doesn't work out?' Ben remembers arguing.

'Sure there are plenty of bands in the country; I'll join another one,' Joe shrugged. A weight had been lifted from his shoulders and Joe was elated. After making his decision, he was now free to follow his dream.

Joe's brave leap into the insecure world of showbusiness forced Ben to seriously focus on the future of The Drifters. 'I knew the band had a lot of potential because Joe, in particular, was getting a great reaction out front,' Ben says. By now, Ben had reduced his own role as one of the lead singers in The Drifters, after recognising Joe's star quality while they were playing at farmers' dance organised by brothers Billy and Dermot Leavy in the Westmeath village of Kinnegad. Up to that point, he had shared the limelight with his sibling, matching Joe song-for-song on stage every night. But at the big IFA social event of the year in Kinnegad, Ben noticed something that hadn't occurred to him before: the packed venue would go wild whenever Joe performed a song. When Ben later reflected on this, he realised there was something about Joe that drew people to him. Joe was also a natural live-wire on stage, he had a great sense of timing and rhythm; and he created electricity in the room.

'I used to fancy myself as a singer, but Joe had no inhibitions. He had total confidence in what he was doing, and I think that's the secret to success,' Ben reflects today. 'If you are worried about what people think, I believe you are doomed. I used to sing country songs in the band, but that night in Kinnegad I realised it was Joe who was the real star. Whenever he'd sing a song he'd get a huge reaction from the crowd. After that, I made sure that whenever I would do a song, Joe would do two. So I always claimed that I "discovered" him,' he laughs.

Legendary RTÉ sports commentator Jimmy Magee recalls seeing one of Joe's raw performances in the early sixties, at St James's Hall in Kilbeggan, County Westmeath. At that time, Jimmy, who compiled the first Irish charts in 1962 (Elvis had the very first official Number-One hit in Ireland with 'She's Not You'), was working for a management group called International Promotions. Their big star was the Irish singer, Maisie McDaniel, and Jimmy was touring around the country with her and MC-ing the shows. 'I remember being in Kilbeggan with Maisie where the support act was a new band at the time called The Drifters,' Jimmy reveals. 'They had a young singer who was just incredible, I thought. He wasn't nationally known then as Joe Dolan. But it was obvious that he was something special. Afterwards, I remember telling a few people about the guy I saw in Kilbeggan. He was sensational. It was like seeing a special footballer for the first time and thinking, Jaysus, he has something, that fella.'

Jimmy was less impressed after he later witnessed Joe's skills as a GAA football player when he togged out for a charity match with the Jimmy Magee All Stars in Ballyjamesduff, County Cavan, some years later in 1966: 'I used to joke with Joe afterwards, "They won't be talking about you around the fire in years to come as a footballer."'

*   *   *

Joe, Ben and their band were rehearsing one night in a shed outside the town when there was loud rapping on the door. Ben went down to check it out and opened their dingy premises to see the familiar face of Paddy Malone, the leader of The Premier Aces showband from Ballintubber, in Castlerea, County Roscommon, standing in the doorway. The Premier Aces was then one of the big bands, featuring a young trumpet player called Johnny Carroll.

They had been on their way to play at a dance in Collinstown, County Westmeath, when their transport wagon broke down somewhere between Ballymahon and Roscommon. Paddy Malone had then hitched a lift to Mullingar where he was told that a band called The Drifters were practising up the road and that they had a wagon of their own. 'I'm Paddy Malone from The Premier Aces,' he said, addressing Ben.

'Sure, I know well who you are,' Ben replied, excited to be meeting the showband bigwig.

Malone poured out the details of his band's predicament and how they were stranded between Ballymahon and Roscommon. He was looking for transport. 'I'd be fierce obliged if you could dig us out of a hole,' Paddy added.

Joe and Ben were happy to come to the aid of the big band and immediately headed off in The Drifters' wagon, with Paddy Malone sitting up front between them.

The Premier Aces then transferred their equipment from the stricken vehicle to Ben's van, and he drove the lot of them to Collinstown. Joe and Ben hauled all the gear into the hall upon their arrival and assisted the band in setting up for the show. Later, as The Premier Aces performed to a packed venue, the Dolan brothers watched with wide-eyed fascination from under the stage. Afterwards, they helped the Aces to pack up before driving them back to Ballintubber and then returning to their own home in Mullingar.

Years later, trumpet player Johnny Carroll would recall the incident: 'Joe and Ben were looking up at us from underneath the stage that night like we were stars. Little did we know that the young singer watching us would himself become one of the biggest stars in Europe.'

Music promoter Pat Quinn from Cloone, County Leitrim, who would go on to launch the Quinnsworth supermarket chain, hired The Drifters as a support band to tour with The Rhythm Boys, a popular showband from Buncrana, in 1962. Joe and the boys were a huge hit on the tour. 'I knew then that we had a real good future ahead of us,' Ben remembers.

* * *

Joe was a car fanatic and he remembers taking possession of his first motoring pride and joy, a VW Beetle, as the band was taking off towards the big time. He often joked about looking for the engine under the front bonnet the day he went to purchase the car.

'I said to the guy, "Somebody has stolen the engine." He looked at me like I had two heads and somehow I kept a straight face,' Joe laughed at the memory.

'The engine is in the boot,' the bemused salesman explained.

'Jaysus, I'd better not plough it into a bullock so,' Joe told him.

* * *

Now that Joe and Ben were going to work exclusively as entertainers they needed to hire professional musicians who would be totally committed to the job. Like every band, players had come and gone through the years, including drummer Eddie Deehy, a lorry driver. Frank Melia from Longford was one of half-a-dozen pianists who literally drifted through the group. Other members had included trombone player Johnny Kelly from

Mullingar and saxophonist Noel Kirby.

As the band started to move up a notch, Ben placed an advert in the papers looking for full-time musicians. One trombone player who answered the ad queried Ben: 'What does "a professional musician" mean?' 'It means you don't do anything else for a living,' Ben told him. Exit, one trombone player. He wasn't prepared to give up his lucrative day job.

As Joe was en route from Mullingar to Swanlinbar in Cavan in his VW Beetle with Ben sitting nervously in the passenger seat, the discussion turned to the next trombone player they were going to audition at his home, a young guy by the name of Joey Gilheaney. 'How are we going to know if this Gilheaney buck is any good if we're not going to see him play in a band?' Joe asked. 'Well, I was thinking if he can play the trombone piece that's in the 'Midnight In Moscow' song then he should be good enough,' Ben said. 'Do you know anything about him?' Ben told Joe that Gilheaney was seventeen years old and lived with his grandmother, as his mother had passed away.

When Joe and Ben finally arrived in Swanlinbar after their long bone-shaking journey on winding, rough, pot-holed roads, they stopped at a bar, seeking directions. A couple of grizzled local farmers, drinking bottles of Guinness in the pub, eyed up the brothers with suspicion. Joe charmed them with small talk. 'It emerged that they did know where "young Gilheaney" lived and Joe took directions,' Ben remembers well.

At the Gilheaney homestead, Joey, a shy, lanky, clean-cut teenager sat embarrassed in the corner as his grandmother complained to Joe and Ben about 'the shockin' auld music Joey plays'. Joe nodded, trying to keep a straight face, as he saw poor Joey squirming in the corner with mortification. 'I do be tellin' him why can't he play the lovely *céilí* music his grandfather and his father before him used to play,' Joey's granny added as she boiled the kettle for tea. Ben recalls that Joey eventually went up to the bedroom to warm up on the trombone. 'That's shockin' altogether,' his grandmother said as she listened with an expression of pain on her face. Joey, it transpired when he finally got the chance to audition, was an excellent trombone player. He performed the 'Midnight In Moscow' audition to perfection. Joe and Ben had found their man.

Ben's friend, Brendan Molloy, who played in one of their favourite local bands, The Merry Minstrels from Delvin, recommended their keyboard player, Des 'The Doc' Doherty from Athboy, in the neighbouring county of Meath. Brendan, a schoolteacher, had been a big help to Joe and The Drifters in their early stages. 'He used to get us bookings and meticulously detail directions to the dance halls, including the locations of tea shops along the way where we could stop for something to eat,' Ben remembers. 'In those days, garages didn't do food and snacks like today and it was hard to find somewhere to get a cup of tea or a sandwich on a long journey.'

The Drifters classic line-up was further shaped by the addition of drummer Sid Aughey from Monilea outside Mullingar. Sid came to the band with rock-star good looks and plenty of experience behind the drums. He had played with Ben's favourite local band, The Merry Minstrels and he subbed for Mike O'Hanlon of The Clipper Carlton at several of their gigs. Years later, Sid recalled that he was cutting barley in a field the day Joe and Ben came looking for him to join The Drifters.

Joe and Ben's Grange neighbour Jimmy Horan had already agreed to go full-time. 'I was the first to give up the day job,' Jimmy recalls. 'I didn't have to think twice about it. I was just music-mad. Even before I joined up with Joe I used to spend my money on my music equipment. There was a hock shop in Mullingar's Mount Street where you could buy things on hire purchase. I was then working in Liptons and during Lent you got a bonus for selling jam. Everyone left the shop with a pot of jam, whether they wanted it or not. On Easter Saturday you'd get your bonus and I remember going down to that shop in Mount Street and putting my bonus down on a guitar. And then it was thirty bob a month, which was a lot of money.'

Bespectacled, silver-haired band member Sean Connolly from Mullingar had stayed with Joe and Ben through all the various line-up changes.

Sean worked as an attendant in St Loman's Hospital, but his true passion was playing the trumpet and he lived for the nights when he got to enjoy the thrill of being on stage in front of an audience. Sean's relationship with the Dolan brothers was like family. They were all brothers-in-arms in the entertainment business and close friends away from the stage. 'When I was living alone and had to undergo a hernia operation, Sean and his wife offered to take care of me in their own home while I recuperated,' Ben recalls. 'I was delighted to accept their hospitality and support and I moved in with the good-natured couple for a short period.'

Ben remembers the terrible dilemma he found himself in the day Sean Connolly informed him that he was going to leave his staff job at St Loman's Hospital, to become a full-time member of The Drifters. Sean was a good musician and a close friend, but Ben was worried about the state of his pal's health. The trumpet player suffered from angina and took a daily tablet for the condition. It had been a running joke between Joe and Sean in the early days of the band. 'Jaysus, Sean, what'll we do if you drop dead on stage?' Joe would say. 'Throw a coat over me and keep on playing,' Sean laughed.

With Joe and The Drifters now going on the road full-time in what Ben expected would be a tough, gruelling schedule of late nights and relentless travel up and down the country, Sean would be under a lot of pressure. Apart from the danger it posed for his health and welfare, Ben felt that Sean was being irresponsible giving up his pensionable job in the hospital at that stage of his life. What if the band didn't work out? 'I'm going to have to tell him he's out,' Ben told Joe.

Sean Connolly was devastated when Ben broke the news to him. He pleaded for his place in The Drifters. Ben stood firm with his decision, even though it broke his own heart. 'It's for the best,' Ben told Sean as they parted.

Even now, years later, Ben says, 'I'll never forget the look on Sean's face when I told him. It was the hardest thing I'd ever had to do in my life up until then. Joe thought Sean would get over it. I really wasn't so sure.'

A young kid called Tommy Swarbrigg from Cootehill in Cavan replaced Sean in The Drifters. Joe, Ben and his friend, Seamus Casey, went to hear his audition at the family home where Tommy, from a family of eleven children, was surrounded by his giddy siblings. Their mother told Ben: 'They're all great singers in this house. Sure Tommy's grandfather there is as fine a singer as you'll ever hear.' Ben said at that point, Tommy's grand-dad launched into a rendition of the song, 'Love Thee Dearest'. Tommy, meanwhile, sat patiently in the corner waiting for his chance to perform while all around the room his brothers and sisters collapsed in a fit of giggles at the shenanigans.

'I still vividly remember them coming to the house that day,' Tommy says today. 'Even though I was only sixteen at the time, I had already been playing in a band for two years, having left school at the age of fourteen. I joined a skiffle group in Cootehill called The Merry Five, but as I was the sixth member they changed the name to The Jordanaires. We couldn't go around saying we were The Merry Five when there was six of us. By this time I had already played in Longford, Mullingar and Tullamore. I couldn't believe it when I got the job with a professional band, The Drifters.'

The memorable Drifters line-up was now in place with Joe the lead singer and guitar player; Ben on sax and vocals; Jimmy Horan on bass; Dessie 'The Doc' Doherty on piano; Tommy Swarbrigg on trumpet and vocals, Joey Gilheaney on trombone and Sid Aughey on drums.

Joe could never have imagined the life journey he would also travel with Ben's music-mad friend, Seamus Casey, when the pair were first introduced in Mullingar. Seamus, then in his mid-twenties, was a popular teacher in a little country school at Dysart, County Westmeath. Like many a young man of the era, he was also fascinated by the showbands. When Seamus went to the dances his main focus at the end of the night was to get chatting with 'a fella in a band,' he recalls. The Clippers, The Melody Aces and The Royal Showband were his favourites at the time, and he soaked up all the information about their business.

As a young man, Seamus, who was well-spoken and wore glasses that gave him a learned appearance, frequently cycled in to Mullingar to socialise on a Saturday night. He often met Ben casually on those occasions and he struck up a good rapport with the young Dolan man who was around his own age. 'I liked the fact that Ben was always full of life and the two of us shared a common interest in music,' Seamus recalls today.

When Ben and Joe started the band, Seamus offered to run dances with them. 'I first convinced Ben to play a dance in Edenderry,' Seamus says. 'We hired a hall and packed it out that night. It was a great success, we made a few bob and I thought the band was just fantastic as well.'

After that night, Seamus became more and more involved in securing dates for The Drifters. 'They're going to be a great band,' Seamus told everyone who would listen. 'They're better than The Clipper Carlton.'

Joe was delighted with all the band dates that Seamus was getting for them. He also loved Seamus's enthusiasm and his sense of humour. 'I've never seen Seamus in bad form,' Joe told me one time. 'He's a lovely man, you couldn't fall out with him. If something went wrong, Seamus would always be the first to say, "I take full responsibility for this." That would cut out all the arguments with anyone else, even if it was feck all good to me. But he was a great diplomat to have in the gang.'

Seamus was holding down his teaching job by day while working as a part-time booker for Joe and the band, travelling around at weekends trying to get them dates. He was still living out in an idyllic rural hamlet with his widowed mother, Rose, in Rathdrisogue, near Castletown Geoghegan, and the phone in the house was the number for the band. While Seamus was sleeping late on a Saturday morning, the phone would often ring with fellas looking to book the band and his elderly mother would answer the call and pass on the message.

Eventually poor Mrs Casey got fed up with this. Seamus remembers her saying, 'I can't take any more of these calls.' That was a turning point for Seamus who realised that he couldn't keep up with the two jobs. But giving up a sensible, pensionable teacher's position was going to be a big decision. Instinct eventually convinced Seamus that Joe Dolan and his band were a good bet. They were creating a huge buzz.

Seamus has vivid memories of taking the plunge and turning his back on on the life of a teacher. 'One day I woke up and I said, "I'm going to do it". Then, after I had a chat with Ben, I packed in the teaching. I never regretted it and I loved the life that followed.'

At the start, Joe, Ben and Seamus were influenced by all the successful bands on the scene, and they learned and copied from them. 'Joe would sing "Boolavogue" in his set at night because Brendan Bowyer was doing it,' Seamus says. 'The Royal Showband were the Number-One band at that time in 1962.'

CHAPTER 8

BRENDAN BOWYER, LARRY GOGAN AND FANMANIA

With his jet-black hair styled in a quiff and his hip-swivelling stage moves, making female fans go weak at the knees, the tall, handsome young showband singer performing in a packed Athlone hotel ballroom reminded Joe of his idol, the American rock 'n' roll sensation, Elvis Presley. Joe was all fired up by Elvis, who had then spread a fever around the globe with hits like 'Heartbreak Hotel', 'Love Me Tender' and 'Are You Lonesome Tonight?' Every night during his own stage outings with The Drifters, Joe would send the excitement levels soaring in the dance halls with a medley of 'Elvis the Pelvis' favourites.

Now Joe and Ben were in The Royal Hotel in the Westmeath town, watching from the wings, as Brendan Bowyer, one of the country's biggest attractions with the Royal Showband, weaved his own magic on stage. Bowyer's gyrations and his vocal style had already earned him the title, 'Ireland's Answer to Elvis Presley'. The Royal had also been the first showband to cut a record. Their song, 'Come Down The Mountain, Katie Daly', featuring Tom Dunphy, another of their stars, had lead the way for Irish bands. Their next single, 'Kiss Me Quick', became the first Irish-recorded Number-One hit in their own country.

Joe was curious to see Bowyer performing live on stage with The Royal, having read reports in the papers about the Waterford-born entertainer's thrilling stage antics. Bowyer was drawing in record attendances to halls and ballrooms in every city, town and village of the country. "'I can see what all the fuss is about; the guy is brilliant,'" Joe told me during the performance, Ben recalls.

After the dance, Joe and Ben got chatting with Brendan Bowyer who remembers being well aware of The Drifters at that stage. He pointed out that they were already 'making a name' for themselves.

'Joe was eager to hear stories from our tours across England where we were also a big attraction on the entertainment scene,' Brendan recalls. 'I told him we had The Beatles supporting us in Liverpool and he was impressed with that,' he laughs. The Beatles were then the hottest band in Britain, following a chart smash hit with their single, 'Please Please Me'.

Ben recalls that later, as they were leaving the hotel, the Waterford heart-throb made an even bigger impact on the two young Dolan men. This time Brendan caught their imagination with his sartorial style, which impressed the Mullingar siblings as much as his stage presence and his gossipy tales from the road. 'We were green with envy as we watched Brendan going off into the dark of night with all the swagger of a Las Vegas superstar,' Ben laughs today. 'We both agreed that he really cut a dash in his fabulous sheepskin jacket.' On the drive home to Mullingar in the VW Beetle, the Dolan boys both decided that if they were going to be in showbiz it was absolutely imperative that they get their hands on a couple of sheepskin jackets.

Brendan Bowyer today recalls that he struck up an instant friendship with Joe. 'We were going for about four years before Joe and The Drifters arrived on the scene, but when we met I liked him from the start,' Brendan says. 'Dickie Rock said to me that the reason myself and Joe always got on so well was because we were both culchies. But I always admired Joe.'

*   *   *

Joe admitted that he wasn't so sure about Ben's sense of style when he saw the colour of the next set of stage outfits his brother had chosen for The Drifters. 'They'll f****in' see us a mile away, that's for sure,' Joe laughed as he examined the new red flannel suits. 'Ben's answer was, "We're in show-business," so anything goes,' Joe recalled in an interview. 'I said to him, "We'll be in St Loman's if we walk down the town in these!" I thought they were a shockin' colour altogether.'

Despite Joe's reservations, Ben was delighted with the suits, which he had purchased in O'Sullivan's of Mullingar for seven pounds each. Mrs O'Sullivan had even agreed to a hire-purchase deal on the outfits when Ben had haggled with her, offering to pay a deposit on the spot and the balance over a couple of weeks. When Joe heard this he reacted with mock surprise. 'And all the lectures you give me, Ben, about buying something before I have the money,' he tut-tutted.

Their manager, Seamus Casey, reserved judgement on the suits when he saw them. 'The deal was done, so I decided to make the most of it,' Seamus recalls. 'I said, "In for a penny, in for a pound," and ordered up a new Drifters' advertising poster, declaring Joe and the boys to be "The Red Devils of Entertainment".'

A few weeks later, Joe was referring to them as 'the wet devils of entertainment' as he discovered the unsuitability of the flannel outfits for stage performances on hot summer nights. 'Those bloody suits would kill ya,' the singer complained while he struggled to peel himself out of his soaking trousers in the dressing room after a show. 'They're a tonne weight with the sweat,' Joe added, as Ben whistled in a corner ignoring his brother's rant.

When The Drifters moved on to a new image, the ever-practical Ben advertised the red flannel suits for sale in the band section of the *Irish Independent* in 1962. The ad was spotted by John O'Dowd, a school teacher in Drumsna, County Leitrim, whose teenage son, Sean, was trying to start a band at the time. He would go on to become a major Irish star from the mid-seventies to the mid-eighties, performing as Sean O'Dowd and Ding-A-Ling.

'I was demented trying to be a rock 'n' roll star at fourteen-years-old, and my poor father indulged me,' Sean laughs today. 'I remember driving up to Mullingar with my father from our home in Carrick-on-Shannon and calling to the cottage where Joe and Ben lived together outside the town. My father negotiated with Ben and I recall a bit of a crowd gathering as neighbours came out of their houses to see what was going on. The seven suits were in reasonable condition and they agreed a price of four pounds each. I remember a pocket handkerchief and a blue tie came with them and it was my father's money that bought them; he was my sponsor.'

Armed with his flash suits, Sean O'Dowd would launch his young band, The Telstars. 'We were a pop band, for want of a better word,' he laughs. 'Each guy in my backing band was given a suit and then whatever alterations they wanted to make, they made themselves. I remember the suits being incredibly heavy with a turn-up on the bottom. They were really red and kind of spectacular. I thought we looked magic in them, but probably nobody else did. The band only lasted a year and I have no idea what became of the suits.'

Sean has never forgotten his first glimpse of Joe in Mullingar that day. 'I remember Joe looked so young and he had his hair in an Elvis style. And that big smile of his, I remember the smile. I was literally star-struck that day just looking at the guy. Shortly before that I had seen him performing at the Cloudland Ballroom in Rooskey. It was the first dance hall I ever went to and that's where I saw The Drifters. I was only thirteen or fourteen and my sisters were older so I was allowed to go with them. I had never heard anything like Joe. Brendan Bowyer was huge at that stage, but I thought this guy is just different.'

Sean would go on to become lead singer with the Donie Collins Showband and then performed with Tommy Drennan, before launching Ding-A-Ling in 1975. Between 1979 and '81, Sean O'Dowd and Ding-A-Ling were one of the biggest attractions in the country, playing to an average of 10,000 people per week. Through meeting on the circuit, Sean became friends with his childhood idol, Joe Dolan. 'I talked to him on a few occasions about the suits,' Sean recalls. 'Joe would laugh over it. I was very fond of him. He was a lovely, lovely guy. In 1980 and '81 I was voted top male pop singer in Ireland, ahead of Joe and Johnny Logan. Joe contacted me and said, "I'll get you next year, Dowdy." That's all he said, but it was nice of him to acknowledge it. I mean, he was a way bigger star than I'd ever dream of being. I reckon only for his love of Mullingar and Ireland, he would have been a worldwide superstar. I'm convinced there will never be another singer in Ireland with that kind of unique voice. Trust me, I've tried to sing his songs over and over and can't get near it. He was in a class of his own. I was in awe of Joe Dolan from the day I met him in Mullingar till the day he died.'

* * *

Joe said he loved Brendan Bowyer and the Royal Showband's big hit, an up-tempo song called 'The Hucklebuck', which was all the rage in 1964. The song had even created its own dance craze. The Drifters were also about to enter the strange new world of the recording studio for the first time. Joe remembered being apprehensive as he prepared to record a track called 'The Answer To Everything', which had been chosen by Seamus Casey and his friend, music journalist and radio broadcaster Ken Stewart.

The sentimental ballad written by Burt Bacharach had been previously released by American singer Del Shannon. 'I remember saying to Ben, "I'd rather have an audience when I'm doing it." Ben just laughed. "You won't fit an audience into the studio," he said.'

Joe and The Drifters piled into a mini-bus, surrounded by their instruments and set off for the Pinewood Studios in Bray, County Wicklow. The recording process was a strange affair for the musicians from Mullingar. Joe and The Drifters performed the song over and over in a downstairs studio, then they faced a steep climb to the top of the building to hear how it sounded in the control booth. Ben remembers declaring, 'It'll do!' as he listened to the track being played back for the umpteenth time. 'Are you sure?' Joe asked, not quite sure if he had achieved the perfect vocals. 'You sound great,' his brother assured him. Ben couldn't face going up and down those 'damn stairs' one more time.

* * *

Young radio disc jockey Larry Gogan was sorting through the new releases for his Radio Éireann show in Dublin when 'The Answer To Everything' landed on his desk. It had been sent to Gogan by John Woods of Pye Records, who were releasing the track for The Drifters. Larry, a handsome radio and TV presenter with a honey-coated voice that oozed teenage enthusiasm and joy for his work, had never seen The Drifters playing in the ballrooms, and wasn't familiar with the sound of Joe's vocals. When he played the track, Larry today reveals his immediate impression was that the singer wasn't Irish.

'I remember saying to John Woods, "That fella has a very unusual voice; he could be black or white or from anywhere in the world." John sounded anxious, "But you'll play the song?" he asked. "Oh, absolutely, it's a great recording," I assured him,' Larry recalls.

Joe and Ben were like kids who'd been given the keys to the candy store when they heard about the radio airplay. Ben has never forgotten how emotional he was on the day of the show as he drove off to a remote rural spot on his own, to listen to it on a transistor radio. Joe and Seamus Casey waited with a growing sense of panic and excitement in Mullingar as Larry played track after track. Then suddenly Joe's voice filled the room. Seamus remembers that Joe was beaming with delight as he listened to the radio that day. 'I think that guy Joe Dolan and The Drifters are going to be very big,' Larry emphasised as the track faded.

Sitting alone in a parked car near the Westmeath village of Moate, Ben was bursting with emotion. He had never been so happy in all his life. The following week Joe and The Drifters went straight into the Irish Top 10 with 'The Answer To Everything'. And overnight the crowds turning up at their shows trebled in numbers.

Joe was truly astonished when he arrived at the Tullamore Harriers in County Offaly, a week later, and saw 2,500 fans filing into the venue for their show. Shortly afterwards, Joe disappeared on a secret trip.

'Where the hell have you been?' a worried Ben asked upon his return to their home in Grange.

'Shopping in Cork,' Joe replied, producing a matching pair of sheepskin jackets.

*　*　*

When Joe used to talk about the moment he met Larry Gogan, he said he knew instinctively that the pair would become friends. They were instantly relaxed in each other's company. 'Larry had no airs or graces about him and I loved that,' Joe said.

Larry confides that he was taken with Joe's easy laugh and infectious sense of humour.

Like Joe, Larry's career had taken off at that time and he was on his way to becoming Ireland's undisputed king of the airwaves. Joe was curious about Larry's background, growing up a city slicker in Dublin. 'You're posh,' Joe teased, when Larry related how he had been reared in a family of eight children on Maxwell Road in the southside Dublin suburb of Rathgar. 'It was kind of posh,' Larry laughed.

Larry's father had gone into the family business, running sweet shops in Dublin's Marlborough Street and Fairview. Gogan's sweet shops had been famous around the capital city for decades. Larry recalled how as a kid he would watch fascinated as the family manufactured a selection of sweets such as bulls' eyes and acid squares in a factory at the back of their Fairview shop. 'At one time my grandfather and his brothers had sixteen sweet shops around O'Connell Street, Queen Street and Dominick Street, but they were blown out of it by the British,' Larry said.

Larry's cosy life in the city seemed to have been a world away from Joe's harsh, rural background, growing up in the Midlands. But as they chatted, the two young men discovered that a similar tragic event had blighted both their lives. Larry's father had also passed away when he was a young boy. 'I was just ten-years-old when he died,' Larry said in answer to Joe.

Both admitted that the memories of their fathers had faded because they had been too young to form a lasting bond. 'I remember that things weren't so good after my father died,' Larry revealed. 'My mother then had to go out to work in the shops and it must have been a frightening time for her with so many of us to rear.'

Joe was fascinated to hear how Larry had left school at the age of sixteen, without completing the Leaving Cert, in order to become an actor. He had gone on to star in productions like *Juno And The Paycock* with theatre luminaries such as Milo O'Shea, Godfrey Quigley, Pauline Delaney and Maureen Toal.

As Joe told of the years he had spent as an apprentice compositor, Larry admitted he had been forced to do all kinds of jobs to earn a living between stage productions. At one point he worked in the CIE garage in Ringsend, taking in the cash from the bus conductors. It hadn't occurred to Joe that Larry had been through such a struggle in his career. Hearing the chirpy disc jockey on the radio, Joe assumed he'd had a charmed life. 'So how did you end up on the radio?' he asked.

Larry explained that when he realised he was never going to survive as an actor, he went to work behind the counter of the family shop in Fairview. An elegant lady called Maura Fox, who worked in an advertising agency that produced sponsored programmes for Radio Éireann, used to come in for her daily newspaper.

One day Larry plucked up the courage and asked her if she could get him an audition to work on the radio. Maura secured him a role in a radio show called 'The District Nurse', which was sponsored by Cussons soap and was hugely popular in Ireland at the time. Radio Éireann producer Bill O'Donovan then spotted Larry's talent and appeal, which led to him working full-time as a presenter on the sponsored radio programmes.

'I see you're married, Larry,' Joe noted on that first meeting. 'Yes, indeed, Joe,' Larry confirmed. He told Joe how he had met his wife, Florrie, after she had been hired by his mother to work in their family shop. 'In fact, Florrie is a big fan of yours,' Larry added.

'It was Florrie who later persuaded me to take her to see Joe and The Drifters performing at The Crystal ballroom in Dublin's South Anne Street,' Larry says today. 'The Crystal was considered to be an upmarket ballroom and it was a shilling dearer into the dances there, compared to the other venues around the city. It was owned by a promoter called Bill Fuller and had a very strict code of smart dress.'

Larry, dressed in a dark, sharp suit with a white starched shirt and a tie, edged towards a corner of the heaving ballroom, to find a good vantage point for Florrie and himself. Florrie, who was the height of fashion in her short dress and neat, simple hairstyle, shuffled excitedly by Larry's side as Joe and The Drifters emerged on stage. 'All around him were screaming girls,' Larry recalls. 'It reminded me of the scenes that greeted The Beatles at their shows, except it was crazier. Every time Joe ventured close to the crowd in front of the stage, a sea of hands reached out to grab him. I was astonished at the hysteria Joe created in the room. Joe seemed to feed off the energy of the crowd and he became larger-than-life on stage. It was in total contrast to his calm, unassuming nature away from the spotlight.' Joe's natural talent, Larry thought, was his ability to be able to turn the showman on. And when he walked off the stage, Joe seemed to leave the showman behind.

Larry had seen many singers perform live, but at that moment he couldn't think of any who had the aura and animal magnetism that Joe exuded on stage. 'Through the force of his mesmerising stage persona and with the power and incredible range of his unique voice, Joe was drawing in his fans, making them a part of the show and turning the dance into one big party,' Larry recalls today. As she clung to Larry amid the fun and the madness of the night, his young wife Florrie was in a state of euphoria watching heart-throb Joe in action. 'Florrie absolutely adored Joe,' Larry says. 'And later after they met, I could see that Joe loved Florrie too.'

* * *

In August of 1963, as Finbar Furey, then a scrawny young teenager, competed in the All-Ireland Championships in Mullingar, playing the uileann pipes, Joe was among his supporters in the audience. The pair were not acquainted up to that point. Finbar Furey recalls that Joe, then aged twenty-three and on his way up the showiz ladder, was friendly with a local family of horse dealers called the Donoghues. The Donoghues were there to support the young Furey brother. And they had invited Joe to come along with them to see sixteen-year-old Finbar bid for glory in the competition. There was wild hollering and cheering when the results were announced and Finbar had been declared an All-Ireland Champ. Joe leapt

Above left: Cheeky schoolboy: Joe had a twinkle in the eye, even as a kid.

Above right: Parents: Ellen and Paddy Dolan.

Below: Joe playing the piano his beloved mother Ellen bought for him.

Above: Brothers-in-arms: Joe and Ben at the start of their career with The Drifters.
Below left: The new band, after the break up of the original Drifters:
L to R: Gordon Coleman, Seamus Shannon, Ben Dolan, Pat Hoey, Frankie McDonald, Ciaran McDonnell, Maurice Walsh and Joe.
Below right: Joe with godson Adrian who grew up to join his band.

Above: The original Drifters: Joe, Sid Aughey, Ben, Des Doherty, Tommy Swarbrigg, Joey Gilheaney and Jimmy Horan.

Below: Talk to my manager: Joe clowning around with the band's manager Seamus Casey in the '70s.

Above: Platforms: Joe shows off his boots in the '70s.

Below: Heart-throb: The idol is mobbed by female fans in the '60s.

Above: Golf buddies: Finbar Furey, Red Hurley, Joe and his tailor Jas Fagan in the '80s.

Below right: Ireland's *Starlight* magazine featured Joe's tour of the USSR.

Above: The Answer To Everything album cover which was photographed by Val Sheehan at Belvedere House, Mullingar.

Above: The new Drifters: Kevin Cowley, Gordon Coleman, Pat Hoey, Seamus Shannon, Ben; and front: Frankie McDonald, Joe and Maurice Walsh.

Below: Freezing in Moscow: Ben, Liam Meade, Pat Hoey, Joe, Tony Newman, Gerry Kelly, Frankie McDonald and Jimmy Mullally in Red Square.

Joe through the decades.

Best Wishes
Joe Dolan

With Love
Joe Dolan

Above: Swinging Sixties: Larry Gogan, Valerie McGovern (Radio Éireann), Joe and writer/TV presenter Pat Ingoldsby at a reception.

Below left: Poster for Joe Dolan US show.

Below right: Ben's wedding in 1963 to Moira. Joe, second from the left, was his best man.

out of his seat and was among the first to congratulate the beaming winner.

Apart from the fact that they had mutual friends in Mullingar, Joe and Finbar's passion for music and song created an instant bond between the pair. As they chatted that August evening, Joe was fascinated to hear that Finbar, who was reared in Dublin's Ballyfermot, had played for American President John F Kennedy in the Mansion House when he had visited Ireland, three months earlier. Joe was a fan of President Kennedy and he was amazed to discover that Finbar had played a haunting tune on the pipes for the great man on that historic occasion.

During the afternoon, Joe also had belly laughs as Finbar regaled him with tales of his own childhood. Finbar's parents, Ted and Nora, were traditional musicians who used to host all-night music sessions in their Ballyfermot home. He told Joe that many a morning he stepped over the comatose bodies of trad stars like Willie Clancy and Felix Doran in the kitchen on his way out to school. 'Felix's false teeth would be in a jar beside him on the ground, and he snoring his head off like a horse,' Finbar recalled.

Joe was in hysterics. 'Me mother would have a big pot of lamb stew on the go on nights like that,' Finbar continued. 'She'd fill up another ladle for Felix and he'd be sayin', "Ah, Jaysus, no more woman!" Me mother'd tell him, "Go on, if you're goin' to be throwin' that auld drink into your body all night you'll need the packaging."'

Joe identified with the music sessions in the home. 'Who taught you to play?' he asked Finbar.

'Me mother taught us to sing, as mammies do; then the auld fella got a hold of us with the instruments and taught me and me brothers, Eddie, George and Paul.'

Joe talked about his own mother, Ellen, and the part she had played in his musical background. 'Oh, me mother is a great singer as well,' Finbar said. 'She can sing and play banjo at the same time like Margaret Barry (a well known Traveller ballad singer). There's only herself and Margaret Barry that can do that.'

Finbar told Joe his father reared them all through playing music. 'He tried real work one time, but he said it didn't suit him.' Joe laughed as his new, young friend took him on a journey into the life and times of his family.

As they parted company that afternoon, Joe asked Finbar to come and see his band some time. 'I will, sure I'm often down in Westmeath as I have a ganzi load of relatives around here,' the Furey brother said.

Four months later, Finbar was among the crowd at a dance in Mullingar, where he witnessed Joe's stage magic for the first time. He was in awe of his new friend. 'You were great,' he told Joe.

Then their conversation turned to a tragic event that had cast a cloud over the island of Ireland and throughout the world: the shocking assassination of President John F Kennedy in Dallas, Texas, a couple of days earlier on 22 November. Finbar was close to tears and he remembers that Joe was equally shaken up by the news.

* * *

Sax player and singer Paddy Cole became a friend of Joe, after their first meeting in the Ierne Ballroom on Dublin's Parnell Square as hot young men back in the 1960s. Paddy, then with the Capitol Showband, turned up out of curiosity to see the new singing sensation from Mullingar that everybody was raving about. 'I loved him straight away,' Paddy recalls. 'I loved his unique voice and what a worker he was on stage. I saw that straight away, from the word go.'

Paddy went backstage that night to meet Joe, and this would be the start of a friendship that grew in depth and strength over the decades that followed. Both young men came from the country and they had an instant bond through their passion for music and life on the road in a band. 'We hit it off, and we became great friends,' Paddy says. 'Subsequently, if The Drifters were playing somewhere in the country and we were close, we'd meet up. And invariably a few scoops would happen and we'd be there till all hours. I remember we were playing one night in Longford and Joe, Ben and the boys were off, so they came to see us. Afterwards, we went back to Joe's place in Mullingar and we were there till eight or nine the next morning.'

As they chatted in the early days, Joe would discover that Paddy was from a poor background, similar to his own experiences. He had grown up in Castleblaney, County Monaghan, the son of a part-time musician who worked in the Post Office, driving the mail van.

'Where did you learn the sax?' Joe asked.

'Me father,' Paddy replied. 'On wet days he used to teach me to play it. Then he'd give me pieces to learn when I came home from school and I'd have to play them for him when he came in that evening. I used to hate it because I'd hear the other boys playing football outside and I wanted to be out having fun.'

Joe laughed, telling Paddy about his own lessons with Molly Carroll.

'Then suddenly I started to like the music when I learned to play the sax,' Paddy said. Joe was amazed to hear that Paddy was allowed to join a local group, the Maurice Lynch Band, and go off on tours of England and the north of Scotland during his school holidays at the age of fifteen.

'Did you ever do any real work?' Joe laughed, as he recalled his own days cutting the turf and picking potatoes.

'Oh, I did plenty of that,' Paddy assured him. 'When I came home from school in the evenings I'd do whatever bit of homework and then go off to serve in the local garage till all hours that night; or we'd go to the Black Island, a wooded area beside us, where we gathered firewood for the fire.'

As his schooldays came to an end, Paddy got the offer of a job working in the local McElroy's Furniture Factory.

'What was that like?' Joe asked.

'I haven't a clue, Joe, as I didn't take it,' Paddy laughed. 'It was ten shillings a week, but at the time I could go and play with Maurice Lynch for the night and get fifteen shillings. So I started doing my sums and staying with the band was a no brainer. Then I got the offer from the Capitol Showband.'

* * *

Tall, slim, amiable Val Sheehan was on his way to becoming one of Ireland's best-known fashion photographers in later life with the *Sunday World* when he met Joe as The Drifters' fame was spreading around the country.

Dubliner Doreen McCormack, a sister of Val's best friend, Oliver, was dating the band's manager Seamus Casey. It was the story of Irish life: throw a stone and you'll hit someone connected to somebody you know. Seamus got to know Val through his girlfriend and he was impressed with the work of the unassuming, but brilliant, young Dublin photographer.

Seamus engaged Val to shoot a series of publicity pictures, which would be handed out to fans at the dances and used on posters, to promote the shows. Large posters were printed up with a photograph of Joe and The Drifters and a blank space at the bottom for the local promoter to write in the date of the band's next appearance at his venue.

Joe, bubbly and full of fun, was like a bold child at the photo sessions. 'He didn't display any signs of vanity or petulance, but he took a childish delight in disrupting my attempts to organise the group in various poses,' Val recalls. Joe would pass a hilarious remark at a crucial moment as the stressed, curly-haired photographer was about to capture their image and this would cause the line-up to collapse amid fits of laughter. 'Ah, behave Joe,' Val pleaded time and again. 'Posing for photographs wasn't one of Joe's favourite parts of life in the world of showbusiness. He hated the idea of just standing around for a camera. He liked to be doing something,' Val says.

One of Val's most sought-after pictures by the fans was a single shot of Joe, which was signed by the heart-throb. Thousands of copies were printed and Joe's female admirers went wild for them when they were distributed after his shows in the country's ballrooms and hotels.

As Joe and The Drifters were creating hysteria at dances all over Ireland, Seamus Casey had a novel idea; he was going to fuel the popularity of the band even more, and ensure that they would become the Number-One attraction, by taking out a series of adverts in the national newspapers informing every child, mammy and granny on the entire island that there was now a phenomenon known as 'Driftermania'. By this stage, 'Beatlemania' in Britain was like an out-of-control wildfire. Professional photographer Sheehan was hired by Seamus to capture this new Drifters' craze in a series of dramatic shots taken from the wings at Joe's live performaces.

* * *

Val remembers directing Joe from the side of the stage one night, beckoning him to move closer to the edge, where besotted women were surging forward and thrusting their hands in the air, to catch his eye. In the flash of a camera, Joe went flying into the crowd after his leg had been tugged by overzealous women. 'He was being dragged along the surface of the audience and across a sea of heads with hands grasping wildly at him from all quarters,' the photographer remembers.

Ben was shocked: 'I got a fright when I saw Joe plunge from the stage. It seemed to happen in slow motion, like you experience in a car crash.' Protecting his saxophone with his left hand, Ben swooped down, grabbed his brother by the ankle and tried to pull him back to the safety of the band in a tug of war with the frantic crowd.

Joe let out a scream as clumps of hair were pulled from his head by young women caught up in a moment of madness. Ben now swiftly off-loaded his sax and went in to rescue Joe with all his might. As his camera fired off round after round of flashes, Val Sheehan couldn't stop smiling at the side of the stage. This was great stuff, exactly what he had wanted. The images were precisely what Seamus had painted when he outlined his plan to Shee-han. If this had been a scene rolling out in a movie, it could not have been more perfect. It vividly captured the astonishing drama Joe was creating in the ballrooms of Ireland.

After the show, Joe was shaken and his stage clothes looked liked they had been attacked by a pride of lions. 'Jaysus, Sheehan, you nearly got me killed out there,' he puffed, knocking back a bottle of fizzy orange.

Val laughed. 'It was nothing to do with me; you were the eejit who let them pull you off the stage.'

Joe gave a wry smile. 'I suppose it serves me right after all the hardship I've given you.'

Val was buzzing with excitement as he checked the rolls of film and care-fully stored them in his camera bag. 'As soon as I get them developed, these photographs will definitely make it into all the newspapers,' he said confi-dently.

'Never mind the photographs, I nearly made it into the obituary column out there tonight,' Joe quipped, as he examined his sore scalp in a mirror.

When the national papers appeared on the news-stands, the shocking scenes of Joe Dolan being mobbed by a wild crowd was front-page news. Above the sensational pictures were headlines declaring the incident to be the result of … 'Driftermania'!

* * *

Tommy Swarbrigg remembers every night in the ballrooms being cha-otic during those heady days in the sixties. 'The women were stone mad about Joe,' he says. 'They would scream their heads off through the entire show. I remember, in ballrooms like The Arcadia in Cork, you literally couldn't hear the band over the sound of the screams. I'm not kidding you, it was like The Beatles. Every night wherever we played around the country, there were hundreds of people at the front of the stage. Half the crowd would be looking at the show and behind them the other half would be dancing. Everywhere we played was stuffed. Anytime we played The Arcadia in Bray (County Wicklow) there would be 3,500 people. The place would be heaving and you'd have people on the balconies watching the show. We'd have over 4,000 people on Stephen's Night in the Jetland, Limerick. And we would be playing Limerick six or more times in the year. A bad crowd would be if you dipped under 2,000 people in a ballroom like the Dreamland in Athy (County Kildare). You'd be saying, "We're slipping." We played five nights a week, fifty weeks a year with a two-week break in May. It was an incredible time.'

*　　*　　*

Joe's second single, 'I Love You More And More Every Day', hit the shops in February, 1965. The release made it to Number Three in the charts. It was the highest entry for Joe and The Drifters and it confirmed their soaring popularity. As they worked towards capitalising on the momentum, they booked the Eamonn Andrews' Studios in Dublin's Henry Street that summer, to follow up this hit with another song called 'My Own Peculiar Way'.

The band was still being shadowed by photographer Val Sheehan who joined Joe and the boys in the studio. 'As the song was being recorded, Joe encouraged me to clap in the background, to add to the sound effects,' Val remembers. During a break in the recording, Val was anxious to capture some new images of Joe. He directed the star of The Drifters to hang out of the studio's open top-storey window as he shot some portraits using a flash.

'The flashing of the camera attracted the attention of people down below on the street,' he recalls. Soon the word spread like sand in a desert storm that Joe Dolan was in the building. 'Within an hour, the street was thronged with giggling young women, hoping to catch a glimpse of the singing star from Mullingar,' Val says.

'Jaysus, Sheehan, look what you've started,' Joe quipped as he stuck his head out the window to the sound of wild cheering and screaming on the street below.

'It's not me that has caused that … it's *you*,' Val pointed out.

Val was excited. 'With Joe trapped in the building, a big scene was beginning to build up,' he recalls. 'The drama that was starting to unfold was a powder keg that could go off at any time, with the potential for more front-page headlines.' Val put a new roll of film in a second camera as he prepared for what was certain to be a turbulent exit from the studios. 'The pictures were already flicking through my mind … Joe being mobbed in the most amazing scenes ever. I was imagining them on the front pages of the national newspapers as we prepared to leave the building,' Val reveals.

'Ah, it'll be grand,' Joe said when one of the band warned him to be careful going into the crowd as he made his way down the stairs to the street. There, his manager, Seamus, was anxiously waiting to collect him in his car.

'The huge commotion on Henry Street had by this point attracted the guards,' Val recalls. They were now mingling with the crowd. Someone had told them that Joe Dolan was coming out of the building. There was a deafening roar from the women and for a split second Joe was visible before he disappeared in the melee. Val was shooting wildly with his camera, having now lost sight of Joe. The guards gained control and started to clear a path for the car. As Val scanned the scene, he discovered that Joe had made it safely into the vehicle. Suddenly there was another surge from the crowd and the car was being rocked from side to side. Val could see the front-page picture of the overturned car flashing in his mind. This was going to be sensational. The guards gained control again and Joe was whisked away, with Seamus maintaining his composure behind the wheel of the car as it snaked towards O'Connell Street.

Shaking with excitement, Val Sheehan slipped away en route to a dark room to process his photographs. The following evening his dramatic shots were splashed across the front pages of both the *Evening Herald* and *Evening Press*.

'That went well,' Val laughed, as he later discussed the incident with Joe.

'Jaysus, that's easy for you to say,' Joe wheezed. 'You were the ferret ... I was the bloody rabbit.'

* * *

In 1965, Brendan Bowyer and The Royal Showband were still pipping The Drifters as Ireland's top band when Joe and the boys left the country, to play in the London ballrooms. As Joe wandered through arrivals shortly after landing on English soil, he heard a familiar voice calling his name. He swung around, to find a smiling Brendan Bowyer waving at him. As coincidence would have it, The Royal Showband was also in town.

Both bands sauntered outside as they exchanged friendly banter. Joe noticed that Brendan and the rest of the Royals had a luxury, state-of-the-art tour coach purring by the footpath, waiting to pick them up for the journey into the city. There was no sign of any transport for The Drifters. Noticing that Joe, Ben and the boys seemed to be stranded, Bowyer generously offered them a lift in their coach.

'Ah, Jaysus, thanks, Brendan, sure we have a bus coming to pick us up,' Joe told him.

'See you around, then,' Bowyer said, with a friendly wave, as he boarded The Royal Showband's impressive mode of transport.

'An hour later, myself, Joe and the lads were still sitting on our band gear outside the building, feeling tired, cranky and dejected,' Ben remembers.

'Someone has really messed up here,' Joe sighed, as he got set to haul their equipment to a train.

'I hope Bowyer and the Royals don't spot us,' Ben added. 'It would be shockin' embarrassing.'

Joe cheered up. 'Ah sure we'll tell them the train was the "Drifters' Express",' he joked.

When The Drifters eventually reached their accommodation in Camden, there was another shock in store. Just two rooms had been booked for the entire crew. 'We should have stayed at home, this trip could be a disaster yet,' Joe said as he realised he was going to be sharing a tiny room with four of the lads. 'I wonder does anyone even know we're playing in this feckin' city tonight?'

* * *

Stories in the Irish newspapers painted amazing pictures of drama and hysteria at the packed London shows, where besotted and overexcited female fans mobbed Joe and The Drifters. News of Joe's success outside Ireland now added more fuel to The Drifters' popularity back home, where they were touring relentlessly to keep up with an ever-increasing demand for the band to play dances.

Ben's pal Sean Connolly was now back in the fold, working with Seamus Casey in the hectic Drifters' office. Although he had remained on good terms with Joe after being dropped from the band, Sean refused to speak to Ben, waving him away with the back of his hand whenever they encountered each other on the streets of Mullingar. Ben was devastated.

Two years later, Seamus, Ben and Joe decided to launch and manage a Mullingar-based pop band, which they called Popcorn. Ben seized the chance to get back on the right side of his old friend, Sean Connolly, by offering him the job as their driver and general minder. Time had healed the wound, and Sean leapt at the opportunity. When Popcorn ultimately flopped, Sean was retained in the office, to man the phone that rang non-stop with offers of dance-hall gigs for Joe and the band.

'Jaysus, Seamus, are you throwing darts at the map of Ireland?' Joe joked when he saw their list of dates for the coming months that would see them zig-zagging across the country.

Jimmy Horan recalls that The Drifters always brought an accordion with them during the early days. 'You had to use all the pianos in the halls at that time and some of them were so bad and out of tune that we'd introduce the accordion instead,' he reveals. 'The equipment was very basic. You'd get out of the van, carry the two speakers in, roll the wires out of the back and plug them into an amp. When we played the marquee dances in the summer, they used to have fridges at the back for selling ice-cream and the minute they plugged them in the sound would go down. There was always a row to get them to plug out the fridge.'

Joe lived for the stage, but he didn't relish the long, tedious hours travelling on bad roads in a bus, to sing in ballrooms tucked away in every corner of rural Ireland in the 1960s. To break the monotony of the journey, he read comics and played cards with Ben and the rest of the band. Poker, Old Maid and 25 were favourite card games in the back of the wagon as they rattled along country roads.

Tommy Swarbrigg recalls Joe being a passionate poker player. 'I was in serious poker schools around Mullingar with Joe, Sid Aughey and a few local people, including a great character called Frank 'Twiggy' Daly, in those days of the mid-sixties,' Tommy reveals. 'We'd get embroiled in poker and you wouldn't leave till six or seven in the morning. We played in different houses, including Joe's flat in Mullingar at the time. Money would be changing hands, so you'd have to have your wits about you. Joe was a good poker player, but probably the best poker player in the band was

Des Doherty. It used to kill time on the bus when you'd be travelling for a long time and bored to tears. In the early days, before he got a car, Joe was always on the bus and he was great craic.'

As well as cards, Ben would host a 'Yes or No' sudden-death quiz to break the monotony of the journey.

'Tommy Swarbrigg first came to Mullingar on a Tuesday. Yes or No, Joe?' Ben asked one time.

'How the feck would I know what day he first came to Mullingar, sure Swarbrigg probably doesn't know himself!' Joe complained.

'Yes or No?' Ben pressed him.

'No,' Joe replied.

'Yes was the answer; you're out!'

'Ah, would you get away with yourself? Sure, how would you remember that it was a Tuesday?'

Ben reveals that the in-bus entertainment on bone-shaking journeys along by-roads moved to a different level when two of The Drifters, Dessie Doherty and Sid Aughey, bought a newfangled invention called a cassette recorder. 'This was a real novelty at the time, as few people possessed one,' Ben recalls. 'Like children with a Christmas toy, the two boys threw coats over their heads at the back of the bus and made hilarious recordings of their commentaries on imaginary football and hurling matches. Then they played them back for the amusement of all on board the wagon. And they'd recite their own poetry which was always very funny. Joe loved it.'

Jimmy Horan remembers that Dessie and Sid were 'our Laurel and Hardy; they were a class act.'

Even funnier was their mimicking of Frankie Byrne, Radio Éireann's famous agony aunt of the time. The husky-voiced broadcaster's 'Dear Frankie' radio show, with its mix of letters, pouring out listeners' personal problems, and its music, featuring the songs of Frank Sinatra, was hugely popular. It was sponsored by Jacobs, who Frankie would declare were 'the people who bake better biscuits better every day.'

Letters from Frankie's worried listeners included queries like: 'Dear Frankie, I've been going out with this guy for eighteen months. Last night at the pictures he put his hand on my knee. Now I'm really worried that I might be pregnant.' Ben laughs as he recalls how the lads in The Drifters had Joe rolling around the bus in fits of laughter with their send-up of those 'Dear Frankie' letters, when they played back their own versions on the cassette player. 'Joe would say, "Ah, lads, I have a pain in me jaw!" Oh, it was hugely enjoyable relief from the boredom of the journeys,' Ben says.

* * *

The Drifters often met other big bands on the road and would stop to chat. Among them were Joe and Ben's early heroes, The Clipper Carlton, who had started the whole showband craze in the 1950s when they became a stand-up band, breaking with the tradition of the sitting musicians in the orchestras and big bands. The Clippers also had a 'Jukebox Saturday Night' set in their show in which they dressed up and impersonated big stars from Elvis Presley to Nat King Cole. Joe had loved them when he eventually got to see them in his teenage years, after his first failed attempt at the County Hall.

'They were big stars to us and the whole country was in awe of them at the start because they were fantastic,' Ben recalls. 'But by the time we got to know The Clippers on the road we were doing fairly well. It was easier for Joe and the rest of us to talk to them, at that stage, because we were getting more confident. I remember meeting them one time and asking one of the guys, Fergie O'Hagan, "How are things going, Fergie?" He put his hand in his pocket and took out a pound note; then in his lovely velvet voice he sang, "We've had our ups–and–downs like all showbands do, but you know in your heart that we worship you." I thought it was hilarious. He was referring to the money."

*　*　*

Joe and The Drifters also passed their down time in the build-up to shows by playing practical jokes on each other. Ben reveals that this shifted to a dangerous level when they were on tour in Northern Ireland and discovered a selection of fireworks on sale in local shops. 'Among the explosives on offer was one called a "Jumping Johnny". When lit, it let off several loud bangs as it exploded while hopping along the ground,' Ben remembers.

'I eventually banned the fireworks after a series of incidents, including band members and road crew having holes blown in their pockets.' The fireworks had been ignited and then dropped into the jacket pocket of the unsuspecting victims by various band members. On other occasions, they were rolled under the doors of cubicles when a fellow Drifter was busy on the loo.

'That's feckin' the end of that, now, lads,' Ben declared one night after a prank back-fired, in spectacular fashion, at a country dance hall. One of The Drifters, thinking his band mate was in the toilet cubicle, lit a 'Jumping Johnny' and threw it under the door. As it exploded, he heard a scream and a man, with a look of terror on his face and his trousers around his ankles, came hopping out of the cubicle like a frog on a hot range. Instead of being confronted by one of his pals, the startled Drifter discovered that he had just terrorised the caretaker of the dance hall.

Joe thought it was an hilarious story when told of the incident, and he struggled to keep a straight face as he apologised to the poor victim on behalf of the band. Later in the dressing room, he couldn't control his laughing while putting on his gear for the show. Tears were still running down his cheeks as he went on stage.

*　*　*

Paddy Dolan's wife, Caroline, ran their early fan club. 'Mammy was their biggest fan,' Kathleen says. 'She used to go absolutely mad when The Beatles would have a song out. They would always have one out at the same time as Joe and she'd be giving out, "Oh, Janey, I hope they don't go to Number One."'

Joe was devastated, in 1974, when Caroline died after a long battle with throat cancer. She was just forty-eight-years-old. 'Joe took it very badly because Mammy had been like a mother to him and he doted on her,' Kathleen says.

* * *

Despite being superstars around Ireland in the sixties, Joe and The Drifters led a modest lifestyle, according to Jimmy Horan. 'When I look back, we'd be on television and on the radio and we'd play somewhere like Bray on a Saturday night to 3,500 people and come home. The next day I'd get a knock on door around noon and it would be Tommy Swarbrigg and Joey Gilheaney, who lived around the corner, calling for me to go to Mass. Joe would call later and we'd go off with the band, to play somewhere else. Monday was our day off and on Monday night we'd go to the pictures. Joe was doing a steady line at the time with a local girl. The boys would come back to my house and we'd listen to a few records. We always had a practice on a Tuesday morning up in the Horizon ballroom. That's all we did. Smaller bands were going up to Dublin and living it up in the night clubs.'

* * *

As a teenager, RTÉ's 'Risin' Time' radio presenter, Maxi, sang backing vocals in the Eamonn Andrews' Studios, in Dublin's Harcourt Street, where she remembers Joe being among the major recording artists in the late sixties. Back then, Maxi was ecstatic when she realised every fan's dream of meeting her idol, Joe Dolan, in the flesh. Later, when she got the opportunity to work with the heart-throb, it was the icing on the cake.

As Maxi tells it, she was hooked from the moment one of Joe's songs caught her attention on the radio at her family home in Dublin's Harold's Cross during her schooldays. It was Joe's voice that stopped her in her tracks from the first second she heard it. 'That happens once, twice or three times in a lifetime,' she reflects today.

Joe's 1965 single, 'My Own Peculiar Way', was the very first pop record that Maxi ever bought. 'It was six shillings and eight pence and I worked so hard to save the money for it,' she remembers. Maxi recalls buying it in Dublin city centre and grasping it like a precious jewel in her hand on the bus home. The journey seemed to go on for an eternity that memorable afternoon. She just could not wait to reach her destination so that she could play the single in the comfort of her neat family sitting room. At home, Maxi put 'My Own Peculiar Way' on repeat on the record player. She played it non-stop, day and night, until eventually it began to annoy the other family members. 'It got to the stage where my mother nearly threw me out of the house, even though she loved the song herself,' she laughs.

The power of the voice that Joe possessed had Maxi in a spell, even at that young age. 'It really was uplifting; no matter what problems you had, you were in a nicer place when you heard that voice,' she says.

In her teens, Maxi was in the Young Dublin Singers choir, doing summer shows and pantos, when Eamonn Andrews arrived in to the Gaiety Theatre one day to hold auditions for three young female backing vocalists. He wanted them to sing on the records that were being recorded in his studios. The three 'voices' chosen were Irene McCoubrey (Maxi), Barbara Dixon (Dick) and Adele King (Twink).

The trio, Maxi, Dick and Twink, were now schoolgirls by day and recording artists in the evening. Maxi recalls how she would jump on her bike from school and frantically cycle up to Harcourt Street, to do her backing vocals. Then she would get back up on her bicycle for the journey home, where she buried her head in her school books for the rest of the evening.

'Every showband in the country was then making a record in the Eamon Andrews' Studios and it was an amazing time meeting and working with all of them,' she recalls.

One evening, out of the blue, her favourite pop idol walked through the door and Maxi got her teenage thrill. 'We were doing backing vocals when in walked the lovely Joe and I went, "Aaaahh!" I was sixteen or seventeen at the time. I'd had the audio for years and now I had the visual, so that was the extra joy.'

Maxi, whose mother came from Crossmolina, County Mayo, and father from Saintfield, County Down, then started performing around the country with her co-singers, Dick and Twink, while still in school. 'We'd arrive home and get the grease paint and lipstick off just in time for school in the morning. Travelling around the country was a big deal in those times and before starting out on the journey, you'd be asking what stops were going to be made along the way. There were no late-night garages then. I think the only twenty-four-hour garage in the country at that time was outside Kinnegad on the Athlone road.'

Maxi's mother, a schoolteacher, was supportive. Mrs McCoubrey and her husband both loved music – she played the piano and he was a violinist – and she told her daughter: 'You can do the performing and the school as long as you do both well. But if your school work suffers, then the music has to go.' Maxi was determined to prove she could do both, and she did. 'I was always wrecked but happy,' she recalls.

CHAPTER 9

BELVEDERE HOUSE AND 'TOP OF THE POPS'

P hotographer Val Sheehan recalls how Joe was on his best behaviour the day in 1968 that he posed for a special photograph with The Drifters. The shoot, with Val behind the camera, would adorn the cover of the band's first album, *The Answer To Everything.* And the setting was the magnificent Belvedere estate, nestling on the shores of Lough Ennell outside Mullingar.

Joe was a personal friend of the then owner, Rex Beaumont, a colourful, dapper and very entertaining raconteur who had offered the run of the estate to The Drifters for this landmark event in their career. 'Rex was a well-known character around town at that time,' Ben recalls. 'He had been an actor at one time, so he loved anybody in showbusiness and he got to know us.'

Val says he noticed that Joe, who would usually be acting the maggot during photo shoots, was very serious and focused on this occasion. It was obvious that the lead singer with The Drifters regarded the imminent release of the band's debut LP as an exciting and major moment in his career. 'In fact, it was set to be the first album of its kind ever to be released by an Irish band,' Val reveals.

'As I wandered through Belvedere House and its beautiful grounds looking for suitable backdrops for the pictures, Joe remarked how it was eerie that a building of such beauty had been created by a man who would tarnish it with his terrible deeds.'

Val remembers Joe then telling him an intriguing story of how the original owner, Robert Rochford, who built the house in 1740, using the architect who had designed Leinster House in Dublin, had become known as 'The Evil Earl'. Consumed with jealousy, Rochford had accused his wife, Mary, of having an affair with his brother, Arthur. Despite Mary's vehement denial of an illicit relationship, Rochford put the mother of his five children on trial for adultery and then had her locked away after a conviction. Mary was banished to another family home, Gaulstown House, where she would spend the next thirty-one years mostly in solitary confinement. Meanwhile, the Earl had Arthur arrested and sent to a Dublin prison where he remained in a tortured existence until his eventual death.

Joe said there were shocking tales of how Mary would sometimes be let out of her room to walk the corridors of Gaulstown House, and staff would find the haunted woman talking to the portraits on the walls.

As he related the estate's history, Joe stopped and then pointed to an old ruin in the grounds. 'That's "The Jealous Wall",' he told Val. Bitter and twisted Rochford had become insanely jealous of another brother George's home at nearby Tudenham. He then built a massive structure, which became known as The Jealous Wall, to block Tudenham from the view at Belvedere. Designed as a ruin, the Earl would pass the wall off to his visitors as the remains of the original house at Belvedere.

'Do you know what became of the Earl?' Val asked.

'He seems to have met a grisly end,' Joe said. 'Some say he was murdered; others claim that he was attacked by wild dogs while out walking at night and that he bled to death. But who knows, sure a fella like that would have no shortage of enemies.'

Val wondered what happened to the Earl's tragic wife, Mary. Joe revealed that she was still alive when her evil husband was taken in death and she was then freed from Gaulstown House by her son, George, who became the second Earl of Belvedere. After a period of recuperation with her daughter, Jane, Joe said that Mary then went to France where she is rumoured to have spent the remainder of her life as a nun.

Despite the unsavoury backstory of the estate's original owner, Joe had insisted on doing the shoot in Belvedere House, telling Val that he wanted the album cover to have a familiar connection with Mullingar. The more benign occupant of the time, Rex Beaumont, who had inherited Belvedere from a male companion, hovered in the background watching the photo session unfold as Ben and the band posed in smart, casual clothes on the grand terraces. Belvedere's fun-loving owner Beaumont was delighted that Joe, Ben and the band were sprinkling his sprawling historic estate with a little bit of modern showbusiness glamour.

*   *   *

The Answer To Everything was a hugely popular album with fans of Joe and The Drifters. It found its way into nearly every Irish home that possessed a record player. But behind the scenes, conflict was brewing in the band. Some might say that the wicked Earl of Belvedere put a curse on them for invading his territory as they were now on the verge of a bitter split shortly after their official photo shoot in the house. In reality, a row over the divying up of earnings among the band members had been simmering for some time.

It came to a head at the Dun Mhuire Hall in Wexford in July, 1968. Joe stayed out of it, leaving all the band's business dealings to his brother, Ben. It was Ben, after all, who had led the way by forming the band in the first place. Ben had always taken care of the business side of running a band. That suited Joe, who was happy to concentrate on the music and who loved being out in the spotlight as the lead singer. Ben was angry and disappointed that the rest of the band were now insisting on the takings being split evenly between every single individual in the outfit. 'Jaysus, lads, whatever about my share, Joe has to be on a bigger share,' Ben argued.

'Joe sat quietly reading a comic in a corner of the room, before a dance, as the row escalated between me and the lads,' Ben reveals. Neither side was willing to concede an inch on the issue of money. Harsh words were exchanged. Ben was angry when someone suggested that he was now too old to be in the band anyway. At this point, his confidence took a blow and he began to doubt himself. Ben could see that the other musicians were not going to back down. They were determined that they would quit unless he acceded to their demands.

'I decided to cool off and have a private consultation with Joe. "What do you want to do?" I asked him,' Ben recalls. He said, "You're the boss as far as I'm concerned; whatever you want to do is fine by me." Then I asked him, "Will you stay with me if they leave?" I wanted to be sure where we stood.'

'Of course I'll stay with you,' Joe responded, in a tone indicating his surprise that the question had to be asked.

'Right!' Ben said as he returned to continue his negotiations with the band, now bursting with the confidence of Joe's support.

When Ben held firm on the existing financial situation and refused point blank on an equal share for every man, the musicians announced that they were quitting.

News of the shock split caused a sensation and made the front pages of every national newspaper when it was announced. Joe and The Drifters would go on play three more dates before their final night in Castlerea.

The *Evening Press* reported on 3 July how:

'The Drifters Showband from Mullingar have broken up after five members quit, leaving lead singer Joe Dolan, along with his brother, Ben, the band leader, and Seamus Casey, their manager. The bombshell came after the band had played at a dance in Mallow last night. Joe Dolan and The Drifters have been one of Ireland's top three bands for the past five years.'

Radio Éireann also broadcast the big showband break-up to the nation. Women were in tears in every town and village around the country as the devastating news filtered through to them. The distraught fans feared that they had lost their idol, Joe Dolan, forever. Overnight, some of the colour had gone out of their lives.

In the immediate aftermath of the split, Joe and Ben also worked through a myriad of emotions. Joe had enjoyed an incredible journey with The Drifters as they rose from obscurity to become the biggest band in Ireland. As he reflected on their life up to that point, Joe recalled all the fun they'd had as a gang.

There was the moment in 1966 when The Drifters heard that they had gone to Number One in Ireland for the first time with their single, 'Pretty Brown Eyes'. That was a memorable occasion for another special reason, as it was the same day that their manager, Seamus Casey, and his beautiful fiancée, Doreen McCormack, walked down the aisle as man and wife.

When Larry Gogan announced on the radio that same evening that Joe Dolan and The Drifters had knocked The Beatles' 'Yellow Submarine' off the top spot, Seamus and Doreen had already left the reception and were at the airport waiting to fly off on their honeymoon.

Val Sheehan recalls how the radio was turned on at the reception to listen to the charts that day. 'I remember the day well and it was a great day. It was a Monday because band weddings were always on a Monday as that was the day bands were off. The reception then stopped to listen to Larry

Gogan and there was huge excitement and cheering when Joe and The Drifters were announced at Number One in the charts,' Val reveals.

A thrilled Joe rounded up the band and assorted friends and they sped off in a convoy of cars from the shindig at Dublin's Crofton Hotel, hoping to catch the happy newly-weds, to break the sensational news to them before they left the country. 'I remember helping Joe to get to the airport because he'd had a lot of champagne,' Val laughs at the recollection.

Seamus Casey today reveals that he had heard through the grapevine that Joe and The Drifters were going to be Number One and the couple decided to leave the wedding reception before the celebrations.

'I had no idea they were going to follow us out to the airport,' Seamus says. 'Doreen's brother, Oliver, drove us out as we were heading off to Majorca on our honeymoon. We were just sitting inside the old Dublin Airport building when suddenly the door opened and in burst Joe and Ben and Jimmy Horan and all the lads. They all came out. There was champagne being sprayed around the place and the next thing Doreen and myself were being raised shoulder high.'

Onlookers in the airport building watched with amusement as the boisterous crew from Mullingar carried the just-married husband and wife around the building, whooping and cheering as they celebrated Seamus's success in steering Joe and The Drifters to the top of the charts.

'I was never as embarrassed,' Seamus admits today. 'Doreen was mortified too. We weren't drinking at that time, so we were sober as well which didn't help.'

As he looked back on his days with The Drifters, Joe also reflected on how the band had enjoyed a rollercoaster ride around Ireland, Britain and even America while their popularity spread far and wide in just a few years. One US jaunt with The Drifters, during Lent in 1967, had taken them from Las Vegas to San Francisco and Nashville to New York. While wandering along Seventh Avenue in New York's midtown Manhattan on that trip, Joe stopped outside Carnegie Hall, to admire the iconic venue.

'Jaysus, Ben, Molly Carroll was right,' he said.

'What do you mean?'

'Molly said that one day, if I practised on that bloody piano, I'd get to Carnegie Hall,' he laughed.

As the brothers reminisced about the good old times in the cold light of their split with The Drifters, there was sadness and regret that a wonderful era in the band had come to an end. But Joe was excited too. 'The future is always better than the past,' he remarked to Ben.

Joe's former band, The Drifters, would go on to enjoy huge success in Ireland with their new group called The Times, which was fronted by Tommy Swarbrigg and his brother, Jimmy. The original Drifters Sid Aughey, Des Doherty, Joey Gilheaney and Jimmy Horan were joined by newcomers Sean Kenny on guitar and sax player Gene Bannon. 'The Times had phenomenal success and a huge following right from the start and we would continue working together up to 1976,' Tommy reveals.

'Looking back on my time with Joe, I couldn't say a bad word about the man. I never had a cross word with him and any time we met after the break-up of The Drifters he was always extremely friendly. I really admired Joe and loved him. I had huge respect for his abilities and his range as a singer. His talent was unique. One unforgettable memory I have is of Joe singing 'Silent Night' at Christmas shows in the Ulster Hall, Belfast. Jim Aiken used to promote it and I remember leaving my home on many a snowy Christmas night and heading for Belfast. There would be 2,500 people at the show. During the night, Joe would step forward and completely unaccompanied he'd sing 'Silent Night' and you could hear a pin drop in that formidable concert hall. He would have to sing it three times on the night because the crowd wouldn't stop clapping. It was incredible.

'I worked closely with Joe in the early days of The Drifters because I was a songwriter and he sang and recorded my songs. I'll never forget one time we were at a party and he came over and sat down beside me and said, "I love your contribution to the band." I grew another six foot that night. Joe made you feel good. My songwriting began when I joined The Drifters and was living in digs in Mullingar. The couple who owned the house, Joe and Josie Reid, were great people and they had a piano. That's when I started teaching myself the piano and the songwriting started immediately.'

After Joe and Ben parted company with The Drifters, Tommy would go on to co-write with his brother, Jimmy, and the pair penned and performed two Irish entries in the Eurovision Song Contest: 'That's What Friends Are For' in 1975, and 'It's Nice To Be In Love Again', which they sang as The Swarbriggs Plus Two, with Nicola Kerr and Alma Carroll, in 1977. It was Joe who had encouraged his songwriting and arranging. 'I started writing these songs and playing them for Joe when I joined The Drifters and he'd say, "Oh, I like that." Now, God love him, the first couple were certainly horrors. But one ballad I wrote for him was called 'I Know It's Over' and he loved it and sang it for many years in the programme. Another one he liked was 'The Wrong Impression'. He was mad into me writing original stuff and he encouraged me like hell. He had an eye on being different and doing original material.

'In 2004, I was in France on a skiing holiday and one night when I sat down to dinner I heard a familiar voice singing in the background and begod wasn't it a CD of Joe Dolan. I went over to look at the album and it was B-sides and lesser-known album tracks and most of them were my songs that Joe had recorded. I never even knew the album existed and he probably didn't know either. There were songs like, 'When You Say I Love You', 'The Wrong Impression', 'I'll Sit On Your Doorstep', 'I Know It's Over' and 'The Work Day Blues'. My biggest regret is that I didn't nick the damn album out of the place because I was never able to trace it when I got home.'

Tommy was in awe of Joe's talent as a singer. 'I used to push him, musically, and get him to do Roy Orbison stuff. He would do a phenomenal job on songs like, 'It's Over' and 'Cryin''; his voice would soar into the heavens. He was so good, in fact, and had such a range that he would be singing it higher than Orbison did. Whenever Orbison brought out a ballad I would immediately get it and copy it and bring it into the band. Joe would lash into it and do a fantastic job. I remember Joe rehearsing one of those Orbison songs in The Royal Hotel in Athlone one afternoon and that night the packed ballroom coming to a standstill listening to him singing it.

'People sometimes forget that Joe was also the lead guitar player in the band during his days with The Drifters. We used to do all The Shadows' hits and he'd play them, instrumentals like 'Foot Tapper' and 'Apache', and he was bloody good. During Lent, when there were no dances, we used to make up shows and go around cinemas with them. They were concerts and we'd have a Shadows set and a Clancy Brothers section and Irish ballads. We'd play places like The Hibernian Cinema in Mullingar and in Castlerea. Joe loved doing those shows.'

Tommy remembers Joe as a man who possessed the indefinable 'X Factor' and it drew people to him. 'Joe attracted people like a magnet,' Tommy says. 'When I joined The Drifters I was only a kid and after a show you'd be changing in a dressing room. I'd be in one corner, Jimmy Horan in another and there would be a crowd around Joe in the same dressing room. They used to inveigle their way into the back room to meet him. If we walked into a bar they would surround him. He was one of those charismatic characters.

'During our time in The Drifters, we all used to go on holidays together in the summer, including Joe. It might seem odd that we didn't take a break from each other, but that's the way it was. I vividly remember one time how all the staff of the hotel where we had stayed in Spain came out to wave us off at the end of one holiday; and I mean the entire staff! In reality, they were actually waving Joe off because he had made such an impression on them with his charm and his good nature. All through the holiday you'd hear them saying, "Oh Joe! We love Joe." It was an amazing sight, all the staff of this magnificent hotel in Torremolinos out on the steps waving us off. They were just mad about Joe. Whatever he had, people loved him. He was great craic, always upbeat and lively and always one for the jokes. I can't personally remember Joe Dolan ever being in grumpy form during my time with him.'

As he reflects on the days of The Drifters, Seamus Casey portrays them as a tight-knit bunch who fought, made-up and soldiered happily together throughout their early years. 'There were various rows about music, even between Joe, Ben and myself,' Seamus reveals. 'In those days, Joe always thought that Ben and I were plotting against him. Ben and myself were into country music, whereas Joe was a rock 'n' roll person. I used to get country songs for Ben to sing in the band. Eventually I persuaded Joe to record a country single himself. It was a cover of the George Jones' song, "Aching Breaking Heart", and it didn't go that well for Joe. We were drinking one night and Joe said, "If you ever bring a George Jones' song to me again you can stick it where the sun don't shine. I don't want to know anything about country music." He used to go bananas about it. But The Drifters was a great period. Every Monday night we all drank together on our night off. We all went on holidays together; it was part of the world we lived in. That went on till '68 when the band split up.'

Jimmy Horan didn't regard the break-up of The Drifters as being a major upset for the band members at the time. 'Lots of bands broke up, The Royal and The Miami, so it was the norm in those days,' he reflects today. 'And it didn't make any difference in the sixties because when you put a new band on the road with a different singer you were playing five or six nights a week again. The business was there and then all you had to do was bring out a record. Our single, "Looking Through The Eyes Of A Beautiful Girl", was a hit pick on Radio Luxembourg and it stayed in the charts that long it was embarrassing.'

Des 'The Doc' Doherty and Jimmy Horan are still performing at weddings and functions today with their own band – and Jimmy reveals that Joe often joined them for a couple of songs in latter years. 'Whenever Joe came in, I'd never put pressure on him to get up and sing. But he always came up, took the mic and did "The Answer To Everything" and "I Love You More And More". He had the original sound with Doc and myself and he loved just doing those couple of numbers. Then he went away happy.'

*　*　*

As he sat chatting with Mick Jagger and the Rolling Stones backstage at 'Top of the Pops', rock 'n' roll fan Joe had to pinch himself. It had all happened so fast. There had been the auditions at the Ierne Ballroom in Dublin, to form another band immediately after his parting from The Drifters. A return to the stage with the new line-up that included Pat Hoey (bass), Gordon Coleman (guitar), Maurice Walsh (drums), Ciaran McDonnell (keyboards), Seamus Shannon (trombone) and Frankie McDonald (trumpet).

Less than a year later in 1969, Joe had become a sensation around Europe where his next single, 'Make Me An Island,' was a Top 10 hit in fourteen countries. After being chosen as the 'power play' song on Radio Luxembourg, which meant that listeners heard it twenty-four hours a day, the popularity of 'Make Me An Island' had taken off across the continent, like a gorse fire in the middle of a long hot summer. To cater for the European markets, Joe also recorded 'Make Me An Island' in Italian, Spanish and German.

Now he was on a gruelling schedule, jetting from country to country, performing on TV shows, then flying home to play with the band in remote ballrooms dotted across Ireland ... and loving every second of it.

Joe took it all in his stride, totally confident in his ability to hold his own among the big singers and bands outside Ireland. At his first 'Top of the

Pops" appearance, Joe discovered that he was going to be singing live and backed by an eighteen-piece band. 'No problem,' he told his manager, Seamus Casey. As they began rehearsing 'Make Me An Island' that afternoon, Joe suddenly raised his hand and shouted, 'Stop!', ten bars into the song.

Today, as he recalls the incident, Seamus Casey says that he was embarrassed by Joe's outburst. 'I remember thinking, "Oh, Jez, why is he telling these fellas to stop?".'

'What's wrong Joe?' one of the English TV crew asked.

'The rhythm is wrong,' Joe replied.

'Okay, let's do it again.'

Seamus reveals that shortly after restarting the song, Joe stopped the show again. 'At this point I was now so embarrassed that I was wishing the ground would open up and swallow me,' Seamus recalls. 'Joe then went to the drummer. He got behind the kit and started beating the rhythm. "This is the way I want it," Joe explained. Then the rehearsals resumed, and this time Joe was happy with the rhythm of the music. "I can't believe you did that!" I said to him afterwards. Joe wasn't arrogant, he was a natural performer with a great sense of rhythm; and he was also a perfectionist when it came to the song, the music and the performance.'

On the night of that first 'Top of the Pops" appearance, Joe chartered a small plane to get him back into Dublin where he was mobbed by the home fans swarming around him as he arrived at his show in the Olympic ballroom.

The following week, the man from Mullingar created a little piece of Irish music history when he became the first Irish artist to reach the Top 5 of the UK charts. 'Make Me An Island' had shot up to Number Three, behind his new friends the Rolling Stones and Robin Gibb.

Before the end of 1969, 'Make Me An Island', an original song written for him by the then English-based songwriters Albert Hammond and Mike

Hazelwood, would also go on to see Joe dominate the charts in Australia and South Africa. He was now a worldwide superstar with a 'Record of the Year' in many countries.

*   *   *

Trumpet player Frankie McDonald, who played with an Athlone band Syd and The Saints, and was also a member of the Western Command Army No. 4 band, remembers how he was 'thrilled' when he got into Joe's new backing group at the age of twenty-two. He would play alongside Joe for the next thirty-nine years. 'Joe, to me, was probably one of the finest singers that ever was in Ireland and musically he was very talented, which is something a lot of people wouldn't have realised. I remember at rehearsals he surprised me on many occasions with his ideas,' Frankie reveals.

'The new band rehearsed for three weeks and my first night with Joe was at the Las Vegas ballroom in Templemore, County Tipperary, on 15 August, 1968. 'I'll never forget the shock I got when I walked out on stage that first night and saw over 2,000 people in front of me; the entire music programme I was about to play left my mind. The crowd went wild. They were all fans of the previous Drifters, so to see the new band and to see Joe back in operation, I'd say they were overwhelmed. I spent the whole night picking Joe up off the floor because he was being pulled off the stage and that's the way it was for that first year … Joe being pulled off the stage and us picking him up. We were his musicians and his security.'

As 1970 came in, Joe had another big international hit with 'You're Such A Good Looking Woman', the song that would become his signature tune forever more. 'It was a great opening number for the show because the brass brought it in,' trumpet-player Frankie says. 'The band would play a little two-minute intro with snippets of different tunes before Joe came on, and the minute we went into "Good Looking Woman" that would really lift the crowd because they knew it was "Joe time". Joe would be coming in on my right and the last thing he'd do was bless himself and then he'd run on to the stage and go into "Oh me, oh my ...." That was very exciting. Joe excited the band when he came on and then the whole thing bounced off the crowd. It was always very exciting with Joe. He was a one-off.'

*   *   *

When Joe talked about his early days as a jet-setting pop star, he remembered that there was very little glamour in it. Joe recalled waking up one morning, shivering with the cold and suffering aches and pains all over his body. In the early morning haze, Joe realised that he was lying on a floor in a corridor, fully dressed and with a blanket covering him. Even his shoes were still on his feet. 'I was thinking, "Where am I? How did I get here?" I was still groggy and struggling to remember.'

Then he realised that he was in Belgium on the morning after a show the previous night. Joe remembered that he was staying in the hotel where he had performed. Ben and the rest of the crew were in a similar establishment next door, but one of their entourage had got so drunk after the show that they had hauled him up to Joe's suite and thrown him on to one of the beds. When Joe later retired for the night, he couldn't get to sleep with the thunderous snoring of his pal on the other side of the room. He coughed loudly and threw a shoe at his crew member, but the snoring got louder and louder. 'I lay quietly fuming under the covers of my bed, wrapping a pillow around my ears but failing to plug out the horrendous noise,' he laughed at the recollection. Finally, exhausted and, in a fit of anger and frustration, he had got dressed again and then bailed out into the corridor.

'I'm wrecked,' he told Ben later in the morning.

'What's up with ya?'

'Yer man was snorin' for Europe when I got to bed last night,' Joe sighed as he explained how he'd then slept in the corridor.

The second resident in Joe's suite hadn't gone unnoticed by the management. They were now demanding that Joe pay double the original price of the accommodation. Ben refused.

Then a diplomatic incident started to erupt. Jimmy Murray, the guitarist on tour with Joe, discovered that his guitar, which had been stored overnight in the ballroom with the rest of the band's equipment, was now missing. Jimmy returned to reception to report the stolen instrument. The manager arrived on the scene and informed him that the guitar was being retained until the outstanding bill for Joe's room was paid.

'There's no way we're payin' that extra charge, sure Joe didn't even sleep in the room,' Ben told an agitated Jimmy.

'Later, I discovered that my saxophone was also missing when I went to retrieve it,' Ben recalls. 'I was thinking, what the hell is going on here?'

Out of the corner of his eye, Ben then spotted Jimmy Murray shaking with laughter and his guitar standing by his side like a faithful dog. 'Jimmy had persuaded the hotel manager to swap it for the saxophone after convincing him that my instrument was more valuable than the guitar,' Ben says today. Now Ben's saxophone was being held to ransom. Joe was laughing so much at the shenanigans, he had to lie down on the bed at this stage.

After some gentle persuasion and diplomacy, Ben eventually left the hotel with his beloved sax in tow.

Ben remembers Joe laughing and asking, 'Did he charge you for that other gobshite in the room?'

'I told him "No, I think he was delighted to see the back of us",' Ben can see the funny side of it all today.

* * *

The loud bang coming from the engine of the band wagon did not bode well for the tour as Joe and the boys were on the move in France.

'That's gas,' Joe laughed when he discovered that the engine had given up the ghost.

Ben didn't see the funny side of Joe's pun. As it was all the rage at the time in Ireland, Ben had converted the bus's engine to run on gas shortly before they'd set off on their European odyssey. Joe and Ben were travelling together in a car when the band's coach broke down.

'We decided that we'd have to hire another wagon and collect our own on the way back after the tour,' Ben recalls. They then towed their broken-down vehicle to a local garage where they left it to be repaired.

At the end of their week-long tour in France, Joe, Ben and the boys made their way back to the boat. Along the route, they stopped off to pick up their wagon. Arriving into town late at night, they decided that they'd stay over until the morning. As they drove around in unfamiliar territory, there was no sign of a hotel on the horizon.

'We were lost, so when we came upon an old Frenchman wearing a beret and cycling along on his bicycle, we stopped to get directions,' Ben recalls. 'Mick Bagnell, who had then replaced bass player Pat Hoey in the band, had a bit of French so he spoke to the old guy.' After much nodding and gesticulating between the two men, Mick announced that the elderly French gentleman was going to lead them to a hotel. For half an hour they travelled at a snail's pace behind the cyclist, only to find themselves in the middle of a small cluster of residential houses. They had followed the bemused Frenchman to his own home. Joe thought this was hilarious.

The following day, after finally finding accommodation for the night, Ben and Mick located the garage where they had dropped off their own wagon to be repaired. Another surprise awaited them.

Joe's tour bus was parked inside the ramshackle building, with the engine still in pieces all over the floor. The mechanic, who didn't speak a word of English, shrugged his shoulders when Ben tried to communicate with him.

'Load the engine into the wagon and we'll tow it to the boat to get it home, 'cause I'm not coming back for it,' Ben said eventually.

They then meandered along mountain roads at a gentle pace, tugging the bus behind. After what seemed like an eternity, they finally reached the boat in Le Havre. Now there was another problem facing them; how were they going to get the bus on to the ferry. Towing another vehicle on board was prohibited. 'We'll just have to chance it,' Ben said.

Mick Bagnell nodded.

'Do you speak English?' Ben asked a crew member standing on guard at the entrance.

'I should do, I'm from Ballyfermot,' the employee said in his thick Dublin accent.

'Jaysus, great, any chance we can tow this auld wagon on?'

'Are ya coddin' me, bud?'

'No ...'

'I'll probably get the sack, but go on, sure it's Joe Dolan,' he nodded, beckoning the driver to move forward as the gang headed home on the final leg of their eventful journey.

When a mechanic arrived from Hamill's garage in Mullingar to pick up the stricken vehicle at Rosslare, he was astonished to find the engine strew across the inside of the wagon.

'It's a long story,' Joe laughed.

*　*　*

Joe regularly sacked his band in the bar of the hotel where they were staying after a show. He was always on a high after his performance and loved to wind down over a skinful of drinks with the rest of the lads. Regular alcohol-fuelled rows erupted on nights like this.

Seamus Casey recalls: 'When Joe would have a few drinks he'd argue with you, but then the next day it was all forgotten about. The fellas would all come into the bar and eventually after numerous drinks you'd hear Joe say something like, "The feckin' band was shockin' tonight, I'm going to sack the lot of yez." Then you'd hear, "You're sacked!" There was many a time he sacked me too. There were plenty of times you'd love to kill him, but the next day it was great.'

The following morning as they tucked into their rashers and eggs, there would be an awkward silence among the band when Joe breezed in with a big smile on his face.

'Jaysus, lads, that was a crackin' gig last night. What's on today?' Joe would announce, full of the joys of life and the previous night's shenanigans completely forgotten.

According to Ben, one of Joe's endearing traits was that he never held grudges or set himself apart from the rest of the band and crew on the road. 'People stayed with us for years and years and that was all down to Joe,' Ben says. 'It didn't really matter what you were doing in the band, everyone was the same as far as Joe was concerned. Joe had as much time for drivers and roadies and stage managers like John Delamere, Tommy Begley, Joe Bustin and Denis Mee, as he did for the musicians. Joe was a team player who understood it was everyone pulling together that made the show work. And he would always insist on everyone staying in the same hotel, even though I used to think that if Joe stayed in a different hotel the rest of the lads might get to sleep sometime.'

* * *

In 1970, Joe became one of the big attractions on the cabaret circuit around Britain. As he started out on this scene, Englishwoman Joy Nicholls suggested to Seamus Casey that Joe should be taught how to dance on stage. Joy worked with the Shaftesbury music publishing company which was now supplying Joe with his hit songs composed by the in-house writing team of Albert Hammond and Mike Hazelwood. As Joe had come from a background of playing at dances, Joy felt that he needed to learn a few new dance steps for his cabaret performances.

'Joy told me that Joe needed a choreographer to get him to move,' Seamus recalls.

The manager then put the suggestion to Joe. 'I was talking to Joy Nicholls and she's going to get you a choreographer,' Seamus said apprehensively.

Joe swung around on his chair. 'For what?' he asked, as a frown creased his forehead.

Seamus coughed. 'To show you how to move on stage at the cabaret shows,' he replied.

Joe was hugely offended. 'Would you tell Joy Nicholls from me to f*** off. Nobody is going to tell me how to move, only me,' he fumed.

'Okay, Joe,' Seamus said, dropping the subject.

When Seamus returned to Joy, he broke the news. 'Joe says he'll be grand doing his own thing,' the polite manager informed her.

Three months later, Joe burst on to the stage in Cardiff for his first cabaret performance in a week-long residency at a local venue. Now he was exposed out front on a big stage, with the band behind him. Seamus watched proudly from the wings as Joe commanded the stage. He even pulled some impressive, sexy moves out of the bag. That night Joe looked like an entertainer who had been doing cabaret shows all of his life.

Joe would go on to become a major star on the UK cabaret scene, where he forged friendships with other superstar entertainers, including Shirley Bassey, Roy Orbison, Englebert Humperdinck, Gene Pitney and Tom Jones. With his disarming charm, warm personality and good humour, the big celebrities were drawn to Joe when they encountered him as he toured the big clubs of England, Scotland and Wales.

He was also signed up by a top-notch British agency called MAM, which looked after big names such as Tom Jones. Joe used to tell the story of how Tom was reminiscing with him one night about his own Irish tours. Jones, who had already enjoyed big hits with 'It's Not Unusual', 'What's New,

Pussycat?', 'The Green Green Grass of Home' and 'Delilah', had been booked for shows in Ireland by Drogheda-born Jim Hand, then one of the country's most successful impresarios.

'Jim called me "Head" the whole way through the tour,' Tom laughed.

As Tom Jones learned, Big Jim rarely called anybody by their first name.

Jim's trademark greeting was, 'Are ya alright, Head!'

As the conversation unfolded with Joe, Tom Jones related how at one point he and Hand had arrived in Drogheda. Jim, who was driving the car, then turned to Tom and said: 'Now, Head, I'm going to take you to see the head.'

'I thought I was the Head,' Jones replied.

'No, I'm going to take you to see the real Head.'

Hand then continued their journey through the County Louth town by car until they reached a local church. Tom told Joe he was mystified when Jim then stopped outside and announced: 'C'mon, Head, we're goin' in!'

'I never took him to be a particularly religious man,' Jones laughed.

Tom Jones stepped briskly by the side of Big Jim that day as they marched up to the church.

Inside, Hand turned to Jones and whispered out of the side of his mouth: 'Now, Head, there's the real Head!'

Tom was astonished as Jim then pointed to a glass case containing a human head. Hand had taken Jones to see the head of Blessed Oliver Plunkett, the Archbishop and Primate of All Ireland who became the last Catholic martyr in England in 1681 when he was hanged, drawn and quartered on a charge of treason. He was later canonised a saint. The martyr's head was preserved in a shrine at St Peter's Church in Drogheda.

'Don't tell me Jim said, "How'ya, Head!" to poor old Oliver Plunkett?' Joe laughed.

'No, in fact, he was very respectful,' Jones recalled. 'But now whenever I hear somebody being called "Head", I instantly think of Jim Hand and the head in the church that day.'

Joe spent the rest of their night bursting into little fits of giggles when he recalled Tom's Irish encounter.

Today, Tom Jones remembers that trip to see Blessed Oliver Plunkett and he speaks fondly of his encounters with Joe on the club scene in Britain. 'I knew Joe to have a chat and a drink with; we Celts, we do like to have a little drink,' Jones laughed. 'Joe was great company and a great singer. He was one of those guys who had a voice. I was always pleased to meet people with a voice because some of the British pop acts didn't all have proper singing voices, and he did. He had come from the showband scene in Ireland and I knew that scene very well, so we had that in common. I had great times performing in the ballrooms around Ireland. The first time I played there was in 1965 at the Boom Boom Room in Belfast. Jim Aiken was my agent and he used to drive me around Ireland in his Jaguar car and I remember one of the gears used to stick. Jim said to me at the start, "Now, look, some of these ballrooms are rough places." I replied, "After performing in South Wales I can't see anything being rougher than that." I wasn't bothered about them being rough as long as the crowd enjoyed it. Joe Dolan said to me that, "The Irish are very similar to the Welsh, they love music and they love a good time. If you give them that then you have no problems." And that's the way it was. You had to walk through the audience to get to the stage, which was alright going on. Getting back out was more difficult because the crowd were now wound up after the show. It wasn't that I was in danger, but people would try to get hold of you in a stampede. That all only seems like yesterday. One of the drags of getting older is that you lose friends along the way and I was quite shocked when I heard that Joe had died.'

* * *

Ben has never forgotten the terrible night that Joe was set upon and subjected to a horrific beating in a Liverpool club. It was the autumn of 1970 and Joe, Ben and the band were on tour in the UK, where they had performed a sold-out show at the Wookie Hollow venue in Liverpool. As he wound down after the gig, Joe stayed on for some late-night drinks. It was a decision that he would regret for the rest of his life.

At some point over the next couple of hours, he became involved in an exchange of words with some local hard men who had been drinking heavily. As they began heckling him, Joe, who was with one of his road crew, Hubert 'Shotgun' Crowley, realised that he had crossed swords with the wrong guys. Sensing the imminent danger he had exposed himself to, Joe made a flash decision to leave the bar with 'Shotgun' in tow. It was too late.

The violence that Joe then endured at the hands of two vicious thugs as he struggled for his life was like a scene from a horror movie. In the vicious, merciless assault, Joe's face was pummelled to a pulp. At one stage in the slow, torturous onslaught the thugs forced the singer's head down a toilet bowl. At this point, Joe feared he might not get out alive.

However, his pal, Shotgun, had escaped his own attacker and had managed to make a frantic emergency call to the police. The sound of sirens brought an abrupt end to Joe's nightmare as the evil gangsters fled the scene.

Although no one was ever charged in relation to the sadistic beating, police in Liverpool believe that Joe had tangled with notorious heavies of the local criminal underworld. In the aftermath, Joe was left hospitalised with multiple injuries, which forced him to cancel an imminent European tour.

Joe's Irish fans were horrified when they saw the gruesome pictures of his battered and bruised face after the sensational story hit the headlines in the national newspapers. His nose had been flattened and his handsome features destroyed.

'I got a terrible shock when I saw him that night,' Ben reveals. 'Joe's face was all swollen and he was in a shocking state. To be honest, I nearly got sick when I saw what they had done to him.'

Although he made a full recovery, the trauma he endured would haunt Joe for years to come. 'It really shook him up and I'm sure it played on his mind for years afterwards,' Ben says. 'But how it affected him I really don't know as Joe buried the incident and never spoke about it after that night.'

CHAPTER 10

JAILHOUSE ROCK

Golfer Joey Purcell from Mullingar became Joe's personal driver in the seventies as the singer juggled a crazy schedule, performing shows at home and on the continent. One of Joey's tasks was to get him to the airport on time for flights.

Joey had a key to Joe's apartment in his home town and he recalls how he would often hear the singer's thunderous snoring when he arrived in the early morning. 'I'd call out his name and the snoring would turn to fits of snorting and then back to a full-throttle snore again,' Joey laughs as he recalls those days.

Joey would sometimes get a jug and fill it with ice-cold water. He remembers one morning stepping into the bedroom and calling Joe. The alcohol fumes told him that his boss had had a good time the night before. From experience, Joey knew that he was waking the dead. 'Joe!' the driver called one more time.

The snoring continued unabated. Early morning calls like this required extreme measures to rouse Joe from his deathly sleep. Joey stepped up to the bed and slowly splashed the ice water over Joe's head.

'Jaysus!' Joe shot up like a wild animal, with his arms flailing.

'Get up, Joe, you've a plane to catch,' Joey told him.

'Yeah, yeah, yeah,' Joe stuttered, pulling the blankets over his head and curling up in his warm, comfortable nest again.

Joey waited for a couple of minutes, then realised that Joe had gone back to sleep. Next he caught the mattress and pulled it on to the floor; then he grabbed Joe by his heels and hauled him across the room.

'Okay, okay, Joey! I'm up! I'm up!'

Joe stumbled out to the car still half-asleep and half-dressed. As Joey shot along the back roads from Mullingar to Dublin Airport, his front-seat passenger was silent for most of the journey. In the early morning and on the traffic-free roads of the early seventies, Joey completed the trip from Mullingar to the airport in just under an hour. By this stage, Joe had come to life.

'Right, Joey, let's get the fry,' he announced chirpily as he strutted into the airport building.

'After a greasy breakfast smothered in brown sauce, Joe was ready to take on the world,' Joey remembers.

*   *   *

Joey Purcell was just a teenager when he first met the singer. The Mullingar schoolboy had displayed remarkable skills as a golfer and was well known on the local scene. Joe's friend Joe Healy, a Mullingar department store owner, had encouraged him to develop an interest in golf shortly after he became a major star with the success of his single, 'Make Me An Island'.

'Playing golf will fill your days, get you out in the fresh air and it'll be addictive, wait and see,' Healy told Joe.

On his first day at Mullingar Golf Club, Joe was introduced to the wonder kid Purcell by Healy. With fifteen-year-old Joey's coaching, Joe soon developed his own golfing skill, and he would carry on a love affair with the sport throughout his entire life.

After leaving school, Joey Purcell went to work as an apprentice mechanic at the local Westmeath Motors garage. Then Joe's manager Seamus Casey and former Drifter Sid Aughey offered to sponsor the teenager and give him the opportunity of developing his golf potential. Joey jumped at the offer, packed in his bid to become a car mechanic and devoted himself full-time to the sport of golf. When he wasn't on the course, the brilliant young golfer helped out in Joe's office, answering the phone and running errands for the singer. Later, when he became Joe's driver, the singer branded him with the nickname, 'The Whizz Kid', for his prowess behind the wheel of a car.

Joey was a non-drinker and a non-smoker, the perfect sidekick for Joe. Whenever the singer needed a driver, he knew he could depend on the young golfer at any hour of the day or night. The downside for Joey was having to spend hours after shows in the bars of hotels and cabaret lounges around the country while the singer relaxed after a performance. There was always a great atmosphere and lots of fun and laughter as the booze flowed and Joe and his entourage entertained each other with jokes and yarns. The craic helped to take the sting out of the long hours tee-total Joey was left hanging around for his passenger. At some point late in the proceedings, Joey would start to gently persuade Joe to call it a night.

'Right, Joey, I'll just have one more for the road.'

Another hour would pass, and then another, before Joe finally threw in the towel.

One night on the homeward-bound journey from Dublin to Mullingar after a cabaret show, Joey was driving to the soundtrack of Joe's snoring in the passenger seat beside him.

It was shortly after 5am when their car reached the sleepy County Meath village of Enfield. As Joey shifted the motor down in gear there was no sign of life, so he put his foot on the accelerator and roared through the locality at 70mph. The car left Enfield like a rocket on its way to the moon and Joey smiled as he reflected on how he'd soon be in his comfortable bed at the family home outside Mullingar. Then something caught his eye in the wing mirror. As he checked it again, Joey's heart started to race. It was the blue flashing lights of a Garda car.

Joey put the pedal to the metal and he could feel the power of Joe's car as it surged underneath him. Joe stirred in the seat, opened his eyes and slowly realised that they were whizzing by trees and hedges at a ferocious speed.

'Jaysus, where's the effin train?' he roared, bolting upright in the seat.

'It's not a train, it's the guards,' Joey replied, staring straight ahead as he piloted the car with his heart in his mouth.

Joe glanced back out the rear window and spotted the blue flashing lights of the vehicle that was in hot pursuit. 'Jaysus, Joey, you'll get the two of us locked up. They'll throw away the key,' he said, the high pitch in his voice betraying his alarm.

'They'll have to catch us first,' Joey smiled.

By the time they reached Kinnegad, the Garda car had disappeared from the rear-view mirror. Joey turned swiftly on to the Galway road and, at Milltownpass, he made a quick right turn on to the by-roads into Mullingar.

'Now, enjoy your sleep,' Joey laughed when he finally dropped Joe off at his apartment in the town.

'Ye mad f**ker!' Joe muttered.

A fortnight later, Joey was driving a sleeping Joe home, after another Dublin show which had been followed by late-night boozing in the bar. As their car entered the village of Enfield, shortly after 7am, Joey was on full alert, this time determined not to get on the wrong side of the law. Upon leaving the village at a snail's pace, he checked his rear-view mirror. The coast was clear and he accelerated. As he came over a hill at 100mph, Joey spotted a car parked up ahead on the side of the road. To his horror he noticed, too late, that the driver was in a Garda uniform and placing a beacon on the roof. As Joey shot past him, the startled garda whipped off the beacon, jumped into his car and swung around in hot pursuit.

Joe woke up. 'Jaysus, where's the fire?'

'There's no fire, Joe, look behind you,' Joey responded.

Joe looked back and saw another car travelling at speed. 'Who's that?'

'The guards,' Joey replied.

'Ah, Joey, what are you trying to do to me?' Joe cried.

By the time they reached Kinnegad, the Garda car had been left for dust.

'See ya later, "Whizz Kid",' Joe said with a smirk when Joey dropped him off in Mullingar.

A week later, as they were having a meal in Harry's of Kinnegad on their way to a show, Joey felt a heavy hand on his shoulder. He swung around to see a garda in uniform.

'How'ya!' the garda nodded.

'Hello, Guard, how are you?' a startled Joey responded.

'I know it was you,' the garda said brusquely.

'What do you mean?'

'I know that was you driving that car on the last two occasions I saw it at Enfield,' the garda informed him.

'I'm not with you at all,' Joey insisted, feigning innocence.

The garda explained that the car had been observed driving at dangerous speeds in the Enfield area on two specified dates. At this point, Joe was shaking inside as he struggled to stop himself from bursting into a fit of laughter. He couldn't look at Joey.

'Ah that couldn't have been him, Guard,' Joe finally interjected.

'And how would you know, Mr Dolan?' the garda asked.

'Sure I'm always with him,' Joe replied.

This seemed to infuriate the garda even more. Turning to Joey, he warned: 'If I catch you one mile over the speed limit from now on I'll have you locked up.'

Joe couldn't finish his steak and chips he was laughing so much after the garda had left.

'You should have seen your face!' he told Joey.

* * *

There was always electricity in the air when home-grown superstar Joe had a show coming up at the Greville Arms Hotel in Mullingar. For weeks, in the build-up to this exciting event, it was the main topic of conversation among his female fans around Westmeath and neighbouring counties. The demand for the precious tickets always exceeded supply as management at the Greville Arms struggled to find space for more and more of Joe's army who came pleading for the hottest ticket in town. Those lucky enough to secure tickets would guard them like they were bars of gold.

It was easy to spot Joe's female followers around the town of Mullingar and in country areas on the day of the concert. They were particularly high-profile on their way to work that morning at a local factory. Joe's besotted factory girls stood out like an alien invasion as they all went about their business in uniformity with curlers in their hair under a protective scarf. The hairdo and dress style was all part of the fun in the lead up to the night's entertainment for the women.

The supercharged atmosphere in the ballroom of the Greville Arms always sparked up Joe like never before, and he unleashed his best-ever performances on those nights. When he looked out at the sea of faces in the audience, Joe would recognise many of them as family, neighbours, friends, fans and casual acquaintances from around the area. Sitting in the front row, watching him like a proud mother, shortly after he became famous, was local resident, Mrs Begley, the poor woman Joe had regularly tormented on his way home from school as a kid. Now Joe was Mrs Begley's favourite local lad done good. She had a smile that stretched from ear to ear as she lapped up the attention of Mullingar's famous son.

'How'ya, Mrs Begley?' Joe addressed her between songs.

Then Joe told his audience about the divilment he got up to as a school-going brat, rapping on her front door before disappearing down the street. 'Remember the time you followed me with the sweeping brush, Mrs Begley?' he laughed.

Joe doted on his brother, Paddy, but he loved winding him up. Paddy recalls that Joe would embarrass him at the shows in the Greville, so he tried to stay out of sight. Joe invariably sought him out and put the spotlight on him. 'He used to make a show of me,' Paddy laughs today. 'He'd say, "There's me brother, Paddy, he must be finished collectin' the money on the door. He's that mean he'd take a fly from a spider."'

*　*　*

Joey Purcell remembers the drama that unfolded on a freezing cold night in March, 1974, as he drove his passengers, including Joe, back to Mullingar after one of the singer's show at the Red Island Club in the seaside town of Skerries, County Dublin. On this particular night, Joe had a couple of friends with him in the car, including a publican and a priest. Drunk and exhausted, he had fallen asleep in the back seat when they started out on their journey in the early hours of the morning.

Joe's yellow car was like a monster canary as it sped along the main road. As well as golf, the singing star had now developed an all-consuming passion for flash motors. His latest pride and joy was an NSU Ro 80 sedan. Joe drove it to the shows and Joey would chauffeur him home. As they were driving through Lucan village, west of Dublin, a garda suddenly jumped out on the road and flagged them down. Joey slammed on the brakes. The garda shone a massive flashlight on the windscreen. As Joey rolled down his side window, he heard a groan in the back of the car. Joe was waking up.

Groggy and disgruntled, Joe barked at the garda: 'What the hell are you doin' there?'

The demeanour of the garda suddenly changed. 'There's no need to be abusive.'

Joe was now in a foul humour. 'Have you nothin' better to be doin' at this hour of the morning?' he sniped in his boozy state.

The garda opened the back door of the car. 'Step out here!' he ordered Joe.

Minutes later, Joe, shattered from the drink and shivering with the cold, found himself locked up in a cell at Lucan Garda barracks. Oblivious to his captivity, Joe's fellow travelling companions were waiting patiently in the car, expecting him to return at any moment, after receiving a reprimand. When there was still no sign of Joe after about twenty minutes had elapsed, the publican got out of the car and went in to investigate the situation. Another twenty minutes passed by and now there was no sign of either Joe or the publican.

Joey decided to go into the Garda station himself, to check what was happening. To his shock, he discovered that both Joe and the publican had been locked up in a cell. By now, Joe was shaking with the cold as he huddled in a corner.

'Will you go out, Joey, and get me auld fur coat from the boot of the car?' the frozen singer begged.

Joey returned with the fur coat.

'Where are you goin' with that?' the garda snapped.

'I want to give it into Joe, he'll get his death with the cold,' Joey pleaded.

'He's not getting that until he sobers up and apologises,' the garda insisted.

'Ah, look, he's frozen ...'

'Right, if you go in with that coat then you'll stay in there with him, is that clear?'

Joey returned to the car with the fur coat and gave it to the priest for warmth. Two hours later, a contrite and wrecked Joe emerged from the Garda barracks with the publican a step behind. He sighed as he curled up on the back seat and went straight to sleep.

Joey shifted the car into top gear and resumed the homebound trip at high speed. Near the Springfield Hotel down the road at Leixlip, the tyres of the car screeched as it careered around a right-hand bend. Joey had spotted two uniformed gardaí jumping out of a ditch up ahead and waving down the car. The two members of the police force checked the car and its occupants. 'What's the big rush?' one garda then asked Joey.

Joe was awake again. This time he stayed quiet in the back of the car.

'We've just been in Lucan,' Joey tried to explain.

'Oh right,' the garda nodded with a smirk. 'You're the guys they had in jail there.'

'Yes, Garda,' Joey acknowledged.

'Right, well, on your way now … and keep her slow.'

As they drove off, Joe mumbled from the back seat: 'This country is gone to the dogs with guards everywhere.'

The following day, Joe heard that the gardaí were out searching for one of the notorious Littlejohn brothers who was on the run from Mountjoy Prison. Siblings Kenneth and Keith Littlejohn were two self-proclaimed British spies who had been jailed for carrying out what was then the biggest bank robbery in the State. They had stolen IR£67,000 in their raid on an AIB bank on Dublin's Grafton Street. In court, the brothers claimed they were British spies who had been ordered to do the robbery, to discredit the IRA. Kenneth was sentenced to twenty years in jail, while his brother, Keith, got fifteen years. During an exercise period in Mountjoy, the brothers had scaled a twenty-five-foot prison wall with handmade ropes while other prisoners distracted the guards. Keith was captured immediately as he had injured his ankle while absconding. Kenneth was still on the run at the time.

As Joe listened to the news on the radio, he realised why the gardaí had been on high alert the previous night. 'We're lucky we weren't shot,' he quipped to Joey.

Kenneth Littlejohn managed to skip the country, but was later arrested in England and sent back to Ireland to complete his sentence.

* * *

Another night Joey Purcell found himself caught up in an embarrassing incident when he went to bed at the Country Club in Kilternan on Dublin's southside. It was the early hours of the morning, after Joe's show in the venue. Joe was staying over, having secured a twin bedroom for himself and his driver, Joey. Around 4am, Joey had left the after-show party, to get some sleep. Joe was still drinking at the bar. Minutes later, Joey rushed back into the bar in a state of alarm.

'What's up with ya? You look like you've seen a ghost,' Joe laughed.

'There's someone in our room, Joe?'

'What do you mean?'

'There are clothes all over the floor and someone is in one of the beds.'

Joe alerted the night porter and the three men went to investigate. As the porter opened the door, Joe noticed various items of women's lingerie strewn across the floor of his room, as well as a man's jacket, shirt and pants. The trail of clothing lead to his own bed. He switched on the light and found a young couple entwined and sleeping. They were mortified when they woke up to the vision of Joe Dolan standing over them.

'I have no idea how they got in,' the porter said later, after he had evicted the intruders.

'They seemed to have had a good time anyway,' Joe laughed.

* * *

A passionate golfer, Joe avidly followed Joey's progress over the seven years he played as a PGA professional on the European tour. Joe was thrilled the day Joey scored his best finish in the Spanish Open when he tied for eight place with British golfer Nick Faldo, whom he'd also played with in the final round.

Joe and Joey participated in numerous Pro-Ams around Europe. Joey believed that Joe had the ability to get his handicap down to a seven or eight. 'He was very strong, but Joe's weakness on the golf course was a short swing, due to his physique, and he struggled with his flexibility,' Joey says. However, the singer impressed the professional golfer on many occasions, particularly during one open week at Headford Golf Club in Kells, County Meath, when Joe shot a 75 gross off an 18 handicap in a singles competition. Joe was cock-a-hoop with his score that day.

* * *

Through the years, Joey got to indulge his love of cars by driving the ever-changing makes and models of super motors that took Joe's fancy. Joe was a great driver too, although there were times when he was reckless and his fast cars would pay the penalty. One beautiful Jaguar ended up embedded in a Limerick telegraph pole.

The yellow NSU Ro 80 got the heave-ho from Joe after a trip home from Dublin one day. This time Joe was driving the flash motor and Joey was in the passenger seat. As he was speeding along the main road and enjoying the thrill of the drive, Joe recognised a car that was tailing him. The motorist, he had noticed, was an acquaintance from Mullingar and he was driving a modest vehicle. It soon became evident to Joe that the other driver was determined to overtake him. 'I'm not going to let this fella have the satisfaction of passing me out,' he told Joey.

Joe stuck the accelerator to the floor and his car shot ahead. He was laughing. Then suddenly the other motorist picked up speed and shot past

Joe in a flash. Joe was raging. 'I'm gettin' rid of this f***in' car,' he said.

'What's wrong with it?' Joey asked.

'Sure, it wouldn't pull a donkey out of a bog hole,' he sighed.

*　　*　　*

Ben Dolan rarely took a drink, and for decades he too became Joe's designated driver. Joe enjoyed the thrill of piloting his latest, state-of-the art motor to the shows, but he relied on Ben to get him home. 'The price I paid for my abstinence was the hours I would spend hanging around for Joe in bars after a performance,' he recalls today. Ben also tried his best to keep Joe on the straight and narrow, particularly during his wilder years in the seventies.

Former Mayor of Galway John Mulholland, who was one of Joe's friends in the west, recalls nights when Ben waited patiently for Joe to finish his socialising in the city. John and Joe had got to know each other in the early 1970s when the singer often dropped by the Mulholland family's Hilltop Hotel and music bar in Salthill after he'd finished a show. 'How long Joe stayed depended on how persuasive Ben was at getting him back out on to the road for home,' John remembers. Joe and John hit it off as, among other things, they shared a common passion for golf. They were also both friendly with the Irish golfer, Christy O'Connor Jnr, from Galway.

John, whose daughter Aoife Mulholland would go on to find fame through the BBC TV show, 'How Do You Solve A Problem Like Maria?', and become a star of musical theatre in London's West End, tells the story of a particular trip with Joe, Christy O'Connor Jnr and a Dublin publican, Brian Lavin, to the Great Northern Hotel Pro-Am in Bundoran, County Donegal in the seventies. 'I had agreed to pick up Joe in Mullingar and give him a lift to Bundoran,' John recalls. 'As we were leaving the house, Ben took me aside on the driveway of his home and warned me: "Whatever you do, don't let that fella drink." I said, "That's a tall order." Ben said Joe was off the drink.'

As they left town, Joe said: 'You're a great man for the oysters, John.'

'That's right.'

'Great,' said Joe. 'There's a very good oyster restaurant about an hour-and-a-half along the way; we'll pull in there for some of them.'

'That's grand,' John agreed.

When they arrived at the bar and restaurant, Joe asked a member of staff: 'Is Mary here?'

'Mary is in the kitchen.'

'Would you mind asking her to come out?'

Mary appeared and Joe had a big, warm greeting for her.

'Now, Mary,' Joe said, 'Will you bring us out two dozen oysters: a dozen for John here and a dozen for me?'

'Okay, Joe.'

'John will have a pint of Guinness and I'll have a vodka and soda as well,' Joe added.

'Joe, I thought you weren't drinking,' John said in a serious tone. He was thinking of Ben's warning.

'Ah, sure, we'll just have the one here now that we're having the oysters.'

'Fair enough,' John reluctantly agreed. He was still thinking of Ben's warning.

Joe had several drinks and before they knew it a couple of hours had passed. John mentioned the oysters at several interjections in the conversation, but Joe insisted that they'd be worth the wait. Finally, John protested that they'd have to get their oysters and head away on the remainder of their journey.

'Oh, aye, call out Mary again,' Joe said to a barman.

Mary arrived a few minutes later.

'This man wants his oysters,' Joe said with a cheeky smile.

Mary looked at John: 'Sure, we don't do oysters. Did you not see that divil winking at me when he asked for them?' she said.

'Well, I should have known better,' John sighed, shaking his head.

John now feared that there could be trouble ahead. When they reached Bundoran, Joe and Brian met up and went off on a drinking session. 'As Christy and myself teed off on the first morning of the three-day PGA Pro-Am, there wasn't a sighting of the other two boys. Christy Jnr was not impressed,' John remembers. At the end of the day, however, John and Christy were six shots behind, despite missing Joe and Brian.

On the second day, as he was heading out to the golf course, Christy spotted Joe and Brian having 'a cure'. John recalls that there was fury in his eyes as he marched up to them. 'I'm giving you ten minutes to be on the tee,' Christy warned them. 'And if you're not on the tee, I'll never speak to either of you again, or never look up if you come into a room.'

Then O'Connor turned on his heels and left the two men standing in shock. Just as John and Christy were about to tee off, Brian came out in a rush, trying to run and tie his shoes at the same time. There was no sign of Joe. The three men teed off, with Christy now fuming in silence. As they walked up the fairway, they heard the singer's distinctive voice shouting in the background, 'Wait for me! Wait for me, I'm coming!

His three golfing companions stopped and turned to see a dishevelled Joe with his shoes still untied. They beckoned Joe to tee off. His ball went flying over their heads and out in front of the other three shots, including Christy's. Joe, who was an eighteen handicap at the time, hit his next shot on to the back of the green before making a 30ft putt into the hole. It was a great start for the team. At the end of the three days, they were beaten by just one shot.

Joe couldn't have been happier, though. Christy O'Connor Jnr had forgiven him.

* * *

Michael O'Leary of Ryanair was one of the young guys who used to caddy for Joe at Mullingar Golf Club. 'Growing up in Mullingar, Joe was a kind of a hero to all of us, since he was the guy with the biggest car, the lifestyle we all aspired to, lots of money and plenty of women hanging off him,' Michael recalls. 'I knew him best from the golf club because if I wasn't caddying there for my father, I'd be caddying for a lot of the other members. I caddied for Joe frequently and everybody wanted to caddy for Joe because he was great craic and he was also a great tipper. In those days (in the seventies), the money was terrible anyway, so you didn't have to be hugely generous to be a good tipper in Mullingar. But Joe was one of the few who tipped. He was a great guy and everybody loved him, even at that stage.'

*　*　*

Joe's goddaughter Kathleen remembers him warning her about booze and boys when she became a teenager. 'When I got to the age where I started going out, Joe would say, "If you're going out you're never to take a drink." That's what he always used to say to me,' she confides.

It was Joe who bought Kathleen her first drink when she turned twenty. 'We were in the Fox's Covert in Ballinafid (outside Mullingar) and he gave me a vodka and Club orange. "Don't tell your father I bought you that drink," he winked. That was the start of going to dances with him. He'd give me a ring and ask if I wanted to travel with him to a dance where he was playing. Daddy would say, "You're not going with Joe. I don't mind you going with Ben, but you're not going with Joe 'cause God knows when you'll get home." I wouldn't say a word to Daddy until I was ready to go. Then I'd tell him, "I'm going to a show with Joe." The horn would beep outside and I'd run out and hop into Joe's car. I remember going to the CYMS in Kildare, Ennis, Moate, Heatherville (Kinnegad) and The Beehive (Delvin), which was an all-night venue. You wouldn't get home till morning and I'd have to sneak in the front door.'

'Oh, you'll be grand, tell your daddy you were with me,' Joe would say.

'If I tell him that I won't be allowed to go with you any more."

Kathleen reveals that Joe was very protective of her when it came to her relationships. 'Oh, Joe vetted the boyfriends alright,' she laughs. 'He'd say, "I wouldn't have anything to do with him. Get rid of him." My husband, Gerry (Oakes) passed the test and Joe sang at our wedding reception. Joe was a great friend as well as being my uncle and godfather. If you told him anything in confidence you knew it wouldn't go any further. I could talk to him and confide in him and he could do the same with me.'

* * *

Legendary Irish songwriter Phil Coulter became a close friend and partied with Joe and his pals in Mullingar during the seventies. 'I had got to know Joe in the sixties after I wrote a song for The Capitol showband called "Foolin' Time". The Drifters were in that same Division-One league during that same era, and I first encountered Joe way back then,' Phil recalls.

The two young men discovered that they had had similar childhood experiences. Phil had come from an ordinary working-class family in Derry.

'It was a time in Derry when things were very tight,' Phil remembers. 'My father was a cop on the beat, so he wouldn't have been making a fortune. There were five kids in the house and we didn't have any great luxuries, but a piano was one of them.

'Like Joe, one of my best recollections from my childhood is that there was always music in the house. My father played the fiddle. A piano was nearly more important than a three-piece suite in the parlour. On a big night, like a party for a birthday or an engagement, it was expected that everyone would do their party piece.'

Phil, whose idol was Buddy Holly, formed a band after getting a scholarship to Queen's University, at the age of eighteen, to pursue a degree in music and modern languages.

'I had no previous band experience, just a passion for the thing. I had that kind of can-do attitude you have when you're a kid,' he recalls. 'Once I started playing in the band, that was it. I knew it was always going to be music. Through all my time in Queen's I was in a band of some shape or form. One of the big ballrooms was outside Derry in a town called Muff and, after lectures on a Friday, I used to hitch-hike there to see the big showbands. It wasn't that I was interested in dancing. I used to stand there, watching and listening. The Capitol showband were heroes of mine and I got to meet them and know them. Then I wrote a song and recorded it with three or four guys for Rag Week in Queen's, as a gimmick, to earn a few quid and I gave it to Butch Moore, who was The Capitol showband's singer. Three months later, I got a phone call from Des Kelly, the band leader of The Capitol. He said they were going to record their first single and would it be okay if they recorded my song, "Foolin' Time", the one I had given them. Would it be okay? Are you kiddin' me! Of course there was only one answer. And it became a hit in Ireland. If there was a defining moment that pushed me towards the music industry, that was it.'

Phil would go on to make a fortune from music, writing hits for everyone from 'The King' himself, Elvis Presley, who recorded his song, 'My Boy', to the Bay City Rollers, Sandy Shaw, Dana, The Dubliners … and Joe Dolan.

Phil had something else in common with Joe back in the early days – he loved his cars – and even at college the money he earned performing allowed him to buy the ultimate status symbol, a babe-magnet MG sports car. 'I was Joe Cool and it's been all downhill ever since,' he laughs. 'I mean, my father didn't have a car. It cost me £150, which was a serious chunk of dough in the late fifties and the fact that I paid for it with what I made in the band was even sweeter.'

In the seventies, Phil would embrace the social life of Mullingar with Joe and their mutual friends. 'I spent many memorable evenings with Joe and the gang in Mullingar … and even more memorable mornings with hangovers,' he laughs at the recollection. 'On New Year's Eve they used to have a Champagne Ball in the Greville Arms and I'd be there with Joe and Joe Healy and their whole coterie down there, all party animals. You were a wimp if you went to bed before daylight. These guys were all like extras from a Tarantino movie. You took your life in your hands going down there. This was not for the faint-hearted; not for boys coming straight out of school, that's for sure. Joe was in the middle of it, of course. That was Joe. He had a zest for life. It was always a great imponderable, "Where the f**k does he get his energy?"'

Whenever they socialised in the seventies, the talk would turn to Joe's idol, Elvis. 'Joe was really impressed by the fact that I had written a song for Elvis,' Phil laughs. 'And, knowing how much he loved Elvis, I used to pull Joe's leg telling him, "Yeah, sure, me and 'The King' hung out together, drinking Jim Beam whiskey and singing songs around the piano." I used to really rub it in. We never did, of course, but Joe lived and breathed the whole showbiz thing.'

It was Joe and Phil's songwriter pal, Albert Hammond, who first heard Elvis singing 'My Boy' in Las Vegas. Elvis had introduced the song that night saying, 'I'd like to sing a song that's close to my heart.'

Phil will never forget the thrill he experienced when Albert phoned him. 'He called me and said, "You f**ker, how did you manage to get Elvis?" It was news to me, but somehow my song had found its way to him and a few months later "The King" recorded it.'

Although he liked to exaggerate his encounter with Elvis to wind-up Joe, Phil's eventual meeting with the legend was a brief one. 'I never got to hang out with Elvis, but I was in a room one time where he acknowledged my presence and that was good enough for me,' he smiles today. 'I was introduced to him as the writer of "My Boy". Although it was at a stage when he wasn't in great shape, it didn't spoil the magic of meeting "The King" in any way. I remember lying in bed that night thinking back to the first time I heard "Heartbreak Hotel" in my terraced home in Derry, never thinking that one day I would meet Elvis Presley, let alone that he would record my song. And that's the magic of this business … the impossible is not impossible.'

Joe and his manager, Seamus Casey, were always sourcing exceptional original songs to record and they chased Phil, whose classics include 'The Town I Loved So Well' and 'Scorn Not His Simplicity', as well as Sandy Shaw's 1967 Eurovision winner, 'Puppet On A String', and Cliff Richard's 'Congratulations'.

'When Joe was looking for songs, there were times when I felt like Dr Richard Kimble in "The Fugitive" and Seamus Casey was that detective that wouldn't leave him alone. Joe had no interest in the business side of showbusiness and he was lucky to have Seamus and Ben taking care of that; it afforded Joe the luxury of being Joe. But he did worry about the songs and would get very exercised about the songs he was singing and what they sounded like. There was never a dull moment working with him. I wouldn't have signed on to work with Joe if I thought there was going to be grief. With Joe you were always sure that it was going to be light-hearted. You were also sure that Joe was the superb professional.'

Phil recalls an amusing incident in London when the pair were working on Joe's 1982 album, *Here And Now*, which featured several of Coulter's songs, including a future hit, 'Deeper And Deeper'. He remembers how Joe was getting increasingly agitated in the studio one night.

'We were recording the vocals and normally Joe was very comfortable in a recording situation,' Phil reveals. 'Joe completely defined "chilled out" when he was performing; he never got hot under the collar and took it all in his stride. That night I sensed that there was something wrong.'

'Joe, are you okay?' Phil asked.

'Yeah, I'm just worried … what's closin' time?'

'Joe, it doesn't matter, this is London. We'll get drink when you're finished, don't worry.'

'Are you sure?'

'Yeah, we'll go to Chinatown for a bite of supper.'

'Ah, Jaysus, great …'

When the recording finished, Phil raced up to Chinatown in his Porsche with Joe, tense and anxious in the passenger seat and Seamus Casey smiling in the back.

'Before we got a menu at all, Joe hijacked this poor Chinese guy and ordered six bottles of wine.' Phil laughs at the recollection.

'You want six bottle of wine!' the startled Chinese waiter exclaimed.

'Yeah, yeah … now, now!'

'Joe was panicking,' Phil laughs again. 'It was hilarious.'

The waiter came out and informed the party that there were only three bottles of the wine Joe had ordered.

'That's grand, we'll drink those, and then I'll get three different ones later,' Joe told him.

Seamus Casey recalls: 'We were eating and drinking and laughing and having great craic and suddenly Joe realised the third bottle was empty. He called the waiter over. At this stage, it was after one in the morning and the waiter said it was past the time for serving alcohol.'

'What!' Joe exclaimed.

'I'll you tell what we'll do, Joe, we'll have a pot of Chinese tea,' Phil said.

Joe reluctantly agreed.

When the tea pot arrived at the table, Joe's face lit up.

He whispered to the waiter as he slipped him some paper money: 'Would you do me a big favour and put a couple of bottles of wine into tea pots and bring them out and leave them on the table, sure nobody will know what's in them.'

The waiter smiled and nodded.

Joe then happily finished off his night sipping wine from a tea cup.

'Joe had the ingredient that, way back in the days of vaudeville, they used to say was crucial to the success of any performer … likeability. You can't underestimate that in any performer and Joe had it in spades,' Phil Coulter reflects.

'If Joe wasn't getting paid for what he did, he still would have done it. Right up to the end, Joe still threw himself into it. From the early days through to the days when I had him in the studio doing songs like "Deeper And Deeper", Joe always had the wide-eyed enthusiasm of a kid that has just been let loose in a toy shop. He regarded himself as having the plum job on the planet. Joe was also very good at picking songs and one of the things that made me happy was that right up to, and including, his very last performance, he was singing one of my mine, "Deeper And Deeper".'

CHAPTER 11

JOE AT HOME WITH BEN AND FAMILY

Ben's spacious, modern home on the outskirts of Mullingar town was Joe's haven away from the razzmatazz of showbusiness. Perched on a hill, the impressive house screamed star status in the 1970s and would have blended in among the opulent dwellings of movie icons in the Hollywood hills. Inside its four walls was the happy, bustling family life of Ben, his wife, Moira, and their young children. Joe had his bachelor apartment in the town, but he enjoyed his home comforts out at his brother's place.

Moira idolised her brother-in-law and treated Joe like one of her children, including him in their meals when he was around the place, and generally welcoming him into the bosom of the family. But, like the children, Joe also knew that, if he stepped out of line with Moira, she'd let him know about it, in no uncertain terms. Joe regularly stayed over at Ben's house, particularly in the winter months as his own apartment had poor heating at the time, turning it into a fridge in the winter months. He loved the company and the fun generated by his niece and nephews.

Joe had been Ben's best man the day in 1963 that he married Moira, a native of Edgeworthstown, in the neighbouring county of Longford. The handsome couple had fallen in love after meeting at a dance in Mullingar's County Hall. Moira was then working as a psychiatric nurse in St Loman's Hospital, while Ben was on his way to stardom with The Drifters. When they left the church that day as man and wife, on their way to a fine reception at the Greville Arms Hotel, the newly-weds passed through a guard of honour, staged by all the members of The Drifters. In keeping with tradition, the best man, Joe, later became godfather to Ben and Moira's firstborn child, a son called Adrian. Four more children would follow: Ray, Michael, Sandra and Colin.

'We loved it whenever Joe arrived home in the morning from a performance at a dance hall in Ireland, just in time to give us a lift to school in his fancy car,' Adrian recalls. 'And my mother loved it as well because she could get a lie on in bed.'

In the summertime, Uncle Joe participated in the fun and games with the family when they holidayed in their caravan at Ledistown around the majestic lake, Lough Ennell, just a short hop from their own home.

'Sandra would be screaming with delight, "Look at me! Look at me!" as Joe carried her around the site, laughing as she was standing on his shoulders with her arms spread out like the wings of an eagle,' Adrian remembers. 'It was Sandra's party piece.' Then he played football with the boys and went cycling with the children. In the evening sunshine, Joe would relax in a deck chair, listening to the buzzing of the bees and the birds chirping as Moira grilled their food on the barbecue.

'We'd then be shouting, "Joe! Joe! Come and play football with us," and he'd kick the ball around with us,' Ray adds.

As night fell, Joe, Ben and the family chatted for hours while they sat around their camp by the light from gas lamps.

Whenever Joe reminisced about those family holidays by the lake, he never forgot 'the feckin' midges' and the hours spent swiping them away as the light fell over the waters of Lough Ennell.

Later, there were summer holidays in a caravan park at the beautiful seaside town of Dunmore East in Waterford. Ben joined the family from Monday to Wednesday before going back on the road with Joe and the band. Throughout the summer, Joe would often drop in to relax for a couple of days. The children looked forward to their father and Uncle Joe's return. 'Although Joe was recognised by the other holidaymakers, they rarely troubled him,' Adrian says.

Despite their privileged background and having an uncle who was famous to their friends, the Dolan children were reared with a good work ethic and it kept them grounded. Their modest pocket money had to be earned. Joe was amused that Ben reverted to the traditions of his own childhood by growing potatoes in the back garden of his impressive home. He'd watch as Ben and his young nephew, Ray, went to dig out a few potatoes for the dinner. Sometimes the entire crop was taken out, picked and then stored in the garage and covered with bales of hay to protect the harvested crop from the winter frost.

Joe watched Ray carrying a bucket for the potatoes as he strolled up the garden by Ben's side.

'Where are you playing tonight, Daddy?' he heard Ray ask.

'Claremorris.'

'Claremorris, that's a great name; where's that Daddy?'

'Mayo.'

'Mayo? Is that a long way away, Daddy.'

'It sure is.'

'We were always excited whenever Joe left the country to do a tour or TV show,' Ray says. 'He never failed to return without the best treat ever in those times ... bars of Toblerone. Joe would arrive in with a big smile, before searching his bags and retrieving five little Toblerone bars for us.' Then he'd produce a giant Toblerone and present it to Moira. Joe knew which side his bread was buttered on.

* * *

Sometimes Joe was guilty of forgetting his godson Adrian's birthday. Upon arriving at the house and discovering the birthday celebration on one such occasion, Joe explained to young Adrian that his present was in the boot of the car.

'"Oh great, Joe," I said, bursting with excitement,' Adrian recalls. '"But, do you know what Adrian, I broke the key in the lock and I can't get it open," he said.

'Oh … do you not have another key?'

'No, I'll have to get the garage to open it for me tomorrow.'

'Alright, Joe.'

A day or two later, Joe slipped Adrian a present, along with some cash.

'You didn't think I'd forget your birthday?' he said.

'He'd never say, "Oh my God, I forgot your birthday." He was crafty and always found a way of turning things around and making them look good,' Adrian says, rembering the story today.

* * *

While Moira doted on Joe, he occasionally tested her patience by arriving home drunk in the early hours of the morning and waking up the entire household as he clattered around the place. He knew by the look on Moira's face when he sheepishly arrived down from the bedroom, late the following day, that he was in her bad books.

'How'ya, Moira!'

Silence.

'Was I a bit loud last night?'

'I'm not saying anything,' Moira snapped.

Joe put his arm around her. 'Jaysus, I'm a shockin' nuisance around the place.'

With his charm and self-deprecating humour, Moira couldn't stay angry with Joe for long. She also mediated whenever Joe and Ben had a falling out. 'Ah, Joe, don't mind him,' she'd say. 'I'll go and have a word with Ben.'

Then Moira would ask Ben: 'Right, what's it all about?' After listening to his side of the story, she'd say: 'Okay, I'll go and have a word with Joe.' And she'd sort it out.

Ben remembers many a night when Moira would wake up to hear Joe and himself chatting in the kitchen in the early morning, after arriving home from a show. 'She'd come down and join us and find Joe slicing up a joint of cold, roast beef, to make a mountain of sandwiches which he smothered with brown sauce. "You can't beat a slice of the bullock's arse, Moira," Joe would say.'

Adrian recalls how Moira would cook Joe his favourite meal when he returned to the house from an afternoon on the golf course. '"You have me spoilt," Joe would say as he devoured his treat of peppered steak and chips.'

*   *   *

Brothers Adrian and Ray both remember having the same complaints when they shared a room in their home with their uncle Joe. His horrendous snoring and smelly socks were the bane of their young lives. It seems that Joe's feet didn't take kindly to being trapped in platform boots during the 1970s.

Ray has a story of waking up one morning to the sound of relentless tapping on his bedroom window. For a few moments the drowsy school kid thought he was in a dream as he heard a raspy voice calling his name. The knocking grew louder and Ray jumped out of his bed, realising it was Uncle Joe. He raced to the door in the freezing cold and let him in.

'Jaysus, sorry, thanks Ray,' Joe said as he stumbled towards the bedroom in a dishevelled state.

The torturous snoring began as soon as the singer's head hit the pillow. 'I tossed and turned in the other bed as I tried to get back to sleep,' Ray recalls. 'It was still a couple of hours before I'd be called for school.' As the snoring grew louder and louder, Ray was getting more agitated by the minute. He coughed to disrupt Joe and the snoring stopped for a couple of seconds, only to start up louder than before. Eventually, in an exploding rage, Ray picked up one of Joe's platform boots and tossed it in the direction of his uncle's bed.

'Oh Jaysus!' Joe roared, as he sprung up from underneath the covers and switched on the light.

'Oh shit!' Ray was horrified; he had hit Joe on the mouth and split his lip.

'What do ya think you're at, Ray?' Joe thundered as he felt his mouth and saw the blood on his hand.

'S-s-s-sorry, Joe, you were snorin' like a pig.'

Ray remembers Joe just muttered away as he switched off the light and disappeared under the blankets.

Then came the crooner's revenge. The snoring started all over again.

* * *

Adrian backs his brother up with the same story of torture whenever Joe slept in his room. 'It sounded like pigs in a trough,' Joe's godson recalls. 'I'd slip out of my bed and then go and hold Joe's nose, but this would only cause him to make gurgling noises through his mouth. Worse than that was Joe's putrid socks and boots on the floor in the room.'

Joe was searching for his boots one morning when he woke up.

'I can't find me feckin' boots,' he told Moira as he arrived down to the kitchen in his bare feet.

Adrian sat red-faced in the corner. He had tossed Joe's boots and socks out of the bedroom window in the middle of the night.

* * *

Ray remembers waking up one winter's morning in his freezing bedroom. The frost had painted a white landscape on the window. As he did on most mornings like this, Ray jumped out of bed, grabbed his clothes and dashed off to the walk-in hot press to dress in the warmth. He stumbled while pulling on his pants, and his bare back touched off something that sent a cold shiver down his spine. He swung around and discovered that he had rubbed up against Joe's sweat-soaked, diamond-encrusted black stage suit that his father had hung up to dry after the previous night's performance. The odour of blended sweat and stale cigarette smoke made Ray feel queasy.

In the bathroom, more of Joe's clothes were soaking in the bath. As well as taking care of business matters and playing saxophone in the band, Ben also looked after Joe's laundry and stage outfits. He did the washing and ironing … and even the sewing in those days. Ray talks of how he and his brothers and sister were fascinated as they watched their father mending or altering Joe's stage pants, jackets and shirts on his Singer sewing machine in the middle of their kitchen, to a clickety-clack soundtrack. And they would frequently see him ironing crumpled items of clothing into crisp, sharp, creaseless outfits for the stage. Ben then taught all his children the art of ironing, instilling attention to detail. The corners of every shirt and jacket were pressed to perfection.

Joe did not do the ironing, but as the star of the show he was working harder than everyone in the band. In the 1970s, it was not uncommon for Joe to do a show in Ireland, return home to Mullingar, catch a few hours' sleep and then leave the country the following morning for a TV show in Europe. Then he would fly back for another performance that same night in an Irish venue. When Joe hit the stage buzzing with energy, the excited fans never had an inkling of the punishing schedule he had just completed in the previous hours.

'Everyone remembers that Joe had incredible stamina in those days,' Adrian says. 'Sometimes he would arrive home to Mullingar at six in the morning after singing at a show with the band. After catching a couple of hours sleep in the car along the journey, Joe was ready to go for a few drinks with his crew in the Greville Arms Hotel. This was followed by breakfast and, when the band went home to bed, Joe then hit the golf course. He would play till three in the afternoon and then have a couple of drinks in the club house before returning to our home at six that evening for his dinner.' Afterwards, he would fall asleep on the couch, watching television, until Ben shook him awake to prepare for another car journey to another show somewhere in the country.

* * *

Joe wasn't a showy person, and in the 1970s his private life was a modest one in comparison to the lives of other international superstars of the era. It was only his obsession with cars that drew people's attention to his status. Joe was the stereotypical man: cars were toys for big boys. With every year that came in, Joe's excited nephews would peer out the windows of their home to see their uncle parking a new, super sleek motor at the top of their drive. In one year, Joe went through two Jaguar cars. After crashing the first one, he replaced it with a similar model. Then he destroyed the engine of that Jag by driving it without oil.

'Joe now has two Jags and can't drive either of them,' an exasperated Ben told pals.

Then Joe borrowed Ben's car and smashed it up in another crash. His five-year-old nephew, Michael, obviously heard his father ranting with rage in the home over Joe's recklessness. 'Feckin' Joe crashed Daddy's car,' Michael told everyone who came through the door.

* * *

It was Joe's super cool Jensen Interceptor sports car that caught the imagination of his nephew, Adrian. Joe fell in love with the golden-brown, eye-catching machine when a friend showed it off to him while on tour in England. The moment he saw the spectacular motor, Joe decided that he had to have it. On the spot, he made his English friend an offer he couldn't refuse. Joe arrived home from the tour, on the ferry, like a child with his new toy. With its electric windows, plush leather seats and wood-trimmed dashboard, this was the car that beat all the cars Adrian, aged ten, had ever seen his uncle Joe driving.

As Joe relaxed on the couch, watching television at Ben's home, Adrian slipped out to investigate the snazzy new vehicle, which was parked at the top of their steep drive. Climbing into the driving seat Adrian noticed the key was in the ignition. He started pressing buttons to make the electric windows slide up and down like magic. This was great fun.

'What the hell are ya doin', Adrian?'

Adrian turned suddenly with shock. It was Joe with a face on him like a bulldog. 'Wha ... at!' Adrian blurted.

'Jaysus, don't be messin' with that feckin' car, will ya get out of it!'

Adrian laughs now as he describes jumping out with the fright when Joe retrieved the key from the ignition. He couldn't understand why his uncle was so angry with him. It wasn't like he was going to drive it down the hill and maybe crash it. And who was Joe to talk, anyway. Hadn't he crashed loads of cars. Adrian cursed his uncle under his breath. Hurt and upset, he mulled over Uncle Joe's sudden outburst when he took refuge in his bedroom.

A week later, Joe was in trouble when a couple of Customs' officers swooped on the Jensen in Mullingar early one morning. In his haste to take possession of the limited-edition motor and to bring it home, Joe had omitted to declare it to Customs and to pay the import duty. Joe tried to plead with the Customs' men as they spirited the sporty motor away on the back of a flatbed truck.

When Adrian later heard about Joe's tale of woe, he can remember secretly gloating and thinking, 'Serves him right.'

*   *   *

Joe and the band rehearsed in the garage underneath Ben's family home; and as the sound of music rang out around the valley, it drew kids and teenagers from all over the neighbourhood, like the Pied Piper. Joe was bringing 'Top of the Pops' to their doorstep. The children and young teenagers congregated on garden walls, fences and ditches, to enjoy the entertainment. There was huge excitement when the band rehearsed the latest pop songs from the Top 20, but the young generation got bored when Joe's own songs were being given a run.

Joe's songs like 'Lady In Blue' and 'More And More' were a big hit with the band's older fans all around the country, but Adrian, Ray and their pals were only interested in the latest pop songs that Joe included in his show. Neither did the kids understand why the band would play a new chart hit over and over as they rehearsed it.

'Why do they keep doing the same song?'

'They're learning it,' Adrian explained.

'They must be thick, they've done that one about twenty times,' a pal quipped.

*   *   *

On days when Joe and Ben were holding auditions in the garage for new band members, Adrian and Ray watched a succession of long-haired musicians parading up and down their driveway. 'There's strange people trying to join the band,' Adrian told his mother.

Moira would jump in her car and drive to town, to escape the noise. Then she'd return later and cook food for everyone.

Their garage was like an Aladdin's cave with all kinds of gear for Joe's band. Sometimes the kids would sneak in to explore and sift through all the strange contraptions.

Ray tells the story of thrashing one of the band's speakers one day when he discovered that there was a magnet inside.

'Look at this,' Ray said to Adrian as he held a nail close to a speaker and watched it jump from his hand.

'There must be a magnet in there,' Adrian said.

'Great, we'll get it out and bring it to school.'

'How will we do that?'

'We'll have to break that yoke up.'

'Joe and Daddy will kill us.'

'Sure it's only junk,' Ray insisted.

The brothers smashed the speaker on the ground and jumped up and down on the carcass. Finally, they retrieved the magnet.

A few days later, Ben came into the house on the warpath. 'Who broke up one of the band's speakers?'

Ray says both he and his brother couldn't get out of the room fast enough. 'It looked like junk to me,' Ray whispered to his brother as they fled.

* * *

Joe played pool in the garage with his nephews after Ben provided them with a home-made table. Using his carpentry skills, Ben built the pool table with a mixture of materials, including rubber from a car tyre and wavin pipes to make the pockets. Then he finished off his masterpiece by covering it with green baize. It was Ben's cunning plan to keep the boys out of the pool halls in town ... and it worked. Their friends now flocked to the garage for pool tournaments. And Uncle Joe was one of the most competitive contestants, enjoying hours of fun on a winning streak.

* * *

Joe watched with both pride and amusement as Adrian and Ray formed their own garage band when they hit their early teenage years. Along with their friend, Ray Bracken, the trio set out for world domination with their rock outfit, Aes Triplex.

Adrian remembers that Joe was amused by their strange name and wanted to know the source of it.

'Ray Bracken saw it on the back of a car window,' Adrian explained.

'The back of a car window!' Joe laughed again.

'I think it's great,' Adrian retorted, in a clearly offended tone.

'Well, it's different, I'll grant you that,' Joe said.

Slim, angular Adrian had chosen to be the bass player, while his more powerfully-built younger brother, Ray, became the drummer. But the only band member who could actually play his instrument was the idealistic young guitarist, Ray Bracken. Joe's bass player, tall, debonair Pat Hoey, agreed to give Adrian lessons; and his drummer, the ebullient Tony Newman, put Ray through a crash course. Little did the boys realise that they were being groomed by two of the finest musicians in the country at that time. Soon the sound of music coming from the Dolan garage had switched from songs like 'You're Such A Good Looking Woman' to Adrian's self-penned, hard rock numbers, 'Punk Teacher' and 'Murder in the Back Row'.

When they had finally gelled as a band and savoured the taste of live performances at their own local shows, Adrian and Ray began pestering their father, Ben, to give them a starring role as the opening act for Joe. Their timing was perfect as Ben was resisting the new trend in dance halls of using a disc jockey to play disco music before the live band came on. 'What do you think, Joe?' Ben asked his brother when the idea was mooted.

Joe remembered telling Ben, 'Ah, sure, they'll probably run everybody out of the place before we go on stage, but it'll be a bit of craic and good experience for the lads.'

As Aes Triplex were warming up before a show deep in the country, Joe stood at the back of the hall, trying to keep a straight face. 'I was really tickled by the very earnest young rockers, performing like they were superstars,' he said. Joe roared laughing at one point when the guitarist, Ray Bracken, launched into a solo, went down on his back legs and then discovered to his embarrassment that he couldn't get back up again.

Later, when the doors opened, a handful of Joe fans trickled in to see the support act. Aes Triplex performed most of their set to an empty hall, but by the time they finished it was full. The crowd had now arrived to see Joe.

'We're after packing the place for you, Joe,' Ray told his uncle in the dressing room after Aes Triplex finished their performance.

'Jaysus, great, Ray, I couldn't have done it without yez,' Joe laughed.

* * *

When Ray left school, Ben insisted that he should go to college and study for a trade. Like his uncle Joe before him, Ray had only one passion. He decided to confide in Joe's drummer, Tony Newman, about his ambition. 'Tony, I have to get into Joe's band one way or another,' Ray pleaded.

'Okay, leave it with me and I'll sort it out,' Tony said, after giving the teenager a sympathetic hearing.

Tony made an approach to Joe, Ray remembers. 'Do you know, I think it would be a very good idea to get Ray in to play with us,' he said.

'Play what?' Joe asked, surprised.

'Play percussion.'

'What do you mean, percussion?'

'Well, freshen up the sound in the band and give songs like 'Good Look-ing Woman' a new lease of life with shakers; a bit of conga work and a bit of tambourine.'

'I don't know …' Joe wasn't so sure.

'Joe, Ray is a young lad who is very keen, he'll be good for the band,' Tony insisted.

'Maybe you're right,' Joe relented.

Joe approached Ben. 'What do you think?'

'Oh, I think it's a great idea,' Ben agreed.

'If I had won the Sweepstake I couldn't have been more excited,' Ray recalls now. 'I said, "Fair play to you, Tony," and gave him a big hug.'

A week later, the singer Brendan Shine arrived at Dolan's bar in Mullin-gar with a set of red congas. Ben had bought them in the UK and arranged for Brendan to pick them up on his way home from an English tour. Ray was now a fully paid-up member of the band.

Adrian had already left school and was working in the bar which Joe and Ben had opened in Mullingar. He was also now playing bass in his new band called Beyond Words. Then Joe's bassist, Pat Hoey, decided that he was leaving to start a new life in America. When Joe and Ben considered their options, there was only one candidate they were happy to sign up. Adrian was now in the band.

The introduction of young blood into his backing band would give Joe a new lease of life in the years to follow as Adrian and Ray steered their uncle down all kinds of music boreens.

CHAPTER 12

THE JET-SETTER

ER LINGUS BANS JOE DOLAN screamed the headline in the
Evening Herald.

Joey Purcell tells the story of how Joe was not around to read the embarrassing newspaper story in October, 1976. He was now stranded without his friends on the Greek island of Corfu, desperately trying to line up all kinds of horrendously expensive flights through various airlines in a bid to plane-hop his way across Europe on a crazy route back home to Ireland.

How had his long-awaited holiday gone so terribly wrong? 'This should have been one of the great memories of his year as he relaxed on a paradise island away from the demands of showbusiness, following his relentless and exhausting touring over the previous months,' Joey points out. Instead, Joe's dream golfing trip with family, pals and colleagues from the band business had been marred by an incident on the flight out from Ireland. Now that confrontation had come back to bite Joe on the backside.

Joe's driver and golfing buddy, Purcell, was sitting in the seat beside him on the flight out. He remembers that after the plane had taken off, Joe decided to open the duty-free booze he'd purchased in Dublin Airport. Several drinks had already been consumed by the party during a long flight delay before take off.

'Would you have a bottle opener?' Joe asked the air hostess as she strolled through the aisle.

'Sorry, you can't drink that!' the hostess responded when she spotted his stash of alcohol.

'Ah, sure we're on our holidays,' Joe laughed.

The hostess wasn't amused.

As she passed by again, Joe now had the bottle open. 'Would you have a glass?' he asked, cradling his bottles of gin and tonic.

'You can't drink that,' the hostess insisted again firmly.

'Ah, would you ever get me a glass,' Joe persisted.

The hostess took exception to Joe's attitude and reported him to the captain. He now came down the aisle to admonish Joe. 'You've just subjected the air hostess to abuse,' the captain told him.

'I didn't abuse anybody,' Joe insisted.

Joey Purcell is adamant that Joe had not used an abusive tone in any way.

By the time Joe arrived in Corfu, he was in a foul mood. To cap it all, there was no sign of his baggage, so he stormed through Customs, without producing his passport and was immediately arrested and put in handcuffs. 'Jaysus!' Joe declared, looking pleadingly at Ben, Seamus Casey, Joey Purcell and the rest of his crew.

'Don't worry, we'll get it sorted,' Seamus assured him.

Joe's passport was eventually located and he was allowed to leave the building to begin his holiday. As the week progressed, Joe was just beginning to get over his annoyance when another incident came around the corner to spoil his fun. He slipped on marble tiles and slashed his arm.

'That's a bad cut, Joe, it'll need to be stitched,' Ben said.

'I'll take you to the hospital,' Joey offered.

'I'm not goin' near any hospital.' Joe was adamant.

'You'll get an infection and then you'll be in real trouble,' Ben argued.

'You know I hate hospitals.'

'You'll end up staying in one if you don't get that cut sorted out,' Ben warned.

Joe finally relented and was taken to a local hospital on the island where he had stitches inserted in the wound.

As the holiday came to an end, Joe couldn't wait to get home. It had been a stressful experience from start to finish. When they settled into their seats on the plane, Seamus noticed that Joe was missing. 'Where is he?' he asked Joey.

'Ah, he got delayed there coming through,' Joey said.

The doors closed and the plane taxied on to the runway with Joe's seat still empty. Aer Lingus had refused to allow him board the plane. Joe had been banned from flying with the national airline. His travelling companions were gobsmacked. 'We'd have all stayed on the ground if we'd known that,' Joey said.

It was two days later before Joe finally arrived into Ireland, after joining the dots on a string of connecting flights across Europe. The trip home had cost a fortune and left him shattered. Worse still, the entire country had now been informed about his embarrassing Aer Lingus ban by the *Herald*, *Press* and *Irish Independent*. It had also made the national radio and TV news. There was only one thing he could do … Joe turned it into a big joke during his TV, radio and print interviews.

His brother Ben's latest foray into the world of fashion was also perfect timing as the saxophonist and band leader had now chosen a set of green suits for the entire group. 'We're sponsored by Aer Lingus,' Joe told his audiences, to loud laughter and applause in the months that followed.

Two years later, Aer Lingus lifted the ban and welcomed the Westmeath Bachelor back on board their flights. Joe was delighted.

*   *   *

The soles of his shoes were frozen to the ground as he stood on the spot, having his photo taken in Moscow's Red Square in the winter of 1978. It was minus 36 degrees, not the sort of weather Joe was accustomed to back home in Ireland. He had dreaded getting out of bed for work at the *Westmeath Examiner* on many a frosty morning in his freezing cottage bedroom outside Mullingar. But he had never felt bone-chilling cold like this.

'Jaysus, will yer man ever finish up?' Joe said to Ben as the photographer hovered around shooting the band from different angles while they were slowly turning into frozen statues.

Drummer Tony Newman was like a bear with a sore head. 'I hope it's not his f***ing career,' he quipped.

Joe laughed. He was on top of the world, despite the cold. This was one of the most exciting moments in his life. He was now on tour in the USSR, performing to nearly 150,000 people. He had known that his songs were hits everywhere from Moscow to Leningrad. But it was only when he touched down behind the Iron Curtain that Joe realised he was now a superstar in this strange part of the world.

The offer to tour in the USSR had come after its ambassador in Ireland experienced one of Joe's memorable performances during a record number of ten sellout shows at The Chariot Inn in Ranelagh, Dublin. Joe's manager, Seamus Casey, had then taken a call from the embassy which asked if the singer and his band would be prepared to go on a cultural exchange to the USSR. Joe had jumped at the chance of a new adventure. He wasn't disappointed.

Joe's jaw dropped when he strutted into Moscow's magnificent Olympic Winter Sports Palace, where he was set to perform to 9,000 people every night. The backdrop on the stage was a forty-foot-high painting of himself. Joe recognised the image: he recalled that it was from a photograph taken by Tom McElroy, who was then chief photographer of the *Sunday World*. 'I feel like a bullfighter walking into the arena,' he told Ben before the show.

Joe didn't know what to expect from the crowd, although Seamus Casey had been chatting with Cliff Richard about the reaction of audiences in the Soviet Union. Cliff had indicated to Seamus that they were 'cool and reserved'. From the moment Joe stepped on stage the audience went wild. The Irish singer was blown away, like a bird hit by an express train. It was an instant love affair between himself and the crowd. Joe became quite emotional when he realised that they knew all the songs: 'Good Looking Woman', 'Crazy Lover', 'Make Me An Island' and 'Midnight Lover'. Besides the hits, they also went wild about the 'Westmeath Bachelor'. Joe charmed them with his one word of Russian: 'Nasdrovia!' he said, as he sipped a drink. It meant cheers.

'Sláinte!', a Russian voice roared from the body of the darkened auditorium.

It threw Joe for a couple of seconds and he could feel tears welling up in his eyes. Everything about Leningrad had a sort of magic for Joe. It was breathtakingly beautiful and he loved the friendliness of the locals. Before he left, Joe played to 99,000 people in the city. Gosconcert, the Soviet state agency which had arranged the tour, laid on a limousine for Joe and a luxury thirty-two-seater coach for his band in Moscow. 'Every time I sit in that car I expect Mr Brezhnev to arrive and hop in beside me,' Joe laughed.

As he savoured the lifestyle of a superstar in Moscow, Joe got a nightly reminder of the matriarch who had sown the seeds for this remarkable success. An old Russian woman popped out of the darkness outside the venue and stopped his car at every performance. 'Joe, your mother is looking after you,' the wizened Russian lady told him through an interpreter.

It was a spooky message that played on his mind throughout his time in the city. Each night the old lady presented Joe with a religious item, including a cross. Then she blessed him and disappeared into the darkness. Joe graciously accepted her gifts, but his mind raced with all kinds of theories about her. At one point, he asked his local interpreters to make enquiries about the woman and her background, but no one was able to provide him with any information. The elderly Russian lady would remain an enigma to Joe.

Another memory that Joe would take from his visit was the severity of the local economy. There was very little on offer for the locals to purchase, including food stuff. Everybody had money, but there was nothing to buy. 'Someone said that if one person stopped in front of you and you stopped behind that person a queue would form, with people thinking there was something to buy,' Ben told his brother.

While there was austerity all around them, Joe, Ben and their band were treated like royalty on the tour, with lavish banquets laid on for the superstar and his entourage. All the local delicacies were provided for the illustrious visitors, including caviar. Ben spat it out the first time he spread it on brown bread and took a mouthful. 'Jaysus, there's an awful taste of fish off that jam,' he declared, scrunching up his face with disgust.

Joe nearly choked in a fit of laughing.

'Sure it's far from caviar we were reared in Mullingar,' Ben quipped when he discovered his faux pas.

Ben's heart was in his mouth throughout the trip for fear that Joe or any of their crew would get drunk and end up in trouble with the extremely strict local security force. 'Next stop is Siberia, lads,' Ben regularly warned them on the tour.

'You're a terrible f***ing pessimist, Ben,' drummer Tony Newman retorted.

'Well, somebody has to worry around here,' Ben said.

'Your biggest worry will never happen,' Tony insisted.

Everyone, including Joe, went drinking to pass the time on an overnight train trip from Moscow to Leningrad. And everyone got very drunk and fell out with each other. At the end of the journey, the train stopped outside Leningrad. Ben and Seamus were told by their interpreter that there had been an incident and that the police were coming on board to have a word.

'Oh, Jaysus!' Ben sighed as his worst fears looked like they were becoming a reality.

Joe wasn't long in bed and was now snoring in his cabin. Fearing that he would kick up a racket and get himself into trouble with the police when abruptly woken up for an interrogation, it was arranged for Joe and his manager, Seamus, to slip away as VIPs. A car was organised and they got a police escort to their hotel.

Meanwhile, Ben and the rest of the band were terrified as they got their possessions searched by the police while being held on the train. It transpired that a member of the train staff had reported them for stealing silverware. The police failed to find any incriminating evidence and much to Ben's relief they were all allowed to go free.

It was some time later before Ben discovered that it was his brother who had narrowly avoided a trip to Siberia. Joe had taken a shine to a set of silver tea holders during a meal on the train, and had slipped them into his pockets as a souvenir. Ben had a fit when Joe confessed.

'Sure how was I to know that they were like the crown jewels,' Joe shrugged.

Joe left Russia with a kaleidoscope of great memories from his travels. He had done twenty-three shows in twenty-three days and soaked up the adulation he enjoyed throughout the Soviet Union. To have made such an impression on the people and to experience such popularity in that strange land gave Joe an enormous boost. It was beyond anything he had imagined.

'I don't think I've ever been so tired in my life before, but then I don't think anything has given me greater satisfaction,' he told then *Sunday World* reporter Sam Smyth, upon his return to Ireland in a blaze of glory that December in 1978.

* * *

Irish Independent journalist and Today FM broadcaster Sam Smyth had forged a close friendship with Joe that began when he was a teenage ballroom promoter in the north of Ireland.

Upon leaving school in the early sixties, Sam started out in life as a messenger boy 'on a bicycle with a basket on the front of it', and as an apprentice electrician. But the good-looking Belfast teenager was soon pursuing his burning passion for showbusiness.

At the tender age of sixteen, Sam was managing a successful band called The College Boys and was now travelling down the country with them and building up his contacts. He also managed Gene and The Gents and, later, Chips. 'Along with my friends in Belfast, I just loved bands and I got to know many of the bigger ones,' he recalls.

While still in his teens, Sam secured his dream job, booking the bands for a chain of ballrooms in the North, including Romanos in Belfast, Milanos in Bangor, The Commercial Ballroom in Dungannon and The Locarno in Portaferry.

Joe and The Drifters was one of the super bands that Sam regularly hired and what would become a lifetime friendship between the pair soon developed.

As a huge fan, Sam remembers he was in awe of Joe on their first meeting in the summer of 1967.

'Joe was then one of the most popular singers and I went down to Mullingar with my best friend at the time, a guy called Donal Corvin, to meet him and the band to try to get them to come and play for me.

'I was a kid, but Joe was so disarming and such an enthusiast; and he had such a love of life. In many ways, that infectious enthusiasm that he had got to everybody. I remember somebody saying that every time you met Joe

Dolan it was like drinking champagne for the very first time. And that was how I felt about him.'

Sam recalls staying in Joe's apartment in Mullingar when Joe and The Drifters were recording 'Love Of The Common People', 'At that time apartments would have been very rare and exotic in a town like Mullingar.' Sam also talks of how both he and Donal Corvin (now deceased) ended up making some sounds on the track in the background.

While working in showbusiness, Sam began his journalistic career writing for a paper called *City Week* in Belfast and he became a director of entertainment for the city of Belfast. 'At the time it was like becoming a director of entertainment for the city of Beirut, except the Troubles in the Lebanon ended a lot quicker than they did in the North,' he reflects. In 1972, following the events of Bloody Sunday, Sam decided to move away. Most of his contemporaries had emigrated to London, but Sam chose Dublin. 'Through showbusiness I had developed many friends in the South and I felt comfortable there,' he explains.

In Dublin, Sam got a job as a writer for Ireland's entertainment magazine, *Spotlight*. From running Joe's shows in the North's ballrooms, Sam now found himself writing about his friend Joe in the popular publication. A year later, in 1973, the *Sunday World* was launched and Sam joined it as a reporter, covering 'showbusiness and "shock horror" and the combination worked out very well, I was very happy with it.'

'My involvement with Joe and the other showbands was such a great advantage to me over many others when I became a journalist because of the contacts it gave me. No matter what end of the country you were sent to, to cover a story, you would probably know a musician, or a promoter or somebody nearby. Other fellas would arrive and not know anybody. People are generally reserved and are not going to tell potentially embarrassing things to a stranger, so knowing somebody in the area was always invaluable. I have always felt privileged to have made those friends around the country. People still ring me up and those contacts are still working for me.'

During his early days with the *Sunday World*, Sam would make his way to Joe's place in Mullingar at every available opportunity. 'If I was down the country on a job, I would always somehow end up in Mullingar,' he laughs.

When Joe was around the craic was ninety. 'Joe would have you out and about,' Sam laughs. 'We'd go to Broder's Hotel in Mullingar, where he introduced me to the B-Specials, a drink that consisted of brandy, advocaat and ginger ale. We'd be acting the eejit half the night in Broder's and it was marvellous there. Joe introduced me to great characters around Mullingar, people like Twirlin' Doyle, a fella who played drums in the town band and who got his name from twirlin' the drum sticks! Fellas like that found their way to Joe's company and they were great, great country fellas. There was very little money around, but those guys really knew how to have a laugh and to enjoy life. It was a learning curve for me as somebody who was brought up in a city because country towns have their own dynamic.'

Joe, Sam and the gang would still be on the town when the sun came up and then they would head out to the country to an early morning pub. 'You have great stamina when you're young,' Sam explains. 'We'd be half-daft at that stage, but Joe would never throw in the towel.'

Sam recalls Joe having strong views on many issues in life, including Serbia. 'I remember Joe sitting me down and giving me a long lecture on Serbia, of which I knew little and I suspect he knew less; but he was wagging his finger at one stage,' he laughs. 'I remember I had to say things like, "Funny, I never looked at it that way before, Joe."'

'But one of his great traits was that he didn't take himself seriously. He took his talent seriously because it was a very serious gift that he had, but he could laugh at himself. That is a very redeeming feature and not a common one among people who achieved the success that he did. And Joe could see the ridiculousness of what he did, whereas so many others had such egos that if they were in a room together they'd be going around like fellas in some kind of Humpty Dumpty suits trying not to bump into each other.

'Joe quietly realised his talent, but he was very, very good at taking a rise out of those other fellas too. He laughed at their pretentiousness. The one thing that made him different, and this is probably unique in that business, is that I don't think he had any insecurities about his talent. He was very confident of what he could do.'

Sam reflects on Joe's appeal and his success: 'Number One, he was very talented; he was a very good singer, he had a very pure voice and he sounded like he meant what he was singing, there was sincerity in it. And, do you know something, he really liked the people he performed for and they could sense that.

'Joe was always thinking about good songs. I remember going through England with him once and him teaching me a harmony line on "Love Thee Dearest", and he sang those great songs too. Joe had a very natural instinct for a good song. He had better taste in songs than most of his contemporaries. He sang better songs and he probably sang them better than most of the other big names of the time.'

*   *   *

As he sat on the plane propelling him across the sky towards the bright lights of Las Vegas in September, 1980, Joe's memories wandered back to his young days cutting turf in the bog outside Mullingar. Then, as he pulled a wheelbarrow filled with the sods of peat, Joe never imagined the remarkable journey that lay ahead in his life. The thought of having his name up in lights in Vegas, the entertainment capital of the world, certainly never crossed his mind as he stacked the turf. His idol, Elvis Presley, had later set Vegas on fire with his shows. Now Joe was about to try his luck in the gambling Mecca and he was buzzing with excitement. Even at this early stage of the trip there had been drama – and Joe was still in the air.

Ben, the perpetual worrier, had been hovering around everyone, like a clucking hen at Dublin Airport, making sure that Joe and the gang all had their passports, documentation and gear in order for the trip. When everybody was checked through to London, where they were getting a connecting flight to Las Vegas, he relaxed. Ben then wandered through the Duty Free and lost track of time. At one point his heart skipped a beat as it struck him that the time had passed for the flight. Ben looked up with the fright, then breathed a sigh of relief as he spotted band members Frankie McDonald and Liam Meade at two different locations. 'Eventually, I rounded up Frankie and Liam and suggested that we should mosey on down to the departure gate,' Ben recalls today. 'It was then that the bombshell dropped. The gate was closed and our plane was about to taxi down the runway.'

A frantic Ben then explained his predicament to the airport ground staff. 'We're on this flight. We're going to Vegas, we have to be on that flight,' he said, nearly in tears.

'That flight is gone, I'm sorry.'

Ben recalls that he was then in a sweat and a terrible state of distress as he poured out his story about their trip to Vegas and how Joe's shows were going to be in jeopardy. Seeing his distress, the staff were sympathetic and organised three seats for Ben, Frankie and Liam on the next flight to London. They also contacted London and arranged for the three musicians to be collected from the plane and whisked to their connecting flight. When they arrived, a van picked them up and took them to the next plane, which they boarded in a state of mortification. Ben then braced himself for Joe's slagging. Shortly after the flight took off on the next leg of the journey, Ben, Frankie and Liam wandered up the aisle to find their fellow travellers.

'Where have you been sitting?' Joe asked.

It was then Ben realised that Joe hadn't missed them, and he couldn't believe his luck. He was going to be spared an embarrassing roasting by his brother. Later, however, Joe did hear about their saga. 'Well, ye're right gobshites,' he laughed.

Joe's trip to Las Vegas had been facilitated by a dapper, teetotal Irish promoter called Joe O'Neill. The Dubliner had a vision that Joe would become a superstar in the adult's playground set in the Nevada desert. Ben wasn't so sure about the offer, so O'Neill brought in two millionaire American promoters to convince him. After watching Joe whip up his audience to a frenzy at a Dublin cabaret performance, the high-powered American businessmen were convinced that Joe would do the same at their Vegas hotel, The Silverbird. A fee was agreed with Ben, including the flights for Joe and the band.

'What about the food?' Ben asked as expenses were discussed.

'My God, you'll get a breakfast in Vegas for fifty cents; food is for nothing,' Joe O'Neill said.

'You have no idea how much those fellas can eat,' Ben insisted.

'Okay, the food is on the house,' O'Neill agreed.

When the deal was sorted, Ben was still dubious. But, some time later O'Neill called to confirm the dates and their airline tickets arrived in the post.

When they touched down in Vegas after their long-haul flight, Joe, Ben and their entourage were greeted like superstars. Two limousines with police outriders were waiting to collect them from the plane, where stunning women dressed as leprechauns welcomed them on the steps.

'I could get used to this,' Joe laughed.

Downtown Las Vegas in 1980 was 'Neon City', a garish wonderland of casino hotels that lit up the night sky in a blaze of colour. 'It was like landing in the middle of a giant movie set,' Ben recalls. Caught up in the magic and the energy of this crazy place, Joe was excited to be playing a starring role as one of its leading entertainers.

When he burst on to the stage at The Silverbird, Joe's dreams came crashing down to earth. His show was starting after midnight, there were only two dozen weary, booze-sodden gamblers and holidaymakers in the place ... and most of them fell asleep. Back home he was used to playing to sell-out show to fans going wild for him.

'It's the bloody graveyard shift,' Tony Newman announced in the dressing room afterwards.

Joe was despondent.

'That time obviously doesn't work for you, we'll change it,' Joe O'Neill promised.

When Joe's shows were rescheduled and moved to an earlier slot the crowds started to build up. Joe O'Neill, who looked every inch a star himself with his healthy tan, slim physique, immaculately coiffed hair and sharp clothes, was delighted that his gamble was now paying off.

Joe also got a boost from the cab drivers who were then playing a major role in promoting shows in Vegas. 'When they collected people from the airport, the drivers were usually asked by visitors, "What's a good show to go to?" Joe got to know several cab drivers when he was out and about, and he made a huge impact on them,' Ben reveals. 'Joe only had to meet someone for five minutes and you'd swear he knew them all their lives.' The cab drivers fell for the guy with the easy charm and started getting all their buddies to recommend the Joe show to people arriving into town. Then Joe's Silverbird Hotel Casino shows really started packing out through word of mouth.

Ben recalls that the food was going down well with the band too. Tony Newman became addicted to the delicious spare ribs. His eyes would bulge with mouth-watering anticipation as a mountain of ribs were place in front of him. Then he'd delve into them. By the time he was finished, Tony's T-shirt would be redesigned like an abstract painting with sauce and speckles of meat. Joe arrived in one day just as Tony had finished off a gigantic portion. He stopped and looked with amusement at the pile of stripped bones that surrounded his wacky drummer.

'Jaysus, Tony, it's like an elephant's graveyard,' Joe laughed.

In the daytime, Joe, Ben and the band often relaxed by the pool at their hotel. One of the chefs would frequently pop his head out through a back door of the kitchen and shout to them: 'Easy money!' Joe enjoyed his sense of humour.

* * *

Joe and Brendan Bowyer laughed heartily as they sailed down the Vegas Strip together, after sharing a boozy afternoon in a hotel bar. Joe was catching up with his old friend, Brendan, who had put down roots in Vegas many years previously. Now they were both on their way to the MGM Grand Hotel, to finish off their evening waching Julio Iglesias in concert.

A private booth had been reserved for the two Irish entertainers at the MGM Grand. At the end of the performance, as Julio Iglesias stood smiling on stage, soaking up the adulation and the thunderous applause from his female fans, Joe and Brendan suddenly stopped snoring. They had both slept through Julio's entire performance. 'Ah, sure he was singing lullabies,' Joe laughed as they slipped away afterwards en route to another bar.

In Vegas, Brendan told Joe the story of the night that Elvis Presley came to see him in concert. Brendan had first met Elvis in Los Angeles, where the American idol was shooting one of his movies. Later, Bowyer ended up performing in The Stardust Hotel, where Elvis and Frank Sinatra regularly starred in the main showroom.

Elvis was in the building this particular night, and on the way out he heard Bowyer singing one of his songs. As he performed in the blinding spotlight, Brendan noticed that there was a commotion in the middle of the room. Elvis had slipped through a curtain at the back of theatre and was rushing up the centre aisle. Now every member of the audience was going berserk.

Joe laughed as Brendan joked how he thought he had suddenly made a wonderful connection with everyone in the room. Then out of the corner of his eye, Brendan spotted Elvis at the side of the stage, waving a cane at him in mock anger. He nearly collapsed with the shock. Then Elvis started laughing and gave Brendan a big wave before disappearing in a flash.

Next, Brendan heard that Elvis had requested the maître d' to reserve a booth for him to see his entire show. 'I want to come back tomorrow night,' Presley had said.

Joe's eyes were now dancing in his head at the thought of his hero Elvis coming to see his old friend in concert.

'Well, of course, the word got out and that night you couldn't get into The Stardust, never mind into our little theatre,' Brendan said.

Elvis, his stunning wife, Priscilla, and their entourage sat at the back of the room, watching Waterford's famous son doing 'The Hucklebuck'.

'What was it like performing for Elvis,' Joe asked, bursting with excitement at the thought of it as he knocked back another shot.

'Amazing,' Brendan nodded, 'Especially when I did some of his songs. I did the best vocal I could, but I didn't try to sound like him. I just belted them out.'

Afterwards, Elvis invited Brendan to join him for a party at his penthouse. A night out with Elvis! It was Joe's dream. Brendan told Joe how Elvis had confided that he had hated most of his movies, but he'd been under contract to do them. Then Elvis asked Brendan about one of the songs he'd sung, called 'This Time Lord You Gave Me A Mountain'.

'Where did you get it?' Elvis asked.

'Oh, that's a Marty Robbins' song,' Brendan said. 'It's kind of a victim song and we've made it more dramatic than Marty's version by adding lots of brass and turning it into a big cabaret number.'

Joe had seen Elvis perform the song on television. 'That's right,' Brendan agreed. 'A year after Elvis came to see me he did the song in *Aloha from Hawaii*.'

As they ordered another round of drinks, Joe marvelled at Bowyer's connection with The King. 'Well, I did a hundred Elvis songs through the years, but at least he got one from me,' Brendan added. Joe laughed.

*   *   *

Joe spent two months in Vegas and while he would return for a second season, the lifestyle did not suit him. It involved two shows a day and he was missing his circle of friends back home. It was even too hot to play golf. Towards the end, Joe was counting down the shows. Whereas before he had always loved the stage, now it was becoming a chore. Vegas had turned singing and performing into a job for him. It was a feeling that was alien to Joe.

*   *   *

Ray Dolan could not believe the turn his life had taken when he found himself touring South Africa with Uncle Joe. 'Just a few months earlier I was sitting in a classroom doing my Leaving Cert,' Ray recalls. Then he had spent two months performing five days a week with the band at Joe's summer show in the Gleneagle Hotel, Killarney. This was followed by a six-week stint at The Belgard in Tallaght. Now he was on an international tour in South Africa with Joe. Teenager Ray felt like he'd been caught up in a whirlwind and he was loving every second of it.

Joe was a superstar in South Africa and had toured there for a decade. Even though he had insisted on playing to a mixed audience, he was eventually forced to join the boycott of the South African regime at the time. 'The 1983 trip would be his last tour in that part of the world,' Ray notes. The pressure had come from all quarters, including Kevin Marron, the then editor of the *Sunday World* who left a blank space in his column 'A Sort Of TV Column' every week, asking Joe to explain why he was still touring in South Africa.

In 1998, Joe spoke to me about his controversial decision to play South Africa against mounting opposition at the time. 'To be honest, when I went there I was thick,' he said. 'I knew nothing about apartheid. I had records in the charts over there and I was thinking of my career. I went to South Africa for music. It was music and not politics that I was involved in, and that was that. I never did respond to Kevin (Marron) because I'm very reluctant to make comments on things. You start a controversy or prolong a controversy by doing that. You give people more ammunition. You're better off saying nothing at the end of the day. And the Lord have mercy on Kevin, he died before we ever talked about it.'

Kevin Marron was killed in a plane crash in November, 1984, along with seven other passengers and the pilot, near Eastbourne in England while taking part in a promotion race to bring back the first Beaujolais nouveau wine from France.

In South Africa in 1983, Ray remembers his father was having second thoughts about bringing him into the touring life of a band on the road. As he mulled it over, Ben decided that Ray should be trained into the more stable family business of running their Mullingar pub. Ray was devastated when his father broke the news to him.

Upon their return, Ray accepted his fate and went to work in the pub. As Joe set off on a series of Irish shows, Ray was now pining for the life he had tasted as a travelling musician in one of the country's biggest bands. Meanwhile, out on the road around Ireland with Joe, Ben was having second thoughts about his decision. 'When he came home he said to me, "Do you know what, there's a fierce emptiness in the band since you left. Joe thinks so too and we want you to come back."'

Ray remembers being thrilled to be back in showbusiness. 'That's great, Daddy.'

CHAPTER 13

DENIS MEE, THE BISHOP AND KILLARNEY

J oe's PA Denis Mee was fascinated by the middle-aged, rugged sailor who rolled into The Green Inn pub in Mullingar in 1977 and stirred his imagination with colourful tales from stopovers in exotic corners of the globe. His seafaring lifestyle, sampling the delights of places like Bahrain and the Persian Gulf, South Africa and Alaska, seemed so exciting compared to the then fifteen-year-old boy's humdrum daily existence in a rural Irish town as he worked part-time in the bar, to earn a few bob during his summer holidays from school. The worldly-wise mariner from the Merchant Navy probably didn't intend it as he sank his pints and poured out his marvellous stories in the pub, but he influenced the direction that Denis Mee would take in life. Young Mee was bitten by the travel bug as he lapped up the seafarer's epic accounts of ocean adventures. Instead of joining the navy, however, Denis would go on to see the world and enjoy some of life's most amazing experiences as a road manager and personal assistant to Joe Dolan for twenty-eight years.

Denis's life journey with Joe happened by chance and seems to have been his destiny. Strangely, the long-haired, well-built, fit teenager initially followed the same path as Joe. After completing his Leaving Cert, Denis got a job in the printing works and book-binding department of the *Westmeath Examiner*.

One day as he sauntered up the street of Mullingar, Denis remembers how he met a man he knew called Tommy Begley. At the time, Tommy was working as one of Joe's road managers. As they chatted on the street, Tommy said he was about to unload the gear from Joe's touring lorry and set it up in The Horizon ballroom for a band rehearsal. 'Would you have a few minutes to spare to give us a hand?' Tommy asked.

Denis was happy to oblige him. 'I was a fan of Joe and the band and many of the other big names then touring on the Irish scene. I would go to see them play at The Horizon, the Greville Arms and at the carnival dances in Clonmellon (County Westmeath),' he recalls. After setting up the gear for Joe and the boys that afternoon, Denis stayed on to watch them rehearse. Afterwards, as he was about to leave, Tommy, a big teddy bear of a man, gave him a nod to come over to where he was working. 'Would you be interested in doing this full-time?' Tommy asked.

'Jaysus, I would,' Denis remembers replying without hesitation.

'Okay,' Tommy said, 'I'll talk to Ben.'

Denis was then hired on the spot. After proving himself as a reliable and conscientious worker, doing general jobs during his two years with the paper, the *Westmeath Examiner* management had then offered Mee an apprenticeship in their printing works. It was a golden opportunity to train up in a secure, well-paid trade. But just like it had done to Joe, showbusiness was now calling him; Denis was being drawn to the bright lights of the band game and he couldn't resist it. His thoughts were with the sailor who had inspired him to travel. Now he was getting the chance to see Ireland as part of Joe's roadshow. 'I might have been going to Ballyhaunis instead of Bahrain, but it was a start,' he laughs today.

In 1983, at the age of twenty-one, Denis fulfilled his dream of the sailor's globe-trotting life when Joe, Ben and the band set off on a three-month odyssey around South Africa. He was finally an international jet-setter as Joe's minder on the trip. It was going to be daunting, but Denis was cool and calm and relishing the challenge.

It was only when the Joe show rolled in to Johannesburg on their first day that Denis realised just how important his role was going to be on the tour. Joe was clearly a superstar in this part of the world, even in 1983, decades after the days of Driftermania.

Denis remembers being highly impressed as he witnessed Joe at a press conference, held around the pool area of an exclusive hotel. There were over 400 media people and the local glitterati of the entertainment business waiting to greet and grill Joe. As his eyes scanned around the area, Denis could hardly believe what he was seeing. A full bullock was being barbecued on a spit and everybody was being served with Irish coffee, despite the temperature being hotter than Denis had ever experienced in his life.

It was part of Denis's role to organise the schedule of interviews for Joe with the local media and somehow he managed to get through that first day with flying colours. The responsibilities he took on for the trip were enormous:

'I was Joe's minder and I was responsible for everything from his toothbrush to his band suits. ... I had to know who was collecting him and what colour the car was in case anybody was misrepresenting themselves. I had to drag him around radio and TV stations and newspapers. I made sure that he was up in time for interviews and that he was in bed in time .... I was responsible for looking after all of Joe's stuff and I took it very seriously.'

Then it all went horribly wrong. As they were moving out of Nelspruit, four hundred miles north of Johannesburg, Steve Quibell, a son of the

Above: Joe with radio and TV personality Gerry Ryan.

Below: Studio wizard: Joe with godson Adrian in their Mullingar recording studio.

Above: Sharing a laugh at a Mount Argus fête with Eileen Reid and Fr Brian D'Arcy.

Inset: The Drifters stamp, issued by An Post.

Right: Joe's tailor Jas Fagan with the last suit he made for the singer. It was never collected.

Above: Drifters: Joe, Des Doherty, Ben, Tommy Swarbrigg, Joey Gilheaney,
Sid Aughey and Jimmy Horan.

Below: Uncle Joe: Joe with his nephew, Colin Dolan, and brother, Ben.

Left: Joe and his pal Paddy Cole, enjoying the fun at the Eamonn Darcy/Joe Dolan Golf Classic.

Below: Joe with radio and TV personality Gerry Kelly, Paddy Cole, snooker ace Ken Doherty and Eamonn Darcy.

Above: Fans: Brigid Cummins and Mags Keating with their shrine to Joe and his hip bone.

Below: A rare photo of Joe, pictured in his beautiful Foxrock home in the '90s.

Left: Female fans showered Joe with knickers at his shows.

Below: Joe, on left, with author Eddie Rowley and Thomas Murphy.

Above: You could hear a pin drop in the room when Joe sang 'Silent Night'.

Below: Paddy Dolan, pictured with the statue of his brother, Joe, at the unveiling ceremony in Mullingar.

South African entertainment promoter Ronnie, offered to help Denis to pack up Joe's belongings from his hotel suite. When they got back to Johannesburg all hell broke lose. Joe's suits were missing – his entire wardrobe for the tour. Steve thought Denis had taken them, and somehow Denis assumed that Steve had brought them. But ultimately it was Denis's responsibility.

'I was in big trouble,' Denis recalls. 'I had been brought out in a highly trusted position, looking after Joe and here I am after messing up. I was only twenty-one and how was I going to do the four-hundred-mile journey there and back to recover the suits? I rang the hotel and, luckily, they said they had a driver going to Johannesburg the following day and they would send the suits with him. I went out to the airport with Steve and we found the driver, so a potential disaster was averted.'

After that fright, Denis personally cleared out Joe's hotel suites when they were moving on. 'There was always a big hamper of fruit in Joe's room when he'd arrive in, enough to feed a small colony of animals in a zoo, and I never left any of it behind,' he says. The drinks cabinet in Joe's suite was stocked with hundreds of miniature bottles of booze. Denis had never seen the likes of it. After the incident with the suits, Denis now retrieved everything from the room, including all the bottles of alcohol.

Their next big trip was ten hours across a desert to Namibia in a convoy of vehicles, after spending a night in African huts at a safari park in Vryburg. Along the journey, Denis produced the bottles of booze and held them out his passenger window to tease drummer Tony Newman who was travelling behind him. Eventually, when there was a break in the journey, Denis shared out the alcohol among the travelling party of fifty people. By the time they had crossed the desert into Namibia all of the three hundred miniature bottles were empty.

In Namibia there was a call from the management at their previous hotel. Staff discovered that the bar in Joe's suite had been emptied, but no one had paid the bill for it. 'I didn't realise they weren't complimentary and that they had to be paid for,' Denis laughs today. 'At that time there was no such thing as a mini-bar in Irish hotels, or certainly the ones that I stayed in.'

South Africa, with its wonderful people, culture and natural beauty, was an incredible experience for Denis. He was astonished by the thousands who attended Joe's big shows.

At the time, Joe's decision not to boycott South Africa because of its racial segregation led to Denis and the rest of the touring party being criticised back home, even though the singer insisted on playing to multi-racial audiences.

'Don't mind them,' Joe would say when he heard of the verbal assaults on his band and road crew. 'People like that have never been a mile from a cowshite in their life.'

*   *   *

Denis says he will never forget his embarrassing incident on an Irish tour in the late 1990s, when Joe's roadshow pulled into the Rochestown Park Hotel in Cork city. The date was 6 January, known as 'Little Christmas' or 'Women's Little Christmas', where it is traditional, particularly in Cork, for men to take on all the household duties and give their womenfolk a day off. It was also traditional for the women of Cork and the surrounding area to spend their special night of the year in the company of Joe Dolan.

That night, as the Rochestown Park Hotel was filling up with excited women, flocking to the Joe show in their finery, Denis was checking out the final schedule in a back room of the establishment when three of the support acts came up, accompanied by a gentleman dressed in the garb of a Catholic bishop. 'As it was a big party night for the women, I looked at the bishop and thought he was a fantastic kissogram. The women were going to love it, I thought,' he recalls.

The 'kissogram' turned to Denis and asked: 'Would you mind if I had a microphone, son?'

Denis laughed. 'Where would you like it, Father,' he replied, making a rude gesture with his arm and fist.

Sudden shock registered on the faces of two hotel management staff who were standing behind the bishop. They were ashen-faced and making cut-throat gestures to Denis, who now realised that he had made a major faux pas. The bishop was speechless.

'Right, Father, c'mon and I'll set you up with a mic,' Denis then said, breaking the awkward silence and still unaware of the identity of the man in the clerical outfit.

Joe thought the whole scenario was hilarious when Denis told him later, and he would tell local journalists about it during interviews for years to come.

'Sure, I didn't know Bishop Buckley, I thought he was a kissogram,' Denis explained that night to Joe. Joe couldn't stop giggling.

Cork's Bishop Buckley was recognised locally as a man of the people. That night he went on stage and welcomed all the ladies out to Joe's show on Little Christmas and wished them a happy night. He was a Joe fan himself.

* * *

The Joe Dolan Love Train would glide smoothly through the country-side packed with party women bound for the Gleneagle Hotel in Killarney, during weekends away at Joe shows through the years. Joe was synonymous with the entertainment and holiday experience in Killarney for decades. As they clinked their glasses and toasted Joe on the specially chartered train, the female revellers sang along to his songs being played on the tannoy through the carriages. Newly-purchased knickers were waved in the air as their excitement built up in anticipation of the fun that lay ahead in the

Kerry town, famous for its lakes, dramatic scenery ... and Joe Dolan shows.

Joe was king of the Gleneagle in Killarney. Hundreds of thousands of Irish families flocked there for his summer residency in the venue through the years, and women lived their lives around Joe weekends in the Irish holiday hot spot.

Gregarious gentleman Maurice O'Donoghue recognised Joe's drawing power in the late 1960s when he performed at the Town Hall in Killarney. Maurice, the owner of the Gleneagle, then set out to woo Joe, Ben and the band to his hotel, eventually making manager Seamus Casey an offer they couldn't refuse, to play a New Year's Eve show. It was the start of Joe's association with the Gleneagle that would span four decades. Killarney became Joe's second home, where he created his own magic for families, singles and married couples alike on summer nights, weekend specials and New Year's Eve – trips they would remember forever.

Joe also became a great friend of the late Maurice O'Donoghue and through the years they would go off on golfing holidays together to America. 'We all took a liking to Maurice as he was such a funny man,' Joe recalled some years ago. 'Maurice was ahead of everybody and he pretty much started the cabaret scene in Ireland. I've had some of the best craic in my life down in the Gleneagle.'

Joe's manager, Seamus Casey, admits the success of their summer residency in Killarney took them all by surprise: 'After we started playing at the Gleneagle, families began rebooking their holidays there for the following year. We were getting literally hundreds of calls from people asking us what date we were going to be starting back in Killarney before we'd even done a deal for the next year. It was a most extraordinary connection that Joe made there with the fans.'

Love stories began at Joe's shows in Killarney, according to Adrian Dolan. And he should know. Adrian met his own future wife, Dubliner Saundra Roc, at a Joe concert in the Gleneagle back in 1982. 'I wasn't in

Joe's band at that stage. I was eighteen and on holidays,' he recalls. 'I saw this girl and got chatting and I got her into the show. And she thought I was great getting her into the Joe Dolan show. Then she told me that she was going home the following day. I only found out later that she hadn't gone home at all. She had just used me to get into the gig. But I was smitten and I had got her address because that night she'd said she was a fan of Buck's Fizz. "I have a great picture of them at home," I said. So she gave me her address to send it to her. The next time Denis Mee went to Dublin, I went with him and we called to her home in Santry. Saundra was as embarrassed as hell with me calling up to the house. But that's how our relationship started. It was out of Killarney.'

Adrian remembers that in 1982, Joe did two months in Killarney, five days a week, and there were lots of other entertainers in the Kerry resort. 'Killarney was like Las Vegas to Joe, except it was better because he was at home. In Las Vegas he had got tired of it and just wanted to come home, whereas in Killarney he still had his golf and all his friends,' he says. "They all went out every Thursday, Friday and Saturday to play golf, including entertainers like Finbar Furey, Dickie Rock and Red Hurley who were also stars of Killarney at that time.'

When Adrian joined Joe's band in '85, they played two nights a week in Killarney during the summer. 'We'd be doing other shows around Limerick and Cork and if we were doing Killarney on a Saturday night we'd arrive late Friday night or the early hours of Saturday morning after a gig. Whatever band had been playing in the Gleneagle would be in the green room and all our band would go in and join the party, with Joe holding court. Joe would be up till six or seven in the morning and then he'd go playing golf at 10am. Bal Moane was the comedian on the show and one memory I have is of Bal standing at the top of the stairs one morning, half-dressed in fisherman's gear and the other half in a golfer's outfit. "I'm between minds today, I don't know should I go fishing or should I go golfing?" he announced. Joe fell on the floor laughing. Everybody was mad down there at that time. You'd get in at three or four in the morning and the night porter would have a banquet laid on for you. It was a different way of living.'

Adrian believes that the Killarney shows boosted and prolonged Joe's career by introducing him to generations of Irish people who might otherwise never have experienced his unforgettable live performances.

'The other venues where Joe played around Ireland weren't family orientated,' Adrian reflects. 'Killarney was a place where the families would go and they knew that at the Joe show nobody was going to be effing and blinding; it was going to be music and just Joe having a good time. The children came to the shows and Joe got on really well with them. He would make a point of taking a kid up on stage and giving him or her a tie. That memory would stay with the kid. So when they got to eighteen, nineteen or twenty they were Joe fans because he had been a part of their childhood. They'd go through their teenage period and maybe go away from Joe, but they'd come back to him then because of those great memories.'

* * *

Joe Dolan was Marie Keating's favourite Irish entertainer. Every summer, Marie, her husband, Gerry, and their five young children, Ciaran, Linda, Gerard, Gary and Ronan, would pile into their old gold-coloured Ford Escort saloon car and set off on their seemingly never-ending journey from Dublin to Killarney for their summer holidays. Invariably, they would hardly be a half-hour out of Dublin when Ronan would pipe up from the back of the car, 'Are we nearly there, yet?' As their car rattled along the roads on the marathon journey there were the usual family rows among the kids. Marie would turn around and warn them that if they didn't behave Daddy would turn back and there'd be no holiday that year. There was no fear of that happening, of course, as Marie couldn't wait to see Joe in concert at the Gleneagle.

Ronan Keating himself would grow up to become a pop star with Boyzone, but back then he was just another kid in the crowd scampering around the place at the Joe shows. His older brother, Ciaran, became friendly with Joe's nephew, Ray, and through the children Marie and Gerry got to know Joe. As he got older, Ronan began to appreciate Joe's stagecraft. Ronan would see Joe over and over through his parents, including performances at The Kilmore Hotel in Cavan where his father came from.

'Joe was the first pop star in my eyes,' Ronan says today. 'He was the one who had the women throwing their knickers at him – not my mother, mind you – but all the young ones up at the front. I guess I took a lot from him, from what I saw of Joe on stage, not that I ever had knickers thrown at me. When I was in Boyzone in the early years, I even went to some of Joe's concerts with my mam. Every time he walked on stage his energy was amazing.'

In February, 1998, Ronan's world fell apart when his mother, Marie, died, following a short battle with breast cancer. He was devastated. Ronan was Marie's youngest child and they had had the perfect mother-and-son relationship. Joe was deeply upset when he heard the news. Marie Keating was a real lady and he had always enjoyed the warmth of her company.

'One of the first people we saw when we arrived at the church on the morning of Mam's funeral was Joe,' Ronan recalls. 'We were all touched to see Joe there and each one of us in the family went up to him and shook his hand. We knew how much it would have meant to Mam, for him to be there.'

In the aftermath of the funeral, Joe spent a couple of days with the Keating family, supporting them through that dark period in their lives. Joe knew the pain of losing a loved one, particularly a mother. During that time, Joe told Ronan that Marie had often talked about him in their conversations and she had been interested in his opinion about her son's career in Boyzone. 'Ronan is a lovely young fella who will always do well in the entertainment business,' he reassured her.

A month after the burial of his mother, Ronan somehow plucked up the strength to celebrate his twenty-first birthday with a big showbiz party at the Red Box club in Dublin. Among the celebrities who turned up was the Keating family's favourite, Joe Dolan. 'I was just so chuffed to see Joe there that night,' he says.

When Ronan and his family later set up the Marie Keating Foundation, to provide cancer information and awareness for Irish people, Joe was one of their biggest supporters. 'Joe came along to all our black-tie events and our golf outings, so I then got to know him very well over the years,' Ronan reveals. 'Joe has been a big influence on me. He was the perfect showman. He never had a bad word to say about anyone. He always had a smile on his face and a joke … and his jokes were just great. It was always good craic to be around Joe. He always had the good side out, and that's what I'll remember about Joe Dolan; and it's a lovely memory, I think, to have of anyone.'

CHAPTER 14

THOMAS'S OF FOXROCK

With his shirt sleeves rolled up, in the late evening Joe was often to be found bringing in the bags and boxes of fruit and vegetables which had been displayed on the stand outside Thomas Murphy's shop, tucked away in a corner of the fashionable Dublin southside village of Foxrock.

Many people in this leafy, upmarket suburb assumed that the food and wine shop was one of Joe's business enterprises because of his regular presence behind the counter where, for three decades, he could be found engaging in jovial banter with his neighbours and the other local villagers and passers-by, as well as the delivery men and women who came through the door.

Thomas's, described as being 'like the pantry in Buckingham Palace' because of the wondrous array of food items from all parts of the world that it stocks, became one of Joe's social outlets away from the stage.

Joe did not, in fact, have a personal financial stake in the shop; it is owned solely by Thomas Murphy, the jolly, larger-than-life character who gives the well-known premises its name and who became one of the singer's great friends in life.

Thomas, who grew up in nearby Cabinteely, had been familiar with Joe the entertainer since the late 1970s when, as a teenager, he had seen him perform at The Horizon ballroom in Mullingar while on holidays with his country cousins from the neighbouring county of Meath. 'I got caught up in the excitement as Joe performed in the barn of a venue that night,' Thomas recalls. 'I was fascinated by the reaction of the crowd and Joe's energy and great showmanship on stage. This was my first experience of a live performance by a superstar in the flesh, as he was to me, and it was an unforgettable memory.'

In 1983, Thomas, then a budding nineteen-year-old businessman, seized the opportunity to open his own shop and bought the Foxrock premises. One of the first customers who came through his door was the very guy he had seen whipping a crowd into a frenzy at The Horizon in Mullingar several years earlier. Shortly afterwards, Thomas remembers how he took a phone call in his shop midmorning one Monday.

'How'ya Thomas, it's Joe Dolan here ...' the familiar voice at the other end announced.

'Hi Joe ...'

'I had a party in the house last night, Thomas, and some people stayed over; is there any chance you could drop up with rashers, sausages, eggs and black and white pudding?'

Thomas was happy to oblige. 'Dressed in my smart, white shop coat with a shirt and tie, I arrived at Joe's impressive home off Brighton Road in my delivery van,' he recalls. It was Joe who answered the door. 'How'ya Thomas, come on in ...'

'Ah, no, Joe, I have to get back to the shop ...'

'Ah, sure come on in for a minute and say hello to the gang.'

At 5pm that Monday evening Thomas was still in the house enjoying the craic that Joe created when he was surrounded by people. 'This was the beginning of our long, close friendship,' Thomas reveals.

Although he maintained his apartment and business investments in Mullingar where, along with Ben, he was co-owner of Dolan's bar (now Mullingar House), Joe made Foxrock his Dublin base when he bought his magnificent, five-bedroom mansion there in 1982.

He guarded his privacy, but in a rare moment in 1994 Joe agreed to do an 'At Home With …' feature, based around celebrities and their homes, for the *Sunday World*. This would give the singer's fans a once-in-a-lifetime peek inside his hall door. The paper's fashion photographer who captured the unique images was Val Sheehan, the man who had chronicled Drifter-mania and shot the cover of Joe and the band's first album at Belvedere House all those years ago. And this author was the journalist who Joe invited over the threshold of his beautiful home that day.

Tucked away in the corner of a cul-de-sac amid a small cluster of exclusive residences, Joe's impressive two-storey house was secured by electric gates. The only evidence of the owner was his Westmeath-registered Merc that sat on the concrete and paved forecourt.

As we wandered through the spacious house, where Joe recharged his batteries amid the demands of live performances on the road, the singer told how he enjoyed the simple things in life, like cooking, reading, watching TV and entertaining family and friends. Joe said he was a big fan of TV documentaries and he loved to switch off and watch the soaps. His favourite was 'Fair City', followed by 'Coronation Street', 'Emmerdale' and 'EastEnders'. 'At least when you're watching 'Emmerdale' you're getting a bit of fresh air,' he joked.

Glimpses of Joe's personal tastes and passions were everywhere to be seen, from his cherished collection of crystal to the set of golf clubs in the hallway. One of his favourite golf courses was just down the road at Powerscourt, where the club manager, Bernard Gibbons, had become a close friend.

Joe's impressive crystal pieces, mostly presents from friends or prizes from golf tournaments, were displayed in a large glass cabinet and on side tables in the intimate designer dining room with its purple colour scheme. Even his telephone in the entrance hall was crystal, similar to one he'd spotted and taken a shine to while watching the American TV soap 'Dynasty'.

Joe's favourite room was a cosy TV lounge with a mint green velvet-covered suite of furniture, lush green carpet and walls painted in warm beige and yellow colours. A life-sized cuddly tiger sat on a mat guarding the marble fireplace, while a stereo player and speakers mounted on the walls indicated Joe's passion for music away from the stage. This room led into a light-filled conservatory that had a view spanning his beautiful, manicured, landscaped garden. It was here that the entertainer enjoyed his relaxation time by reading his newspapers and books. His Foxrock pad oozed opulence – the luxuries included a sauna and a Jacuzzi – and, along with the neighbouring homes, it gave the area a Beverly Hills-style appearance.

While he valued some quiet time out of the spotlight, Joe was outgoing by nature and he was never going to be happy living a hermit-like existence, locked away behind closed doors, even if it was in luxurious surroundings. He loved the company of people, so whenever he became restless in his empty home, Joe would set off down the road to Thomas's end-of-terrace shop where he would hold court behind the counter. He would make himself a cup of coffee and chat with Thomas in his office down the back of the popular premises, passing shelves stocked with fine food, wines and Champagne en route. 'When he spotted a neighbour or some local acquaintance on the security cameras, Joe popped up like a jack-in-the-box, to engage in a bit of banter, catch up on the goings-on in their lives and to tell them his latest jokes,' Thomas reveals. He never actually served customers, but people coming and going left with an impression that Joe Dolan was working in the shop.'

Although Joe kept his life in Foxrock low key from the general public during the 1980s, with most people assuming that Mullingar was his main base until his newspaper feature in '94, the singer often promoted Thomas's shop in the early days from the stage and in the media.

One night while they were participating in a charity bowling competition in Stillorgan, Joe told Thomas that he would not be staying on for a late-night drink. 'I have to take it handy tonight, I'm doing the Gay Byrne radio show in the morning,' he said.

Some of Gay's family shopped in Thomas's. 'Drop into me on your way to RTÉ in the morning and I'll give you a rhubarb tart for Gay,' Thomas said. 'He was saying on the radio last week that he loves rhubarb tart.'

'Oh, yeah, no problem,' Joe agreed. 'And sure I'll mention the shop as well.'

'Well, that was sort of the idea,' Thomas laughed.

When Joe arrived in to the studios the following morning, carrying the rhubarb tart, a member of Gay's radio staff informed him that there were no plugs allowed for products on the show.

'Fair enough,' Joe nodded.

During a commercial break, Joe said to Gay: 'I believe you love rhubarb tart, or so you were saying on radio the other day? I was in Thomas's of Foxrock on the way in and he gave me this to give to you.'

Gay was 'delira and excira'. 'Oh, I know Thomas, bring up the story when we go back on air,' he said.

When the interview resumed, Joe said: 'By the way, Gay, I believe you love rhubarb tart.'

'Oh, I do, indeed,' Gay replied.

'Well, I have a nice rhubarb tart here for you from Thomas's in Foxrock; he told me to call in and collect one for you on my way here,' Joe said.

'Oh, well, how kind of him, sure I know Thomas well, indeed I do, and he has a great little shop out there in Foxrock,' Gay responded.

Thomas remembers being thrilled as he listened to the interview on the radio. 'You couldn't buy that kind of publicity,' he said.

Today, Gay Byrne has fond recollections of his encounters with Joe through the decades. 'I always thought Joe was a lovely fella, who was very funny,' Gay remembers, 'Joe would always be smiling, laughing, having a bit of craic and enjoying himself. He had a great sense of his own place in showbusiness and he knew exactly what he was about. I remember seeing him performing in Limerick one time and he was fantastic the way he got the crowd going. He had a set of vocal chords made of cast iron, judging by what he put them through. He worked hard and he was on the road all the time, keeping it going. I always knew he was very fond of me, as I was of him. But I didn't get to spend a lot of time with him because I'm not a golfer, so I missed out on that.'

* * *

In the journey of life, Thomas Murphy met his wife, Trish, whom Joe doted on after he too got to know her. Joe was among the guests at their wedding reception and, as the celebrations got into full swing that night at the Killiney Court Hotel in Dublin, he went up on to the stage and joined the band, featuring his old friend Paddy Cole. Over the course of an hour, as Joe thrilled guests with all his hits, including 'You're Such A Good Looking Woman', which he dedicated to the bride, the wedding party seemed to double in size, packing out the ballroom. It was virtually impossible to move in the room at this time. Shortly after Joe finished his set and the gathering had dispersed, it emerged that most of the guests attending another wedding in the hotel had left their party downstairs to watch Joe Dolan in action, after the word spread that he was putting on a fantastic show.

When Thomas and Trish became parents to David, Niamh and Elizabeth in the years that followed, Joe was a regular presence in their home life, as he was in the lives of his own nephews and nieces. He laughed heartily at their childish expressions and their naïvety; and he played along with their sense of fun. 'The kids adored him,' Thomas says. 'In many respects Joe was a big child himself. He was often to be found at the kitchen table in our house, helping the children with their homework in the evenings when they started primary school. Joe would sit and work with our young daughter, Niamh, particularly on her Irish lessons which he enjoyed.'

Joe's favourite time of the year was Christmas; it was a period when the child inside him truly emerged. He loved the ceremonies, the presents, the fun and the laughter. Joe even hosted dinner one Christmas in his home for the Murphys. Thomas remembers that in the middle of the festivities, as everyone tucked into his delicious meal of turkey and all the trimmings, he sat back in his chair with a beaming smile, looked around at the happy faces and declared with huge joy in his voice: 'Isn't it great to have kids sitting around the table on Christmas Day?'

Although he never married, Joe always insisted that his life was fulfilled. He told me one time: 'People say, "You never had kids." My answer is, "I've always had kids. I have nephews and nieces to beat the band and I absolutely love them. I've always enjoyed my nephews and nieces. They're grown up now and it's even more fun because I can socialise with them. I'll get a call, "Are you home, Uncle? Can we call round?" It's not a lonely life by any means. I have great people in my life. I have a great family and friends.'

Through the years one of Joe's traditional shows was a performance at the Gleneagle Hotel in Killarney on New Year's Eve. When one year in the late 1990s he was forced to break with this annual event because his voice was hoarse, Joe took up an invitation from Thomas and Trish to join their house party. 'Other than his voice not being up to scratch, he was feeling fine,' Thomas says. As the wine flowed that night around the table, someone asked: 'Joe, gives us one song.' So Joe duly obliged, after warning that his voice wasn't in great shape. His performance was enthusiastically received by the appreciative gathering.

'Ah, Joe, go on, you might do another one,' somebody else egged him on, as more wine and Champagne was poured.

Joe sang again. Then there was another request. 'Jaysus, I'd be better off in Killarney, at least I would have been earning a few bob,' he laughed.

* * *

Joe was in great form as he lapped up the party atmosphere in the corporate box at Leopardstown Racecourse in July, 2007, when Thomas Murphy hosted a gathering of his family and friends to watch his horse, *Rivoletto*, compete in one of the evening's races. The horse had been a winner in Sligo, a couple of months earlier, and there were high expectations for the night that lay ahead.

'Do you want to come to Leopardstown and see how a real horse runs?' Thomas had asked Joe in the build-up to the event.

Back in the early 1990s, Thomas had been Joe's guest in a corporate box at Leopardstown when the singer's horse, *Goodbye Venice*, was competing in a race. Joe was buzzing around that afternoon, literally walking on air with excitement in the build-up to the race. Surrounded by family members and his pals from all walks of life, he was in seventh heaven. A couple of wins on tips in some of the previous races had added to his elation as the Champagne flowed. As *Goodbye Venice*'s race came up, Joe was now on tenterhooks. Watching from the box, surrounded by his supporters, Joe's excitement suddenly went south and his heart sank while a nightmare story unfolded out on the racecourse. *Goodbye Venice* trailed the field through the race and finished in last place.

'Does anybody have a number for Albert Reynolds?' Thomas Murphy announced among the gathering.

Joe shot him a glance as if to say, 'Stop right now!'

'What's Albert Reynolds got to do with anything?' another pal asked.

'Albert owns a pet-food factory down in Longford; he might buy that donkey off Joe,' Murphy replied, and Joe now joined in the laughter.

Despite hosting the expensive reception in a private box for his pals, Joe was subjected to unmerciful slating over the rest of the evening at the racecourse. But he took it in good spirits; that was Joe. Later, several of his friends, including Thomas, joined Joe back at his Foxrock home, where the party went through the night and into the following day when the Champagne corks were still popping. 'Jaysus, what would we have done if *Goodbye Venice* had won?' Joe laughed.

In the years that followed, whenever the topic of horse racing was raised, Thomas Murphy says he loved to remind Joe of the 'donkey' he used to have.

It was Joe who had driven his pal, Murphy, up to the races to watch *Rivoletto* perform that evening in 2007. Thomas was full of the joys of life as he brandished his owner's and trainer's badge on the way in to Leopardstown.

'You used to have an owner's and trainer's badge one time Joe,' he slagged.

Joe was quick to tell Thomas where to go.

The owner's and trainer's badge allowed the car to make its way through the throng, but it was only a special pass up to a point. As the car was being stopped, a steward recognised the driver.

'Is that Joe Dolan?'

'It is,' Thomas replied.

'Right, follow me,' the steward said as he opened a gate and escorted Joe's car into an exclusive VIP section.

'Now, you know what you can do with your owner's and trainer's badge!' Joe laughed, unable to resist the chance to slag Murphy.

Joe backed a couple of winners in the build-up to the race featuring *Rivoletto*, and he was thoroughly enjoying the evening's entertainment. Thomas, meanwhile, was hovering around like an expectant father outside a maternity ward. With an insider in the camp, his pals were pumping him to find out if *Rivoletto* was going to be a sure-fire winner. The trainer had assured the owner that the horse 'won't embarrass you'.

'Put a couple of bob on each way,' Thomas told his friends who asked.

Just before *Rivoletto*'s race, Murphy's nerves got the better of him and he slipped away to watch it on his own. Joe stayed in the box to observe the race with Thomas's guests. *Rivoletto* started well, but as the race progressed the horse lost pace and it soon became obvious that Thomas Murphy's worst nightmare was about to become a reality. The last horse home at the finish was *Rivoletto*. At that moment, the familiar sound of loud, raucous laughter filled the corporate entertainment box. Joe looked like he would have to be resuscitated, he was laughing so much.

'The shite I've had to put up with for years about *Goodbye Venice*; it's the last time I'll hear anything about that,' he guffawed again.

It was hard not to feel sorry for the clearly embarrassed and sheepish horse owner who arrived back to the box where guests were enjoying the fine food and drink at his expense. But Joe succeeded in overcoming his sympathy for Murphy. 'People in glass houses should never throw shite,' he told him.

Just like Joe had done over two decades, Thomas now took his slagging and laughed it off.

'I have that number for Albert Reynolds,' Joe added, only to be told in no uncertain terms what he could do with that suggestion.

Later, as they discussed the race, Joe asked: 'What did the trainer say?'

'He said the horse hit a wet patch,' Thomas replied.

Joe collapsed again in a fit of the giggles.

* * *

Despite his passion for golf, snooker, rugby and boxing, Joe was not an avid follower of our national GAA games or of soccer. Thomas Murphy would jokingly tell the singer that the reason he had never been to an All-

Ireland Final in Croke Park was because he came from Westmeath. Murphy, a passionate supporter of the Dublin Senior Football team, was the holder of a couple of corporate seats in Croker. He had tried, and failed, on several occasions to persuade Joe to accompany him to matches. Finally, Joe relented and agreed to tag along with Thomas, to watch his native Westmeath take on the mighty Dubs.

'We'll have a small wager,' Joe suggested.

Even though he didn't follow the sport, Thomas remembers that Joe regularly had a bet on a Sunday game with him. He would call into the shop that morning. 'Who are you going for today?' Joe would ask his pal. Then he would put down a wager on the opposing team. 'It was for small money, but it was one of Joe's simple kicks in life,' Thomas says. The following day, Joe would call in, to collect his winnings from Thomas, or to pay up. 'If Joe was the loser, he would try to discreetly hand over the cash,' Thomas laughs at the memory. 'I wouldn't let him off the hook, though. "Joe lost on the match yesterday and is here to pay up," I'd announce to the entire shop.'

On the day of the Dublin-Westmeath tussle, Thomas arrived in his Dublin jersey to pick up Joe. 'Where's your jersey?' he asked Joe.

'I don't need a jersey to tell people where I'm from,' Joe quipped.

'Just as well you're not wearing one, at least you won't be embarrassed on the way home.' Thomas was quick to reply.

'What do you mean?'

'Sure, we're going to slaughter Westmeath.'

When he arrived at Croke Park, Joe got a great reception from the Westmeath fans. There were several of his friends among the crowd, including Lorcan Daly, owner of a Mullingar petrol station.

'Are we going to win today, Lorcan?' Joe asked.

'In your dreams,' Thomas chipped in.

As the final whistle sounded, Joe was already on his feet, cheering.

Thomas was sitting shell-shocked in the stadium. Suddenly, he spotted familiar faces heading in his direction. It was Joe's friends. Thomas winces today as he recalls how he was then subjected to a barrage of good-natured slating by the jubilant Westmeath fans.

The following morning, Joe arrived into the shop. 'Westmeath beat Dublin yesterday and I'm here to collect from Thomas,' he announced to the amusement of customers.

*   *   *

Down through the years, Thomas Murphy was a firsthand witness to Joe's big heart, his generosity and his innate kindness to people in need. Thomas's wife, Trish, had worked with Respect, an Irish charity which caters for people with an intellectual disability. They were desperately in need of funding and when Murphy mentioned this to Joe in the late 1980s, the singer immediately offered his services. Joe and Thomas then approached Bernard Gibbons, the general manager of Powerscourt Golf Club, and Irish golfing legend Eamonn Darcy. Out of their discussions emerged the Eamonn Darcy/Joe Dolan Golf Classic in 1987, the year that Darcy had the winning putt for Europe in the Ryder Cup. It was Joe who insisted that Eamonn Darcy should be given top billing for the event. 'He's the golf star,' he pointed out. Joe then personally phoned his celebrity friends, including UTV presenter Gerry Kelly and sports stars DJ Carey, Ken Doherty and Nicky English, appealing to them to support the event.

Joe had built up a close friendship with towering media celebrity Gerry Kelly through the years and would go on to make several appearances on the Kelly show. 'I loved Joe's company; he was one of life's great characters,' Gerry recalls today during a round of golf. 'I used to dance to him in my young days, but I didn't know him at that stage. To me, he was then Joe Dolan the superstar. I went dancing to him all around the North in places like Canon's Hall in Downpatrick and The Central ballroom in Newcastle, never in a million years thinking that one day we would be treading the fairways together. It was through golf that we really got to know each other.'

Like Joe, Gerry played with the Links, a charitable celebrity golf society based in Dublin and one which raised millions for good causes since its launch in 1966. 'We played on a fairly regular basis with all the other guys like Dickie Rock and Red Hurley,' Gerry recalls. 'That's how I became very friendly with Joe. We'd sit and talk into the wee hours of the morning, once there was a vodka in your hand; and the craic was mighty. It was just that type of relationship, enjoying somebody's company. Joe was very easy to be around. It wasn't Joe Dolan the superstar. It was just Joe Dolan. He was like a fella you met down the road.

'Joe, of course, would always be telling jokes. If you had none of your own it didn't matter, Joe had enough of them to last the night. But he also had a serious side and was fascinated with the North and the political scene going on here. He had a very good knowledge of it and would ask me hundreds of questions. It was a genuine interest. It wasn't just small talk. He wouldn't expound to the Northerners what should be done; he just asked the questions for his own knowledge.

'Joe also loved a good argument on an intellectual level. I was absolutely knocked back one night to discover that he was an authority on the British royal family. I don't know what his fixation was, but Joe seemed to have a huge interest in them for some reason. He knew all the connections within the family. That's one argument I didn't win because I knew very little about them, to be honest. Joe really did love them.'

The Eamonn Darcy/Joe Dolan golf classic was a huge success in 1987, raising over IR£40,000 and more in the years that followed. Joe also starred in two concerts for Respect at the National Concert Hall, Dublin, giving his services free of charge in aid of the charity.

'There were many individual cases where Joe helped to alleviate the financial pressures of people who had been diagnosed with life-threatening illnesses or contributed to charities in their name,' Thomas reveals.

In 2003, when Thomas told Joe his personally devastating news that his uncle, Tony Murphy, was terminally ill with a brain tumour, was unable to work and with his first child on the way, the singer's instant response was: 'If there's anything I can do, I'll do it.'

Joe then waived his fee to star in a fund-raising concert for Tony and his family, a short time later at the Arklow Bay Hotel in County Wicklow. He also personally visited Tony at St Colman's Hospital in the Wicklow village of Rathdrum. Tony, a passionate music fan, was thrilled that the Irish celebrity had come to see him. It was a massive morale boost as he bravely battled his illness. He was so excited that he began pressing his buzzer for the nurses to pop in to meet his famous visitor. The singer was unaware of this, as he was then using the ensuite toilet in Tony's private room. Emerging from the tiny bathroom, Joe was mortified to find the nurses waiting to say hello to him as remembered his sound effects that were like Niagara Falls.

Later, as he sauntered through the hospital's television room, the hearts of several elderly female patients skipped a beat when they recognised the Irish entertainer.

'Ah, well, I declare to God if it isn't Joe Dolan!' one said with obvious delight.

'How are you?' Joe laughed as he went to hug the women.

There was music on the television and Joe said: 'Okay, who's going to give me a dance?' Suddenly, to laughter and cheers, Joe was waltzing around the room with his female fan club. For a few moments at least, the old ladies had miraculously forgotten about their worries and ailments.

Tragically, Tony, passed away a short time later in May, 2003, at the age of forty-nine. It was just a week before his wife, Lisa, gave birth to their first child, a baby daughter called Toni. Joe's kindness has never been forgotten in the family.

One night in 2000, as Thomas was chatting with Joe, he told him that he was going on a visit to Beaumont Hospital to see a friend, Tony O'Reilly, who had been diagnosed with lung cancer. 'Tony worked in the Dublin Fruit and Vegetable Market, where I got my supplies for the shop. Joe said he would like to go along,' Thomas recalls.

In the hospital, Joe talked to Tony like they were old friends. Later, when Thomas suggested organising a fundraising night for the hospice in Tony's name, Joe instantly volunteered to be one of the entertainers. Sadly, Tony O'Reilly passed away just a week before the concert in Killiney Castle. Tony's family, including his mother, attended the show in his memory and, when his part in the performance was over, Joe spent the evening with them at their table. 'I met Tony; he was a lovely guy,' Joe told his mother over and over.

On stage that same night, Joe was his usual ebullient self. The celebrity backing band included his friend, RTÉ presenter Ronan Collins, on the drums.

'This is the worst band I've ever had behind me,' Joe told the crowd to a burst of laughter.

'And this is the worst singer we've ever had in front of us,' Ronan responded in a flash, sending Joe into a fit of laughing.

*   *   *

Thomas Murphy's abiding memory of his old pal is that there was always laughter when Joe was around. And there was fun at every turn. Thomas joined Joe and their mutual friends on numerous golfing trips to Spain.

'What are you having to drink?' Thomas asked the gang after they had checked in at Dublin Airport on one their outings to the south of Spain. Four pints were named. Then it came to Joe. 'I'll have a glass of Champagne,' he said.

Thomas ordered the pints, including one for himself, then he asked for a glass of Champagne. It only came by the bottle, he was told. He duly ordered a bottle of Champagne and asked for six glasses. He was shocked when he was presented with the bill.

There was time for another round. 'I'll get this one,' Joe said, 'What are you having?' Pints were ordered. 'I'll have a glass of Champagne,' Murphy said.

Joe arrived back. 'They only have it by the bottle.'

'I know,' Thomas replied. 'Who had to buy the last one?'

Joe returned with a fresh bottle of Champagne. 'That just cost me a hundred quid,' he said, addressing Murphy in mock outrage.

'I know, it cost me the same,' Thomas laughed.

While they were enjoying a meal at the Valparaiso restaurant in Mijas on that same trip, several Irish fans came over to their table to say hello to Joe.

'Let me get a hug from Ireland's Numbe-rOne entertainer,' one well-heeled and well-oiled lady said, grabbing him in a bear hug.

Joe laughed. 'Dickie Rock wouldn't be very impressed to hear that,' he said.

Later, after some encouragement from his friends, Joe sang a song called 'If I Could Put My Life On Paper'. More Irish tourists came to the table to greet him and shake his hand. Later, some English tourists stopped by on their way out. 'You must be somebody famous, but we don't know who you are,' one of the gentlemen said.

'Yes,' Joe replied, 'I was the first Irish footballer to play for Barcelona.'

One of Joe's friends, Brian Farrelly, then piped up: 'Joe, tell them about all the greats you played with.'

The Brits stood staring in awe, waiting for Joe to regale them with fascinating tales of matches played with soccer's legends. Joe glanced at Brian. If looks could kill. Farrelly was now chuckling. Knowing that Joe hadn't a clue about soccer, Brian enjoyed watching him trying to squirm out of the spoof he had started.

'Ah, too many greats, too long ago,' Joe then said enigmatically.

*　*　*

'Despite his celebrity status, Joe didn't have any airs or graces about him. He was professional about his singing and performing, but he didn't take himself seriously,' Thomas says as he recalls the night that Joe asked him for a lift down to a black-tie function at the upmarket Berkeley Court Hotel in Dublin's Ballsbridge.

'No problem, I'll drop you in to the Berkeley when I close the shop,' Murphy said.

'That'll do grand, Thomas.'

Later that evening, Joe and Thomas arrived at the plush hotel where Mercs and BMWs were dropping off party-goers, dressed to the nines in their evening gowns and suits. As Murphy drove up to the hotel entrance there was a look of horror on the face of the doorman, and he began frantically waving their vehicle around to the rear of the building.

'What'll I do?' Thomas asked his front-seat passenger who was clearly enjoying the commotion they were causing.

'Drive right up,' Joe laughed.

Thomas pulled up outside the front door in his shabby old delivery van. As the doorman, now in a state of sheer panic, came rushing over to move on the offensive vehicle that was lowering the tone of the occasion, Joe opened the passenger door and hopped out, dressed in his tux and with a big smile.

'Oh, g-g-good e-evening, Mr D-D-Dolan,' the flustered doorman muttered, taken by surprise.

'How'ya?' Joe said, laughing and shaking the poor man's hand.

Then, with a look of divilment in his face, he slapped the side of the van and shouted after Murphy: 'Come back and pick me up later.'

* * *

In the evenings, when the shop was packed up and the shutters had come down, Joe and Thomas often shared a bottle of wine while shooting the breeze at the end of the day. On one such evening, Joe was talking about a conversation he had had that day with a friend from the world of showbusiness. His pal, a well known singer, had been complaining about a IR£200 mobile phone bill he'd run up on calls to his mother.

'I'd love to be able to spend two hundred quid to talk to my mother,' he told Thomas. Joe had often mentioned Ellen on nights like this, reflecting on how much he would have loved her to have seen and enjoyed what he was doing in life. Mostly nights like this, though, were some of Joe's happiest times; there were jokes to be told and people to be slagged.

CHAPTER 15

FATHER BRIAN

Father Brian D'Arcy recalls the time when, as a young student priest, he was racing through the night on his bicycle, quietly muttering a prayer amid short puffs of breath. As he frantically pedalled along the deserted, dark streets from Dublin city centre to the sleepy suburb of Kimmage, Brian was praying that he would not be caught by his superiors in the Passionists while slipping back into Mount Argus after his curfew. His heart was racing with a mixture of apprehension over his return to base, and the adrenaline rush of seeing his favourite entertainer singing live on stage that night. 'I had absconded from the monastery and sneaked into the city to watch Joe Dolan performing at a dance,' he reveals.

As well as having a vocation for the priesthood, young Brian D'Arcy, who grew up in the village of Bellanaleck, about five miles from Enniskillen, County Fermanagh, was passionate about music and was a fan of all the big bands that were popular at the time. Just two years earlier, in 1963, the then eighteen-year-old novice had masterminded a similar escape from the same monastery to see The Beatles performing at The Adelphi Cinema in Dublin. With the precision planning of a convict plotting a break-out from prison, Brian had orchestrated to leave a ground-floor window ajar that evening. 'The bicycles were locked up at night, so I had hidden one of them close to the window for my transport to town,' he recalls. When the Mount Argus hierarchy had retired to bed after their prayers, he then scarpered out of the monastery, as swiftly and silently as a professional thief, making his getaway in the night. 'I was in raptures as I had the once-in-a-lifetime experience of hearing John, Paul, George and Ringo that historic evening in the capital, even if it was just on the street outside the venue,' he says today. 'Afterwards, with my heart in my mouth, I made it safely back to Mount Argus and into my bed. To my relief, my superiors were none the wiser about my escapade.' As he rose early for prayer, Brian says he could barely concentrate on his religious meditation; his mind was racing with a rollercoaster of thrilling memories of The Beatles. It might have been a sinful act, but it was a great night out for the teenage priest in the making.

The moment he heard The Drifters' first hit, 'The Answer To Everything', being played on the radio in 1964, Brian says he loved Joe's voice and he instantly resolved to see the band performing live at the earliest opportunity. He just had to figure out how to escape from the monastery to catch this new entertainer from Mullingar at a Dublin show. 'A charity event shortly afterwards provided me with a golden chance to fulfil my dream as it was a Sunday afternoon performance,' Brian reveals.

The Drifters were one of the big bands, including The Miami, The Mighty Avons and The Pacific, playing that day at The *Herald* Boot Fund concert in the city. This annual show was sponsored by the *Evening Herald* newspaper, and it raised funds to provide boots and shoes for underprivileged children. 'It was a spine-tingling experience for me, in 1964, as I watched Joe and The Drifters in action during that afternoon,' he recalls. 'And I was determined in the aftermath of the performance to go backstage and try to meet the amazing lead singer of The Drifters.' Neither

Brian nor Joe realised then that this would be the beginning of a lifetime friendship between the pair.

Joe was intrigued by the shy, nervous young man in the clerical outfit who approached him. 'The first time I met Brian, I saw this mad, young cleric in his black garb and I didn't know what to make of him,' Joe laughed years later.

From that moment on, Brian would frequently slip away from the austere monastery at Mount Argus, to see Joe and The Drifters whenever they were playing in Dublin. As he had no money, the student priest was reduced to blagging his way free into the dances.

Apart from disappearing out through a window to see the bands, Brian often used the Legion Of Mary as his excuse for a trip into town. 'As well as going to UCD, you'd get permission for a visit into the city if you needed to get a book, or something like that, but you had to be back in for night prayers at half-nine. If I was going to a Legion of Mary meeting I'd say, "I mightn't be back in time for prayers," and that would be accepted. But you'd still have a curfew of 10pm at the latest. So I'd go out to take a Legion of Mary meeting, and then take in Joe on the way home. There was no way then that I was going to make it back to Mount Argus for 10pm, but I had a good chance of not being caught out upon my return because of the late hour; it was the later the better at that stage. I'd sneak in and then tip-toe up the back stairs, praying that no one was up and about. I never told Joe about this at the time because he would probably have mentioned it in some interview and got me into trouble.'

Brian also had a flair and a passion for writing, and later he began penning articles for the *Dancing Gazette*, an Irish entertainment magazine owned by Albert Reynolds and edited by a colourful character called Jimmy Molloy. At the time, Brian was not supposed to listen to radio or read newspapers, never mind report all the happenings on the Irish showbiz scene for a magazine. Eddie Masterson, a solicitor friend who had penned the song, 'A Tribute To Jim Reeves', which became a hit in the UK pop charts for Larry Cunningham and The Mighty Avons, came up with a soloution to Brian's problem. At the time, priests who were talented footballers were togging out with top teams, using someone else's name. Masterson suggesed that Brian might write under his father's name. Soon readers of *Dancing Gazette* were enjoying in-depth interviews with all their favourite Irish stars, written by a fella called 'Hughie'. Working with the magazine gave Brian easy access to all of the major entertainers of the era, and the young cleric soon became a familiar figure on the dancing scene.

The Belvedere Hotel on Dublin's Great Denmark Street was a popular meeting place for the bands, and Brian, who was studying scholastic philosophy at University College Dublin, would drop by on a late afternoon, to catch the big acts before they checked out and headed off around the country for their shows that night. He laughs and jokes at the humorous suggestion that he was a groupie of the showband stars at the time. 'Well, if I was, then I was a very ugly-looking groupie. I was never a danger to their chastity, shall we put it that way. I was the kind of groupie that would scare the real groupies away.'

With their friendship cemented over a few years, Joe was one of the cherished people Brian invited to his ordination in 1969, the year 'Make Me An Island' turned the Irish showband singer into an international pop star. It was with deep regret that Joe had to miss out on his friend's momentous occasion due to his own showbusiness commitments at the time. But with his insight into Joe's hectic world, Brian understood his friend's dilemma.

Enormous fame then came tumbling on to Joe's shoulders with his success in the British and European charts, but watching from the sideline Father Brian observed that it did not change Joe's personality and he never allowed it to put up a barrier between himself and ordinary folk.

'Joe never changed,' Brian reflects today. 'He was always the same guy. Even though I was a nobody – and I was a nobody – Joe would always have time for you. He'd sit and chat with you. And I grew very close to him after my ordination. He was never competitive in the sense that he had to be bigger than everybody else. Joe was convinced that he could be big, but that didn't mean that everyone else was small in his eyes.'

While Brian was a fan of all the major Irish bands of the era, it was Joe who really captivated him, particularly after one show where he watched the Mullingar maestro masterfully hold an audience in the palm of his hand while performing in cabaret at the Old Sheiling Hotel in Raheny. It was the moment Brian realised that he was in the presence of a true superstar.

'Joe was one of the first Irish singing stars to do cabaret – they were all doing dances at the time – and he was out of this world; he was fantastic that night,' Brian recalls. 'I knew then that Joe had something different. There was no question about that. And such was his popularity that he used to do a week at a time in the Old Sheiling.'

They were now on different journeys in life, but Joe and Father Brian maintained a close relationship through the decades. A common connection between the two men was their involvement in the entertainment world. Father Brian became chaplain to the Irish entertainers and, consequently, a popular and respected member of this colourful community of people. He did their marriages, baptisms and funerals and was with them through their good and bad days. In times of crises, Father Brian was a valued confidante, adviser and a rock of support.

Father Brian recalls one particular night he tapped on the door of Joe's dressing room backstage at the Old Sheiling Hotel.

'How'ya, Brian? God Almighty are Ben and myself glad to see you!' Joe declared.

'What's up?' Brian asked, noticing that Joe was slightly agitated.

'That fecker McDonnell is talking about leaving us, to go off and join the priesthood,' Joe said.

'And what's wrong with the priesthood?' Brian laughed at Joe's outburst.

'There's not a thing wrong with it,' Joe smiled, 'but McDonnell is a great musician and he'll do more good in our band than he will locked up in a parish somewhere.'

'Will you have a word with him, Brian?' Ben pleaded.

'Ah, sure, of course I will,' Brian agreed.

'Their keyboard player, Ciaran McDonnell from Strabane, had often spoken with me about the Church and how he would have loved to have been a priest,' Brian remembers. 'So Joe's news had not come as a major surprise to me.'

Father Brian took Ciaran aside for a quiet chat in a corner of the band's dressing room.

'Ciaran, the boys are not happy with you going,' he told the keyboard player.

'I know they're not, Father Brian,' Ciaran replied, 'but you know yourself, once you have the calling you have to go.'

'I know, indeed, Ciaran,' Brian agreed.

The priest and the band man chatted for some time, but Father Brian did not attempt to dissuade Ciaran from leaving Joe and Ben, to join the priesthood.

'Well?' Joe asked with great expectations, when Brian returned.

'Ah, Joe, the fella wants to go and you can't stop him,' Father Brian replied.

'Fair enough,' Joe said, 'but I'm glad you had the chat anyway, to make sure that he's taking the right decision.'

Father Brian remembers that Joe was totally supportive of Ciaran McDonnell when he realised the musician had discovered his true vocation. 'It was Joe who drove Ciaran to the seminary in one of his flash cars on the day he entered St Patrick's College in Thurles, County Tipperary. As the two men shook hands and said their goodbyes, Joe presented Ciaran with a beautiful guitar as a parting gift,' he reveals.

Father Ciaran McDonnell is still a committed priest to this day and is based in a parish in England.

When Father Brian became the parish priest at Mount Argus, Joe regularly dropped by for a visit and would chat about everything under the sun. Brian describes Joe as being 'a very intelligent man who was well read and up-to-date on politics, religion and current affairs. Joe could have a conversation with anybody about any of that. Maybe it was the auld bachelor thing, but he also understood me and I understood him. We'd have serious conversations where we'd talk about our doubts and about where we were going in life, but then we'd have a laugh and a joke as well. Joe, of course, had a bottomless well of jokes and sometimes you had to choose the company you could repeat them in.'

Father Brian was friendly with many of the big names of the sporting world and he introduced Joe to them. Barry McGuigan became a friend. Irish rugby ace Tony Ward often called in to see Brian in Mount Argus, and if Joe was around they'd give him a call to join them. 'It was just guys relaxing together and having a chat,' he says.

Daniel O'Donnell arrived unexpectedly one day, to find Father Brian in conversation with Joe and Tony Ward. 'At this stage, Joe did not know Daniel very well, but the pair were soon chatting like they were long lost friends,' Brian recalls. 'Joe told jokes and Tony was involved in the conversation. Then Daniel provided Joe with the biggest laugh of the afternoon. About an hour into their get together, Daniel turned to Tony and asked: "What do you do yourself?"'

Joe nearly had to be picked off the floor, he was laughing so much.

Poor Daniel was mortified when Father Brian filled him in. 'That's shockin', sure I should have recognised him,' Daniel said later.

Tony wasn't offended, as no offence was intended, and he laughed about the incident. Joe thought it was hilarious. From that first meeting, Joe recognised Daniel's sincerity and his sense of fun – even if he was unintentionally funny that afternoon – and the two singers would go on to become good friends.

'We were friends and I met Joe numerous times, but because of our busy careers I never got the opportunity to really get to know him, which I regret,' Daniel says today. 'But to even know Joe in passing and to see him on stage was a delight. One of his shows that stands out in my memory was at the Gaiety Theatre in Dublin. Seeing Joe in that amazing setting with his audience was quite incredible. Joe was born to be on a stage; you could see that from the way he was completely comfortable up there. And he loved it, judging by the way he performed.'

Father Brian had an open invitation to visit Joe at his home at any time. The popular priest was often among Joe's guests from every walk of life who joined him in his Foxrock home on Christmas Day. It was a small gathering of family and friends, and Father Brian recalls that, on many of those occasions in the 1980s, Joe welcomed young Traveller boys and girls into his exclusive home.

'I think they were from a campsite in nearby Shankhill and they would come begging,' Father Brian remembers. 'Joe would have them sitting in the best chairs in the house beside the fire in their smelly wellingtons. Then he'd be busy packing up food – pieces of leftover turkey and bits of this and that – and he'd say: "Go on, bring that home with you now." And he loved drawing them out. "Now, can you sing like Joe Dolan?" he'd ask. And they'd start singing, "It's you, it's you, it's you ..." They'd have bits of all the songs learned off: "Take me and break me and make me an island ..." And Joe would be in kinks of laughter listening to them.'

Joe had huge empathy with people in need, according to Father Brian. 'He was no saint and he could be volatile and he could fall out with anybody, at any time, but Joe was one of the most compassionate guys I have ever met. As he went along through life, he grew from being a volatile young fella to reaching a lovely level of maturity. He was a frequent Mass-goer in his middle age. He went to Foxrock and he came to Mount Argus quite regularly. He was very much a believer. Joe never had any hassle with the Church, even in its worst times. He would say, "Sure, you get bad eggs everywhere." Then there was his enormous generosity to people.'

Father Brian is aware that Joe would not want him to divulge all the details of his good deeds. So he tells just one story to illustrate his own experiences of this side of Joe. In the early days of his career, Joe heard a rumour doing the rounds that an individual in the entertainment business had fallen on hard times. Married with young children, it seemed likely that he was going to lose the family home amid mounting debts.

'Joe came to see me and asked, "Is this true?" And I confirmed to him that it probably was,' Father Brian recalls. 'Joe then handed me a thousand pounds in notes, which was probably a fifth of the price of a house at the time. He told me to pass it on to the individual, but under no circumstances was I to reveal to the person where the money had come from. Joe didn't want to embarrass the man. I took the money and I passed it on and it was the making of that person and that family. It got him back on his feet and it saved the family home. And that was all down to Joe and his kindness and generosity to others. There was rarely a time when I met Joe that he didn't slip me the equivalent of a hundred Euro to give to the poor. He'd always say the same thing, "I'd rather you keep it for yourself but I know you wouldn't. But you know who the poor are, give it to them." Joe had a social conscience.'

Joe had a deep, religious faith and as a singer he was devoted to St Blaise, a martyr who has had the curing of many throat illnesses attributed to him. Every year on 3 February, the feast day of St Blaise, Joe never failed to visit Father Brian, to have his throat blessed when he was based in Mount Argus. On that day, Father Brian would also bless oil, which Joe then carried with him through the year. And for twenty years after he had left Dublin, Father Brian would continue to bless Joe's throat on that day.

'Joe always asked me to bless his throat,' Father Brian reveals. 'He knew that when the "Hobson's Choice" (rhyming slang for "voice") wasn't right, he couldn't give his fans value for money. It was the only sickness which frightened him and he always asked me to pray that he'd never lose his ability to sing.'

While Father Brian started out as a fan of Joe the singer, it was Joe who would go on to become an admirer of the work of Brian the priest. In a 1998 interview, Joe told me: 'I'm a great fan of Father Brian D'Arcy, not just as a writer or a broadcaster or a priest, but as a person. I've always found him to be an absolutely brilliant gentleman. He's such a genuine bloke and I really do believe the man is a saint. No one knows half the things he does for people. It doesn't matter whether you're Joe Dolan or Joe Bloggs, Brian is someone you can depend on in your hour of need. On a personal level, Brian turns up at my house every St Blaise's Day with St Blaise's oil and a candle to bless my throat. I have the highest regard for him.'

CHAPTER 16

THE WHITE SUIT AND
THE TURKEY

The immaculate white suit was hanging majestically in Joe's dressing room at Dublin's Vicar Street venue, like a celebrated star in its own right. It was the iconic sartorial ensemble that had become synonymous with the entertainer. Like Johnny Cash's all-black attire, the white suit had been Joe's trademark over several decades.

In was the autumn of 2005 as I joined Joe backstage before he began the ceremony of transforming himself into 'The Man In White'. Downstairs the male and female audience of all ages, including several hen parties, were already in a jubilant mood as the excitement built up in anticipation of the night's entertainment that lay ahead. This was Joe's return to the stage, following his ten-month lay-off, after an operation to replace his hip.

Joe was apprehensive as he slipped out of his dark trousers and pulled on the white pants of the suit. There was uncharted territory ahead of him. After the hip replacement, the singer wasn't sure how he was going to react when he re-entered the spotlight for the most eagerly awaited comeback of any Irish entertainer. Would his innate sense of rhythm and timing be the same or would he now be more hesitant and restricted?

'I'd be telling a lie if I said that I'm not apprehensive, because I don't know until I get out there whether it's going to be the same as before,' Joe said as we chatted. 'I've been away for nearly a year. I've had a hip replaced. I'm bullin' to get back out there on the stage, but will it be the same? I don't know until I do it.'

His excitement was palpable, but Joe was also anxious: 'Yeah I'm nervous, but I'm always a bit nervous before I go on stage. But the nerves go after the first couple of numbers and hopefully it'll be the same tonight.'

He did up the buttons of his crisp, white shirt, then added with a laugh: 'I know one thing for certain, I won't be doing any Irish step dancing on stage tonight.'

Joe went to the dressing-room mirror and fixed an ear piece that performers use on stage so that they can hear themselves singing and stay in pitch. Then there was a knock on the door. It was his PA Denis Mee. 'Joe, it's stage-time,' he said.

Next, Joe slipped on his snow-white jacket, gave a little shake of his upper body and checked his image in the mirror again. His face was now glowing with excitement as he suddenly morphed into the live-wire character we know from the stage. The transformation was instant, like he had been suddenly plugged in to an electric charger. He was now a different Joe to the more subdued man who was earlier sitting quietly in a room playing cards with his brother, Ben.

'It's the white suit,' Joe said as he left the dressing room and carefully made his way down steep stairs towards the intimate auditorium, where the crowd was cheering wildly as the band cranked up and got ready to segue into the opening number, 'You're Such A Good Looking Woman'.

'Don't ask me why the suit has that effect,' Joe added as he disappeared into the spotlight. 'Jas Fagan knows. He's the guy who makes the suit.'

* * *

Joe's friend, Jas Fagan, was steeped in showbusiness. A tailor by trade, Jas had swapped his sewing machine for a trombone in the 1960s, to taste showband stardom as a member of The Cadets with Eileen Reid. With the release of their single, 'Fallen Star', Eileen became the only Irish female singer in that decade to have a Number-One hit. The Cadets were now in the major league, performing on TV with the Rolling Stones and touring Ireland with Johnny Cash and June Carter.

Apart from the music, Eileen and The Cadets earned instant recognition for their unusual dress sense, which included smart, colourful military-style jackets. Eileen also set a fashion trend with her distinctive blonde beehive hairstyle. When The Cadets scored a big hit in 1964 with their most famous song, 'I Gave My Wedding Dress Away', she would captivate audiences at live shows by performing the number while wearing a wedding dress.

After his exciting life and times in showbusiness with The Cadets, Jas returned to his original trade as a tailor. He was in demand, making stage outfits for the stars of the Irish music world, as well as First Communion, Confirmation and regular clothes for the general public at his modest shop on Thomas Street in the heart of Dublin.

Joe was among the famous faces who came through the door of his friend's premises in The Liberties, to be kitted out for the stage, causing huge excitement among the surprised customers who happened to be in the shop at the time.

'You should pick one colour that suits you and make it your trademark,' Jas told Joe in the early days.

'Jaysus, sure how would I know what colour to pick?' Joe said as he collected a blue suit with bell-bottoms.

Joe's style changed with the times, but he always wore suits on stage, as did the band. Ben had convinced Joe at the outset that this was the way to go. 'If you tell fellas to wear whatever they like. it could get out of hand,' Ben had argued.

'What do you mean?' Joe asked.

'Well, some fellas might be slick dressers and then you could get fellas who'll turn up in jeans with the arse out of them,' Ben explained.

'You're the boss,' Joe agreed.

There was one personal problem that ruined Joe's sartorial style on stage every night. Sweat would seep out of every pore of his body from early into the performance, and the damp patches spread all over his smart suit. Some might say that Joe was sweating out the alcohol from a session the previous night, but the singer insisted it was his body temperature.

'I'm hot-blooded,' Joe explained. 'Even when I'm driving I'll have the cold air on in the car. Ben is always complaining that it's like a fridge.'

Ben agreed. 'Singing is very hard work on the body, too, and Joe does twenty songs in the show,' he pointed out. 'And when you put a lot of people into a room with no air conditioning you'll find that everybody is sweating.'

One day Ben announced that he had a solution to the problem. 'I was thinking we could line the inside of the suit trousers with plastic and then the sweat won't show on the cloth, it'll run down your leg.'

Ben was serious. Joe laughed all day.

Jas Fagan was a fan of the white suit from the time Australian singer Frank Ifield, famous in the 1960s for hits like 'I Remember You', performed on stage with The Cadets.

'Frank Ifield really stood out in his white suit that night when he sang with us, as we were all wearing royal blue jackets and it was a fabulous contrast,' Jas told Joe. Jas was planting the seed, nudging Joe towards choosing an all-white outfit.

When Johnny Logan won the Eurovision Song Contest in 1980, singing the Shay Healy-penned song, 'What's Another Year?', he was wearing a white suit made by Jas Fagan.

It was the early eighties before Joe finally adopted the colour that would become his most enduring image. In the decades that followed, Jas made twenty white suits a year for Joe. It's an ill wind that doesn't blow someone some good: Joe had to regularly replace his suits because they were ruined by sweat stains. Jas also enjoyed a steady trade making Joe's famous stage ties with his signature stitched into them. Joe now had a ritual at every performance where he slipped off the tie and threw it into the audience. Some fans would spend years flocking to his show in the hope of going home with a much sought-after and highly-cherished Joe tie.

* * *

Dustin The Turkey wore one of Joe's ties when he represented Ireland in the 2008 Eurovision Song Contest, singing 'Irelande Douze Pointe' ('Ireland Twelve Points') in Belgrade while sitting in a souped-up shopping trolley.

Joe and his feathered friend, Dustin, went back a long way. Dustin's handler, Johnny Morrison, had a connection with Joe and Mullingar. Johnny's late father, Jackie, was one of the Morrisons who lived next door to the Dolans in their council cottage at Grange. It had been in Morrisons that Ben found Joe playing cards the night he got him his first gig with a local band.

In a strange twist of fate, Johnny's alter ego Dustin would go on to give Joe a career boost by introducing him to a new generation of fans in November 1997, when the pair went to Number One in the Irish charts with their Barnados charity duet single, 'Good Looking Woman'. They had also recorded 'Make Me An Island' as a track on Dustin's album.

The success of the Dustin single led to Joe sealing a new record deal with the high-powered EMI record label in Ireland and the recording of some incredible new albums like *Joe's 90s*, *21st Century Joe*, *Home Grown*, *Double O-Joe* and *Let There Be Love*.

'I have to deny all me culchie connections. In theory I've never heard of those people (the Morrisons),' Dustin says today. 'But Joe was the biggest culchie of them all. He was a big, dirty culchie. I mean, he was Richie Kavanagh with coleslaw on. That's just culchie modified. When we were shooting the "Good Looking Woman" video, all the culchies came up to Dublin with him. They insisted that it be done on 8 December because apparently they wanted to make a double day out of it and do Clearys and Arnotts and stuff like that. When Joe turned up with the band, I actually thought *One Flew Over The Cuckoo's Nest* was being made. And the bang of cabbage off them, I'm not jokin'! On me first album we did, "Make Me An Island", which is another song he didn't write. We recorded it out in Bally-brack and I actually was amazed that he could sing, in between telling all his bad jokes. But he was brilliant and I said to him that if I was ever doing a single again, because I had done one with Smelldof (Bob Geldof), "I wouldn't mind doing one with you, Joe, because you make me look good." So we did "Good Looking Woman".'

Dustin has happy memories of shooting the video for 'Good Looking Woman', which featured Irish model and TV presenter Amanda Byram. 'Oh, yeah, I remember that day well; I'm trying to blank Joe out of me mind because yer wan Amanda "Bimbo" Byram was in it, dancing around in a skimpy dress. Joe was too, but I'm not supposed to say that. Joe was whispering in her ear, "I've got a chalet down in Mullingar." And I had the Hi-Ace out the back with a mattress in it, ready for all sorts of things. It was a great fun day when the smell of cabbage disappeared into the air and we got down to shooting the video. We had no idea it would get to Number One. We actually knocked "Barbie Girl" off the top of the charts. Joe phoned me that day and said, "We got to Number One!" I said, "Joe, please don't phone me again."

'But it was good that we raised a lot of money for Barnados and stuff like that. Joe wanted his share, but I gave mine to charity; that's between us. He was a bit mean. That white suit was his Confirmation suit and it was lined with all the punts and Sterling from his showband days in Ireland and England; it was lined with fivers and tenners.'

Despite the slagging, Dustin misses his friend Joe today: 'Overall, I have to say, Joe was the Irish Elvis; he could sing and, besides the boring jokes, he was actually a bit of a mate. And Joe's fans were great to me; the good thing about his fans is that most of them are hard of hearing.'

* * *

At the EMI label, Joe now found himself working with a son of his old pal, Larry Gogan. Just like the Dustin connection with his childhood neighbours the Morrisons, life had come full circle again when he met EMI's marketing manager, David Gogan.

David and the company's MD Willie Kavanagh realised that with Joe's huge audience, great voice and passion there was the potential for him to produce more hit albums, particularly if they could match him with the right songs. 'We sold it to him on the basis that we didn't want it to be a karaoke album; it had to be songs that we felt Joe could make his own,' Willie reveals. Several CDs of suggested songs were sent to Joe via his manager, Seamus Casey. They included a song called 'The Universal' by British band Blur, which Seamus passed on to Joe.

The next day Seamus's mobile rang; it was Joe: 'How'ya Seamus, did you make a mistake and give me the wrong CD?'

'What do you mean?'

'I've listened to these songs and they're a heap of shit.'

'Joe, they're not.'

'Well, I don't like them.'

'You are in with the boys recording next week, so you'd better learn them,' Seamus insisted.

'Joe did not rehearse them, but when he was recording he would get a feel for a song after singing it three or four times.' Seamus reveals. As the recording went on, Joe began to love the songs, particularly 'The Universal'. It became the single backed by a moving video, featuring Joe as a puppet.

He also recorded songs by artists and bands like Pulp, Radiohead, Reef, Elvis Costello, Neil Young, Suede and Rainbow for his new album. Although Joe was not familiar with all the original performers, he loved the tracks and put his own stamp on them.

EMI's then media promotions' chief Darren Smith sat down with Joe to discuss the interviews that were lined up. They both agreed that Joe would not pretend that he was a fan of all the acts he had recorded. He was sure to be caught out as a fake if he suggested that he had been listening to bands like Suede since their early days. Joe agreed that his argument and line should be that a great song is a great song and it can be done by anybody whether it's a pop act or a rock act or Joe Dolan.

The first big interview was with Tom Dunne (now with Newstalk radio) for a TV music show. Tom introduced Joe as the 'King of the Showbands'. The he said: 'You're now doing these songs by bands like Oasis; how did that come about?'

Darren Smith remembers listening in the background as Joe talked eloquently about how great songs always stand out no matter who is singing them. Several times throughout the interview, Joe mentioned the great songs that Oasis have written and recorded.

When the camera stopped rolling, Darren said: 'That was brilliant, Joe.'

'Ah, Jaysus, thanks Darren,' Joe responded, delighted.

'There's only one problem, Joe,' Darren added.

'What's that?'

'You haven't ever recorded an Oasis song.'

Joe laughed. 'Oh, Jaysus.'

Then he turned to Tom Dunne. 'Right, ah sure we'll do it again. Turn on that camera.'

Dunne laughed, and Joe took off, this time singing the praises of Blur and their great songwriter, Damon Albarn.

Albarn's song, 'The Universal', was a big hit with the most listened to and influential radio DJs throughout the country. Suddenly Joe was back on daytime radio. He was trendy again and a big star to a new generation of fans. Gerry Ryan on RTÉ's 2fm radio loved Joe, went to his shows and arranged for the singer to do a private performance in the home of a fan. The lucky Joe fan who won the Gerry Ryan show competition was Angela Nolan from Pollerton in Carlow.

As she drove into Angela's housing estate in Pollerton on the morning of Joe's visit, Gerry Ryan's roving reporter Brenda Donohue (now with Derek Mooney's afternoon show on RTÉ Radio One) entered a carnival atmosphere as the entire neighbourhood turned out for the special event. 'Even more striking were the decorations on the trees, shrubs and lamp posts. The estate was festooned with a colourful array of knickers, bras and other items of lingerie,' Brenda laughs at the memory.

Inside, there was bedlam, with fans hanging out of the staircase and packed into the small hallway. Brenda squeezed through the bodies in the hall and eventually found Joe being mobbed in the kitchen, which was heaving with people.

'"Ah, Elizabeth Taylor, how are ya?" Joe said with a big laugh as he hugged me in the crowd,' Brenda recalls fondly. 'It was his pet name for me and I loved it.'

'Keep calling me Liz Taylor and I'll hang out with you all day,' Brenda told Joe.

When she glanced out the back window Brenda saw the fans vying for a vantage point on the garden walls, to catch sight of Joe. 'A couple of fields away, in the distance, employees of a local factory had climbed on to the roof of their workplace and were trying to view the action in the Nolan home through binoculars,' she recalls.

The entire country got the opportunity to enjoy the shenanigans that day when Joe's performance in the house was broadcast live to the nation on the Gerry Ryan radio show. RTÉ also despatched one of its top TV news reporters to Pollerton, to do a special report on the showbiz event for the 'Six-One News'. Joe thought this was hilarious; he fell around the place laughing when he watched the news that evening and saw a very serious broadcaster filing his report as a big pair of knickers flapped in the wind from a tree behind him.

Brenda, a native of Newbridge, County Kildare, had grown up listening to the music of Joe Dolan in her home as her parents were fans. 'I never imagined then that one day Joe would become a part of my own life,' she says. Joe would go on to take Brenda on a trip down memory lane around Mullingar as he regaled her with tales of his life and times when she visited his hometown for her radio series, 'Going Home'.

'You never knew where you were going to end up when you met Joe,' Brenda laughs today. 'I'd go down to Mullingar, to do a story, and the next thing I'd find myself at the Kilbeggan Races with him going, "How did that happen, Joe?" There was just something about him that you can't explain. He'd say, "C'mon", and you were off. If he was big on stage, he was as big off stage, personally, with people. I always felt welcomed wherever I went to meet him; whether it was in Mullingar, a gig or doing a story; you always felt that he was glad to see you. And, obviously, as a performer he was something else. He had an amazing ability to connect with a crowd on every level and to get them off their feet. That's why people feel a void with him gone, because he did emotionally connect with the audience. They always walked out of his show thinking they just had the best night. And I love the fact that everyone from nuns to hip young things loved him.'

*　*　*

Larry Gogan launched Joe's '90s album with a live broadcast of his 2fm radio show outside the Virgin Megastore on Dublin's Aston Quay in 1998. The two old pals were now in the fourth decade of their successful careers. As Larry interviewed him that day live on the show, Joe had no idea of the terrible trauma and heartache his dear friend was suffering at that moment. His darling wife, Florrie, had discovered a lump in her breast and was in hospital for a biopsy. Larry had been by her side in the hospital that morning before leaving her with their daughter, Gráinne, to do his lunchtime show and Joe album launch. He had not been expecting the results of the biopsy to come through so quickly when Gráinne phoned during the one o'clock news break. Then Larry's worst fears came to tear apart his perfect life. Florrie had been diagnosed with breast cancer.

As he went back on air to chat with Joe, Larry maintained his composure and kept his troubles buried deep inside. Joe would leave that day without a hint of the dark side of life that Larry was now experiencing. Ever the professional, the legendary radio DJ had turned on his sunny side for the radio.

Joe's fan Florrie would battle bravely for three more years. Larry tells how one day she turned to him in the hospital ward and beckoned to four other patients who had terminal cancer. '"They're all going,' Florrie said, pointing to the heavens. Then she added: "And I'll be next."'

Larry choked inside. 'Not at all,' he whispered.

His voice cracks with emotion as he remembers Florrie's reply, '"Well, I hope I don't have to spend my life with a bloody mask and oxygen," she said.'

In a cruel twist of fate, Larry himself took ill while Florrie was fighting the cancer and he had to undergo a life-saving heart by-pass operation. During his recovery, he made daily visits to his seriously ill wife in hospital. Florrie was worried about Larry, fearful that the stress and exhaustion would cause more damage to his health. One evening, after he'd been by her bed for some time, Florrie insisted that Larry should go home to rest. Larry finally relented.

'Okay, I'll see you tomorrow,' Larry told her. Then he gave his darling Florrie a goodbye kiss.

It was to be the final act of love between the husband and wife who'd been married for thirty-nine years. Florrie took a turn for the worse after Larry left and peacefully slipped away.

Joe was out of the country when he heard the sad news, and he immediately phoned Larry to offer his support. 'Joe was so kind,' Larry says today. 'He really did have a wonderful human touch and, of course, he loved Florrie. Joe was one of the most genuine stars I have ever met.'

* * *

Joe was shocked and heart-broken in 1998 when Ben's wife, Moira, died suddenly after suffering a brain haemorrhage at their holiday home in Dunmore East, County Waterford. The pair had worshipped each other. Her husband, Ben, was devastated. 'It was an awful shock because Moira was never sick,' Ben recalls. 'Moira was on her own at our holiday place in Dunmore when it happened. She got to know a lot of people down there and if the weather was good she'd stay on after a holiday. Moira would sometimes complain about a bad headache, but other than that there was no warning. It was a terrible time for all of us.

'It hit Joe hard too because they loved each other. Joe always bought his personal clothes in Galvin's menswear in Mullingar and he'd get Moira to shop with him. If he was going on holidays, he'd ring Moira and say, "I want to get a few things for the holidays," and he'd come down to Mullingar and the pair of them would go off shopping. She had also been such a big part of everyone's life through the band. I remember how one time Moira even drove the band's bus up to Dublin airport, to meet us off a flight. Moira was such a wonderful person and we remember the happy times we had when she was with us.'

*   *   *

The success of Joe's modern albums gave him an enormous thrill in his fourth and fifth decades in the business. 'When I look at all the new pop stuff and rock stuff and R&B stuff that's in the charts and, after all this time I'm still in the middle of it, it's absolutely fantastic,' he told me. 'It's a great thrill to be still played on the radio and to be on the TV; to be getting an hour-long Gerry Ryan show and to be performing on the new Ryan Tubridy TV show, as well as being played on all the local radio stations, that's been a massive lift.'

Joe admitted to me that in the seventies he didn't fully appreciate the golden opportunities he been presented with: 'I didn't take care of business in the early days. I was a bit boisterous then. I made a lot of mistakes. There were things that I shouldn't have done, like missing a plane to Spain to do a TV show because it would be there tomorrow. I neglected things and was a bit dizzy. I'd say I didn't have time to go to France or to Germany. That all happened and that was purely all my own fault. Now I take care of everything as I go along. I'm more aware of the responsibilities of it now. I'm excited that a big record company like EMI would be interested in me for starters. It has got me excited. When they asked me to come into the office, I was in before them.'

*   *   *

In his final promotion, Joe proved that he still possessed a healthy ability to laugh at himself when he jumped at the chance to strip off and hop into a hot tub for a highly entertaining Meteor phone company TV advert.

For Joe, the advert appealed to his sense of fun, but he was also conscious that the TV campaign for Meteor would connect him to a new generation of fans. 'When the concept for the advert was devised, we wanted somebody who was very well known, really popular and a bit of a legend in the music industry; and who better than Joe,' Amanda Carroll of Meteor says. 'We were really delighted and honoured when Joe Dolan agreed to do it. It was brilliant to get Joe. He was a much-loved Irish personality and everybody knows his songs. Everybody would identify with him straight away.'

The advert centred around a bridesmaid about to sing 'Good Looking Woman' at a wedding reception. She forgets the words and then phones Joe to ask: 'Is it Oh Me, Oh My? or Oh My, Oh Me?' Joe, who is in the bath tub, then breaks into a rendition of the song as a jazz band appears playing behind him.

Meteor staff and the crew who shot the advert enjoyed the experience of working with Joe. Amanda says: 'You never know what to expect with celebrities, but Joe was great fun and so easy-going to work with. Nothing was a problem, he was lovely. And it was a very successful ad campaign for us. People really liked the ad; they were talking about it and you can't ask for better than that. The concept was fun, the line, "Oh Me, Oh My", tied in quite well. And even though it was a Meteor advert, it was still a Joe show. Even in the ad, Joe had that cheeky smile that was just lovely.'

CHAPTER 17

FINBAR FUREY AND
THE FINAL SHOW

S inger and piper Finbar Furey did not know it then, but November 2007 was to be the last time he would see Joe alive. The life-long friends were out on the golf course in Castleknock when Joe was forced to throw in the towel on the seventh green. He just did not have the energy to go on. As on many other occasions, Finbar had been partnering his pal Joe in a round of golf with several showbusiness pals, including Dickie Rock, Syl Fox, George Hunter and Gary Power, whose son, Glen, is now an international star with Irish pop group The Script. When Joe indicated that he was unable to continue, Finbar made a mobile call for a buggy to come and pick up his dear friend. Then they all adjourned to the clubhouse where they sat with Joe, drinking tea, eating sandwiches, reminiscing and, of course, cracking jokes, until a nephew arrived by car to take him home. Finbar stood by a window, waving Joe off as he left the clubhouse that afternoon. He was deeply worried about his old friend.

Finbar recalls how Joe always kept in touch with him, even when he and his brother, Eddie, emigrated to Scotland in the sixties. Joe was delighted to hear that they were doing well there as entertainers. As the 1960s came to a close, they were drafted in to the Clancy Brothers, following the departure of Tommy Makem, and this led to them touring America.

By the late 1970s, they had become The Fureys & Davey Arthur; and in 1978 they were Number One in Ireland with 'The Green Fields Of France'. Joe was on the phone immediately to congratulate Finbar and the lads.

'There was no auld bullshit with Joe,' Finbar says today. 'He wasn't walking around afraid to take off his mask in case people found out what was underneath. Joe wore his heart on his sleeve and I loved him for that.'

Joe was on the phone again in 1981 when Finbar, along with his brothers and Davey Arthur, got a spot performing on 'Top of the Pops', after going to Number 14 in the British charts with 'When You Were Sweet Sixteen'.

Through the decades, Finbar played a major role in Joe's social life. 'What are we going to do, now, Furey?' Joe would ask after a round of golf.

'I don't know, what are we going to do?'

'Will we go on the tear for the day?' Joe would then suggest.

'You're an awful man; you're always bullying me into these things,' Finbar would say in mock protest.

Then, as they got set for a marathon session, Finbar would add: 'I'd better ring Sheila and tell her I won't be home for dinner till tomorrow night.'

Finbar recalls how their sessions would go on for twenty-four hours, with Joe always ending up singing. And he never heard anybody sing a better version of 'Danny Boy'. 'To hear Joe singing "Danny Boy", or the "Derry Air" as I like to call it, would make the hair stand up on the back of your neck.'

Finbar marvels at how easily Joe created entertainment in a room, even by producing a pack of cards. 'Joe would get a table going in a flash and the craic would be ninety. And he would be in his element if there was a snooker table on the premises.'

There was endless laughter on the golf course with Joe. Finbar recalls that he would set everybody up for a slagging, to spark off the fun among the gang. And Joe always played for money; big or small it didn't matter, but there had to be a bet.

Finbar partnered Joe in a four ball. 'How much do you want to play for?' Joe asked the other players on the day.

Then he turned to Finbar. 'How much do you want to play for?'

'Joe, I'm your partner!'

'I don't give a shite, how much do you want?'

Finbar laughs. 'He'd take on the field, that was Joe.'

* * *

Many's the time Finbar found himself in Johnny Fox's pub up in the Dublin mountains with Joe after a round of golf. Their pals like Red Hurley and Paddy Cole would call it a day after their golf outing, but Joe was always eager to keep the party going. 'Do you fancy Johnny Fox's?' he'd ask Finbar.

Another mutual friend, George Hunter, was a non-drinker, so he became the designated driver. Finbar recalls the scene. 'After a couple of hours in Johnny Fox's, we'd be going out of our minds with the music on the PA: Christy Moore singing "Only Our Rivers Run Free", or The Wolfe Tones's "We're On The One Road" or "Sweet Sixteen", The Fureys. We'd get the barman to switch it off, then we'd be there for the long haul, having a few drinks and breaking the day. And Joe was one of the funniest characters to be with.

* * *

Despite his reputation as a hard drinker, Joe appeared to be an iron man. As he entered his sixties, his voice had lost none of its power or pitch – even though he never did a vocal warm-up in his life before a performance – and he was still packing in the crowds and sending them home with the most fantastic memories.

Coming up to the new millennium, Joe met his showbiz friend Brendan Bowyer in Cork's Rochestown Park Hotel. As they chatted about old times, Brendan turned to Joe and said: 'It's just dawning on me that you've been performing now for thirty years and you're still amazing. You are totally indestructible.'

Joe was particularly taken with this description. 'Bowyer says I'm indestructible,' he told pals afterwards, with great delight.

Although Joe knew that he could not hold back the sands of time, he never contemplated retirement. 'The future is always better than the past,' was his motto.

'I'd be happy to live out the rest of my days in showbusiness,' he said. 'I know too many people who retired and who went down hill and were only half the person they used to be. I have spent all of my life on the road and I don't think I could live without it.'

However, Joe would gradually discover the he was not indestructible. The first sign of his mortality was his hip replacement operation in 2005, which put him off the road for ten months. It was the first time in forty years that he had been absent from the stage for such a long period.

'When I was off the road, there were times when I was pining to be back on stage, and it's great to know that the hunger is still there,' Joe told me as he made his comeback at Vicar Street,

Back in his dressing room after that night's performance in one of his all-time favourite venues, Joe was in a jubilant mood. It had been just like old times. Just seconds after he had launched into 'You're Such A Good Looking Woman', his ecstatic female fans were showering him with knickers and thongs. If he had had any doubt about losing his sex appeal and animal magnetism during his enforced absence, Joe got an instant answer with the arrival of the sexy lingerie that Thursday night in February, 2006.

It was obvious from the highly excited women who thronged Vicar Street – one even dressed in Joe's trademark white suit – that they had been starved of their favourite entertainer. They were up for a night of unbridled fun and frolics and Joe did not disappoint. The singer, who had an incredible thirty-three chart hits in Ireland, gave the fans value for money, including all the old favourites like 'Make Me An Island', 'Sweet Little Rock 'n' Roller', 'The Westmeath Bachelor' and 'The Answer To Everything'.

Drenched with sweat in his dressing room afterwards, he was like an excited teenager himself. 'I wish I could bottle what I got off that crowd out there,' he told me.

As for the effects of his hip replacement, Joe said it had given him a new lease of life: 'I can play golf again, I'm back on stage and I feel great. I didn't know anything about hip replacements until last year, but now it seems, from talking to people, that half the country has had it done.'

That night Joe insisted that he was now going to cut back on his stage work, another indication that he was beginning to acknowledge his diminishing physical capabilities. 'I'm not going to burn myself out from now on,' he added.

*   *   *

Joe was never one to seek sympathy when he was feeling unwell. 'When we were working, he might be in agony on the stage, but he'd never complain,' Ben says. Through the decades, Ben had tried to warn Joe about burning the candle at both ends and running the risk of damaging his health. But Joe would cut him short.

'You're not looking great today, Joe,' Ben remarked one time.

'Are you some sort of a doctor?' came the curt response. Ben learned not to meddle.

Joe always had his sunny side out, even if he was hurting inside. He had no time for whingeing and moaning. He had a positive approach to life. He might have a pain or an illness today, but, so what, it would pass. He did not burden people with his complaints and he did not welcome their prying. But a complex series of health issues began to take their toll on Joe in the aftermath of his hip operation. He had been diagnosed with Type-2 Diabetes. Ben believes that his brother failed to manage this problem. Then it was discovered that he had a low blood platelet count, which required regular blood transfusions.

Joe's nephew, Ray, has a vivid memory of how pale his uncle was before a show in his last couple of years. To expressions of concern, Joe simply replied that he was booked in for a transfusion the following day. 'Wait till you see me when I get the blood!' he laughed.

'He was like Dracula,' Ray says. 'He'd always be in great form after a transfusion.'

Ben describes his brother's rapid decline over 2006 and 2007 as like a car crash: 'Joe was healthy and then suddenly he hit a wall and it was one thing after another.'

His summer tour in 2007, including what would be a final performance at his old haunt, the Greville Arms Hotel in Mullingar, was a real struggle for Joe as he battled desperately to cope with his failing health.

Finally, on 27 September at the Abbeyleix Manor Hotel, the moment Joe never dared to contemplate arrived to bring the curtain down on his show for what would be the last time. As he prepared for the stage, Joe confided in his loyal PA Denis Mee that he simply did not have the energy for the performance that night.

'Then why are you killing yourself? You just weren't ready to go back,' Denis said. 'If you don't feel like doing it, don't do it.'

But Joe insisted he would go on. As was the norm, Denis walked Joe to the stage and helped him up the steps amid the blinding lights. As Denis watched from the wings, he could see Joe struggling through the opening songs. Then Joe's fears became a terrifying reality when he nearly collapsed while performing the fourth song, 'Ciara'. In desperation, he looked over at Denis and gestured that he was pulling the plug; then he turned around to Adrian. His nephew will never forget the look of heartbreak and bewilderment in Joe's face as he indicated to him that he could not go on. Joe then apologised to the crowd as he explained that he was unwell. He got a standing ovation from the supportive crowd as he left the concert room. Backstage, Joe was devastated.

'He burst out crying into my face,' Denis reveals. 'He said, 'Feck it, Denis, I let everybody down.' I told him, 'Don't be actin' the bollox; you let nobody down.' Then I ordered tea for him and after a while he left for home.'

Joe insisted on driving himself back to his Foxrock home in his new Merc that night. He was admitted to Dublin's Mater Hospital the following day, Friday, for tests. Whether he was in denial or just did not know the seriousness of his condition, Joe was up-beat and positive when I phoned him at the hospital on the Saturday morning, to get an update for a *Sunday World* news story.

'I went on to do the show on Thursday night and I just got as weak as a kitten,' Joe told me. 'I did four songs, but I was overcome with the heat and I realised I couldn't go on. I had to tell the audience that I wasn't feeling well, that if the mic stand wasn't there to support me I'd be out on top of them. I told them that to continue wouldn't be fair on them, and it wouldn't be fair on me. I'd never do a show unless I could give it a hundred per cent, but in this case I wasn't able to do it anyway. The crowd were just unbelievably understanding and they gave me a standing ovation. To be honest, the warmth of their reaction made me feel even more lousy that I couldn't do the show for them. I owe them one and I'll do it for them in the future.'

Joe then painted a positive picture about his health. 'They've done tests and there's no sign of anything major,' he told me. 'I feel fantastic now, thank God. Obviously I'm still in here, but while I feel fine to leave, I have to wait until someone tells me I'm free to go. I expect to be out in a day or two. I think the problem was probably down to the fact that I've been over-working, to be honest with you. Even when I was on a break from perform-ing, I wasn't resting. I've just recorded a brand new album (*Let There Be Love*) and I did that in two weeks. It'll be out at the end of October. After that, I went straight back into touring, so really I've been burning the candle at both ends.'

Joe then had to cancel several shows, including a sold-out concert at Dublin's Vicar Street the following night, Sunday. 'I'll have a couple of days to judge my fitness when I get out of hospital, but I expect to be back on stage next weekend,' he added.

*   *   *

Just a few days before his concert in Abbeyleix, Joe had phoned me about doing a feature in the *Sunday World* on the family's latest business enter-prise in Mullingar. Ben's second wife, Helen, had opened, Joli's, a state-of-the-art hair and beauty salon in the town, and Joe was really proud of this new venture.

Stylish Helen had worked for the Dolan brothers since the seventies as a secretary and book-keeper in the office, and the warm, good-natured woman had become a family friend through the decades.

Ben, who was living alone in the years after Moira's passing, invited Helen to accompany him to a function one night. 'We went to a few things then and the relationship developed from there,' Ben reveals. 'Later, I couldn't have been happier when Helen accepted my proposal to settle down together. My family was delighted, as was Joe. My children had grown up with Helen and she used to babysit them when they were young.' When the couple married in September 2000, Joe was Ben's best man for the second time. It was Helen's first marriage. 'The day we got married Joe had champagne at the church. It was a great day,' Ben recalls. 'Helen kills me with kindness,' he adds.

Helen would go on to launch Joli's, which added to the Dolan's business portfolio that included the pub, Mullingar House; a nightclub, Mojo's, and recording studios. Joe agreed to pose for exclusive photographs in Joli's for the *Sunday World*. We had arranged to meet in Mullingar on the Tuesday after his collapse. Joe was discharged from the Mater on the Monday and, true to form, he drove himself to Mullingar that Tuesday to do the promotion for Helen.

Remarkably, although pale and with obvious weight loss, Joe was in great form that day. On the way down, he had stopped off at Joe Bracken's pub in Kinnegad to have soup and a sandwich with his niece, Sandra, who was working in the local bank. He was a real family man.

As he posed for photographer Liam O'Connor in the chic Joli salon, Joe was game for a laugh while pretending to give one of the female staff a full-body massage for a fun shot. Joe also posed with his brother, Ben, and Helen. 'I have a home in Dublin, but I've never really left Mullingar,' he told me. 'I have my own apartment over the bar, as well as a recording studio, but I'm down here for days at a time.'

Later in the evening, Joe drove the short distance from Joli's to the Greville Arms Hotel for a light evening meal. He sat on the inside of the table wearing a baseball cap, telling jokes and greeting locals who said hello on their way past. Afterwards, I was admiring his new Merc in the hotel car park and he offered me a drive back to my own motor parked up at Mullingar House. Along the way, we passed Ben sauntering up the street on foot. We chatted for a while in the car for the *Sunday World* article I would later write.

'Is that a recorder?' Joe asked when I produced a tiny digital audio recorder.

Joe remarked on its miniature size; then we laughed about our changing world, where big is no longer impressive and how now we brag about our gadgets being tiny in size.

As we shook hands and said goodbye that evening, I did not realise that this was to be my final time meeting Joe in the flesh, or that he had just done his last ever media interview.

CHAPTER 18

THE KING IS DEAD

Popular radio personality and former singer, Maxi, now one of our national treasures, was relaxing in her comfortable Dublin home on the afternoon of St Stephen's Day in 2007 when she was jolted out of her reverie by the sound of her phone ringing. It was distraught friends calling in tears from America. They had just heard on the grapevine that Joe was dead, they blurted out, heartbroken.

The presenter of RTÉ Radio 1's early morning show, 'Risin' Time', was dubious about this turn of events. This was news to her; she immediately cast doubt on the accuracy of the information her friends were passing on. 'It's probably just another "Paul McCartney is dead" rumour,' she responded, referring to the false reports of the legendary Beatle's demise that regularly do the rounds.

Maxi's friends insisted that they had heard the devastating news from a reliable source. As difficult as it was to believe, Joe had just passed away.

Still doubting the accuracy of the rumour, Maxi suggested she would check with the RTÉ news staff and call them back. 'I really did not believe what I had been told. It was impossible to imagine a world without Joe. My mind went into turmoil when an RTÉ colleague confirmed the dreadful news that my favourite Irish singer and long-time friend had indeed passed away,' Maxi recalls today. As she put down the phone, Maxi was now slipping into a state of devastation. Then the tears came.

Maxi, who eases early risers into a new dawn with her soft vocals on the radio, and lights up the lives of the truckers and taxi drivers who have been working through the night, had personal experience of Joe's kindness and generosity during a low time in her showbiz career.

As one-third of Maxi, Dick and Twink, the singer had enjoyed a great career touring the UK, America and Canada, before the trio split up in 1971. Afterwards, Maxi worked with Danny Doyle and Music Box. Then she went solo and represented Ireland in the 1973 Eurovision Song Contest with 'Do I Dream'.

Joe came to her rescue when Maxi then hit a low point in her career as a solo artist. 'I was used to being managed and being handed my gigs, but when you were solo you had to hustle for stuff yourself and I soon realised that it was leaving me in a precarious position. Suddenly the phone was silent and there was no work coming in. I told Joe that I found it very isolating. You could talk to Joe. He knew the dips of the business and he knew the marketing end of things.'

Joe was about to do a TV show from the National Stadium and he immediately offered Maxi the role of backing singer in his band. 'It's a television show, you'll be in view and it'll let people know that you're still here and interested in working, otherwise they forget,' he said.

Maxi never forgot Joe's thoughtfulness and support in her time of need. 'Joe was a gentleman in that respect, because there were quite a few entertainers who were exactly the opposite and who would block you from moving up the next step of the ladder. He was unselfish and that's what I loved about him. He was very confident about his own appeal and his own talent. But he also understood that we are all only as good as the team we have around us.'

Joe gave Maxi the lift she needed to keep her singing career on track. She would go on to enjoy showbiz success with another girl-group, Sheeba, who represented Ireland in the 1981 Eurovision Song Contest singing 'Horoscopes'. Sheeba also worked with an Italian songwriter and producer called Roberta Danova, the man behind some of Joe's biggest hits, including 'Sweet Little Rock 'n' Roller', 'Lady In Blue', 'Crazy Woman', 'Sister Mary' and his live show finale, 'Goodbye Venice, Goodbye'.

And Joe also became one of Sheeba's biggest supporters. It was always a special night for Maxi when he would turn up at their shows to see them perform. 'We would go to Joe's gigs all through the years and he came to our gigs and that was a huge compliment because the buzz went around, "Oh, Joe Dolan is in the audience!" You knew by the wave of the crowd that there was something happening and you'd look down and you'd see Joe and his big grin. At the end he'd be shouting , "Encore!" and "More! More!" That was a massive endorsement for us, because people thought, "Well, if Joe Dolan likes them that much then they must be good." Then he'd meet us afterwards and we'd spend the night swapping stories and having a laugh. Joe loved every inch of the business.'

* * *

In Joe's mind, he was always going to make a return to the stage after that night in Abbeyleix, in September 2007. Even as his health went into an accelerated breakdown, Joe was positive about the future. He had ordered a new white suit from his friend and tailor Jas Fagan for the Christmas shows that he had rescheduled. 'I'll be okay, Jas,' Joe said. 'I'll be in to collect the suit from you next week.'

The week came and went and the iconic white suit was left hanging in a back room of Jas's shop on Dublin's Thomas Street.

Father Brian D'Arcy, one of his closest confidants, was in regular contact with Joe all through his illness, visiting him both at his home and in the hospital. One particular personal call was at Joe's special request. 'Joe was looking for a blessing in the hope that it would do something to help him get through his illness,' Father Brian revealed.

Even at that stage, Joe was still maintaining his optimism that he could get back on his feet. Joe never, ever said to Father Brian that he knew he had a fatal illness. The only indication the priest had of what was going on in Joe's head, amid his desperate battle for survival, came a week before Christmas when he asked Father Brian to anoint him. 'I did anoint him, but even then Joe didn't say to me that he was dying or that he feared he was dying.'

At this point, Father Brian himself suspected that his old friend was now knocking on death's door. He could see that Joe was very weak. 'I had come to the conclusion then that Joe wouldn't survive. Later that week, I was surprised to find that Joe had got out of hospital for Christmas. But I never, ever thought that death was going to come so quickly for him.'

In mid-December as he was preparing to close his Foxrock shop, Thomas Murphy's phone rang. It was Joe. He was on his way back from the country and was calling to see if Thomas was in. Joe wanted to call to the shop.

Thomas remembers Joe asking, 'Will you be there for a while?'

'Yeah, sure I'll wait for you,' Thomas assured him.

Later, Thomas would learn that Joe had spent the day visiting his family, including his brother Paddy, and friends spread over Westmeath. A nephew drove his car because Joe was too debilitated to get behind the wheel. One of his close pals, Mullingar garage owner Lorcan Daly, recalls Joe's Mercedes pulling in to his petrol station. Lorcan was busy doing a car wash at the time. Joe tipped his cap to him, then his car drove off.

When he reached Thomas's shop that night, Joe broke with tradition by refusing a glass of wine. 'Do you mind if I have a coffee and you have a glass of wine?' he asked.

Thomas made him a coffee and poured a glass of wine. Joe was exhausted and didn't stay long. Before leaving, he picked up Thomas's glass. 'Cheers!' Joe said before taking a sip of the wine and handing back the glass.

Thomas visited Joe at his Foxrock home on the following Sunday morning as he prepared to go back into hospital. When it was time to go, Thomas helped him to his car, as Joe was now barely able to walk.

On the way out, Joe caught his reflection in a mirror and declared: 'Jaysus, Joe, you look shite.'

Thomas remembers he tried to lighten the mood by adding: 'Joe, you've looked like that for the last forty years.'

Joe rewarded him with a last laugh. The singer's sense of humour was still intact. A car then took him to hospital.

Although he was very ill, Joe pleaded with medical staff to be allowed out for Christmas. His wish was granted and Joe came home to Foxrock again the day before Christmas Eve. By now he could only stand with the support cf a Zimmer frame, but when his brother Ben phoned him Joe painted a rosy picture. 'You know, I'm feeling great today,' Joe said chirpily.

'That's great,' Ben said, surprised at how good Joe sounded on the phone.

'Ah, you know, maybe in a month's time I'll be back to normal,' Joe insisted.

As he recalls their conversation today, Ben says: 'That was only four days before he died. In Joe's mind he was still in showbusiness. He wasn't saying it's all over. He never said that to me.'

The family members who spoke on the phone with Joe that Christmas Day were alarmed by his mood. Joe had always been like Father Christmas, big and jolly on that day throughout his entire life. It had been his favourite day of the year and nothing could ever dampen his spirits for the special occasion. This time, however, Joe couldn't hide his pain. Ben, his beloved niece, Kathleen, or 'Goggeen' as he called her; and his dear friend and lifetime manager, Seamus Casey, all sensed from their brief conversation with him that Joe really was troubled.

His friend, Thomas Murphy, also had a short phone conversation with him at around 4pm on Christmas Day. As they talked, Joe said he'd have to go. 'I'm knackered,' he said. They were the last words Murphy would ever hear his old pal utter.

Joe had been due to return to hospital on St Stephen's Day for more treatment. As his condition deteriorated through the afternoon, Joe contacted his doctor and it was arranged for him to go in that night. While he waited for an ambulance to arrive, he phoned Ben. 'I'm going into hospital in about ten minutes, Ben,' Joe said.

Ben was surprised. 'I thought you weren't going in till tomorrow,' he replied.

'I don't feel great,' Joe admitted. 'Whatever they are going to do for me tomorrow they can get it started.'

'Is there anything you want to tell me, Joe?' Ben then asked his brother.

'What do you mean, anything?' Joe replied in a tone which indicated that this particular conversation was not going to go any further.

Ben dropped the subject. He knew his brother too well to press him on an issue that was not up for discussion. If Joe knew the gravity of his situation at that moment, he was not ready to acknowledge it. As their conversation ended, Ben said he would be seeing him.

One of Joe's lifetime friends, Isabella Fogarty, was in the house and accompanied him in the ambulance that evening. She clutched Joe's hand as the ambulance raced across the city. Along the journey, Isabella felt Joe squeeze her hand and in that moment it is believed he had a brain haemorrhage.

Joe was immediately put on a life-support machine at the hospital and his family was contacted with the devastating news. A scan on St Stephen's morning confirmed that Joe had suffered a brain haemorrhage and was now being kept alive by the machine. In a decision no family every wants to face, Joe's loved ones now gave their consent for the machine to be switched off. Joe's immediate family, including his brothers, Paddy, Ben and Vincent; his sisters, Imelda and Dympna, and a number of close friends were then invited by the medical staff to say their goodbyes to the man who had been a light and source of great fun and support in their lives.

Then the machine was switched off and, with his loving sisters, Imelda and Dympna, each gently holding one of his hands on either side of the bed and his eldest brother Paddy chatting to him, telling him to 'Go on now, Joe,' the singer slowly and very peacefully slipped away.

Everyone in the room felt that Joe was now gone, but then a strange incident happened. Joe lifted each arm lying by his side and crossed them on his chest. It's a pose that his family and friends were familiar with. Joe would fall asleep on a couch in front of the telly with his arms crossed on his chest. It was then that he was in his most relaxed and most comfortable state.

Shortly after 3pm on St Stephen's Day, 2007, Joe Dolan, Ireland's first international pop star, the nation's much-loved entertainer and a man idolised by his family and friends, was officially pronounced dead.

CHAPTER 19

RATHGAR TO MULLINGAR

Shock, disbelief, bewilderment and unbearable loss were the myriad of emotions that Joe's devoted fans at home and abroad experienced on that black St Stephen's Day in 2007 as the news filtered through that their favourite singer and lovely friend was gone.

* * *

Broadcaster and journalist Sam Smyth was in South Africa at Christmas, 2007, with his partner, Angela Ryan when he received a text from his daughter, Faela, that Joe had died. 'Faela had met Joe with me and she knew we were friends. I was extremely proud to be a friend of Joe Dolan,' Sam says. 'I knew he had been ill, but I didn't know how ill he was and I just could not believe that he had died. I was devastated.'

His partner, Angela, was deeply upset too as she had got to know the singer when she made the 1999 RTÉ TV documentary, 'The Mullingar Mojo', which joined Joe and the band on the road. The programme featured behind-the-scenes footage and interviews with Joe, his crew and the fans, as well as a live performance, and it was screened by RTÉ on the night of his removal.

Today Sam Smyth reflects on Joe's passing and says of his old pal: 'I have nothing but the fondest memories of Joe Dolan. I never had an awkward moment with him, nor an ugly moment and nothing but good times. And now, looking back with the benefit of a bit of space, I can see that as hard as it is for his family and those who loved him, and while he was taken from us too soon, at least he didn't suffer the awful indignities that sometimes follow a serious illness. More than most of us, Joe's whole life was his work and he was still on top of his career when he died.

'Joe will be missed but he will be there forever for us like President Kennedy, both frozen in time looking well; and certainly that's how I will remember Joe. And I think in this country, of his generation there was nobody who was more fondly regarded or highly regarded than Joe Dolan. He was a magnificent artist.'

*   *   *

Mags Keating had been enjoying a pleasant afternoon at home with her family in Mitchelstown, County Cork, when her mobile rang. It was her sister-in-law, Brigid Cummins, barely able to speak on the other end. As she struggled to compose herself, Brigid finally broke the news to her. She had just heard on the radio that 'our Joe is dead.'

Vivacious mother-of-three Mags, in her early thirties, began to tremble. 'Surely there was some mistake?' she questioned. Maybe the radio had got it wrong. Mags and Brigid both knew that Joe had been unwell, forcing the cancellation of several of his shows. But just the previous night the sisters-in-law and best friends were talking about how they had expected him to return to the stage in February, 2008. They were looking forward to a great night out in his company once again.

Finally, Mags was forced to accept the terrible reality that Brigid's phone call had changed her life forever. As she glanced around her room in floods of tears, Joe was everywhere to be seen in the photographs, album sleeves and huge collection of memorabilia that formed her personal shrine to the man in the white suit. And proudly displayed among her Joe collection was one of his white suits, which Brigid had given her as a present, having purchased it at a charity auction in 2004. The singer then wore the jacket on stage at a concert in the Silver Springs Hotel in Cork, and there was wild cheering from the crowd that night as Joe removed the item of clothing before passing it over to Mags. Everyone had grown accustomed to Joe giving his tie away, but getting a jacket took his affection for a fan to another level in the eyes of the audience that night. Mags was beaming with pride.

The suit is now a treasured part of Joe that she holds dear to her heart; but displayed in a glass case was an even more personal souvenir of the singer. Mags is also the proud owner of surely one of the most unusual keepsakes that any fan has ever acquired ... Joe's hip bone.

She had forked out 69Œuro for the ultimate Joe souvenir, after he had kindly allowed his body part to be auctioned on eBay as a fundraiser for Boyzone and 'Coronation Street' star Keith Duffy's autism charity. The bone is autographed by Joe and popular Irish TV puppets, Podge and Rodge, on whose RTÉ TV show the auction was launched by the man himself.

With the passing of time and the abating of her grief, Mags now looks back at the great days and nights she and Brigid and their families shared with Joe and the rest of his fans. Joe was more than a singer who entertained them of a night; he became part of their lifestyle and they regarded him as a friend. It was a unique connection that Joe made with tens of thousands of fans through the decades. Joe was a superstar who never erected a barrier or placed a velvet rope between himself and the people who followed him.

Mags, who was just thirty-two when Joe passed away, had been reared to a soundtrack of his music. Her mother went to Joe's dances when she was a young woman; and she constantly played his records in the house when she got married and began to raise a family. Mags recalls her mum dancing around to 'Make Me An Island' over and over as she busily polished the house with Brasso. It was inevitable that Mags herself would become a fan of this music from her childhood.

As fate would have it, Mags met and fell in love with a Joe Dolan fan – her husband, Mike. His sister, Brigid Cummins, was also a devoted follower of the 'Westmeath Bachelor'.

'We used to go to the Gleneagle in Killarney for weekends away to see Joe and it was a great time in our lives,' Mags recalls.

Her relationship with Joe became more personal after she met him by chance in the car park of the Firgrove Hotel in Mitchelstown, where he was due to perform that night in 1995.

'I went out to my car to get something just before the show,' Mags recalls. 'On my way I ran into him in the car park and he was wearing his white suit. I got the chance to have a quiet chat with Joe, during which I told him about my aunt in London who ran a pub and a B&B. Joe used to play in the pub and he stayed in the B&B. My aunt had sent me photos of her and Joe together. Joe remembered her. It was just a brief conversation because he was due to go on stage.'

Back at the show, Mags then had the most thrilling night of her life, as any fan would when singled out in the crowd by their favourite entertainer. 'Joe sang down to me all night long from the stage. From then on, I went to see him in concert at least once a month. There was one year when Brigid and myself went to over forty shows. I was lucky that my husband, Mike, understood my addiction to Joe.'

At various stages through the years, Mags and Brigid were joined by dozens of other Joe fans as they pursued the electric entertainer from show to show, hiring coaches, mini-buses and, on a number of occasions, limousines. One day they travelled six-and-a-half hours from Mitchelstown to Bundoran to see Joe in concert.

There were other tests that Mags had to face, to prove to herself that she was completely devoted to Joe Dolan. One of those personal challenges happened on the day that her brother got married. The family wedding celebrations that evening clashed with a local Joe show, posing a major dilemma for the sister of the groom. In those circumstances Mags had to make one of the most difficult choices of her life – she left the wedding celebrations and went off to see her Joe. 'I was the black sheep of the family that day,' she laughs.

Just as Mags had grown up to the sound of Joe's records being played in the family home, the Mullingar singer would go on to become the soundtrack to the lives of the next generation – her own young children. Mags constantly played his music in the home and in the car. The doting mum then brought her eldest children to see Joe live in concert as soon as they left the cradle.

'Joe would always make a fuss of my daughter, Chloe, who is now a teenager,' Mags says. 'He'd take her up on stage and put his tie around her. When my son, Danny, was four I got him a white suit and shoes just like Joe. Then I entered him as a mini-Joe in a local tiny tots competition … and he won. Later, I took him to one of Joe's shows in the suit. Joe brought him up on stage and made a fuss of him. He was just absolutely wonderful with children and they adored him.'

Over the years, Mags amassed an eclectic collection of Joe Dolan memorabilia, including rare records that were only released abroad. 'Joe was amazed at some of the stuff I had,' she reveals. 'I had records that he had never seen, but he signed everything that I have. They are all so precious to me now. Like the rest of his fans, Joe brought so much joy and fun into my life and the lives of my nearest and dearest. He will never be forgotten in this family. But life goes on and I'm sure Joe wouldn't want us to be crying over him. So we'll remember the good times and all the laughs he gave us, and we'll keep on smiling and listening to that wonderful voice that he has left behind. Every time I put on one of Joe's songs, it brings me back to some of the best times of my life.'

*   *   *

In life, Joe always had a full house at his shows. It was no different in death. Ten thousand family, friends, neighbours, celebrities and fans from at home and abroad flocked to his native Mullingar on Saturday, 29 December 2007, for the biggest send off Ireland had ever accorded one of its illustrious entertainers. Joe would have been proud and humbled that so many had interrupted their Christmas festivities to be present for his final moment in the spotlight.

In a eulogy to his dear friend, Fr Brian D'Arcy told the hundreds of mourners who were packed into the magnificent cathedral of Christ the King, where Joe had attended Mass and received the sacraments as both boy and man, that the singer and himself often had a conversation about death. 'Joe used to say to me, "If you go first I'll sing at your funeral and if I go first, give them a laugh."' Then Fr Brian broke down as he told the congregation how he never thought he would see the day when he would have to say a final farewell to his pal Joe.

When Joe was around there was always laughter and applause and, fittingly, the cathedral did resound to both that day as Fr Brian spoke of the fun they shared and the jokes 'of doubtful taste' that they exchanged. 'I'd tell Joe jokes that I could tell nobody else, if you get my drift; and he'd tell me jokes and I'd give him absolution,' he said to a burst of laughter.

Joe always said there was no such thing as a dirty joke, only people with dirty minds, he laughed. Father Brian also spoke of Joe's devoted fans and what they meant to him. 'For Joe, the most loyal group he had were his fans for forty-five years. Joe loved his fans and knew them personally.'

In a parting tribute, Fr Brian added: 'Joe was a true superstar who was at home in his own skin. He was able to be happy with the rich and the poor. It didn't matter to him – all he saw were human beings like himself.'

There wasn't a dry eye to be seen in the cathedral that afternoon as Joe's remains were carried shoulder high down the aisle by family members to the sound of 'Goodbye Venice, Goodbye', the song that had brought the curtain down on all of his shows. It was performed by his band member Frankie McDonald on trumpet, and sung by his niece, Ben's daughter, Sandra.

There was a final round of applause for the man in the white suit as he left the stage for the last time. Then Joe's remains were driven in a black hearse on his final tour through the thronged streets of Mullingar, the town he loved so well; and on to the cold, country graveyard at Walshestown where he was buried close to his beloved parents, Ellen and Paddy, his brother, Michael, and other relatives and friends.

In the aftermath of Joe's funeral, his brother Ben found humour amid his deep grief when he related how one local came up to him and inno-cently declared: 'That was a fantastic funeral Joe had. It's just shocking that he had to die for it.'

Joe would have loved the comment. It fitted his own sense of humour to perfection; he would have been texting it to family and friends and re-telling it on the golf course and in the bar.

* * *

Standing outside the windswept graveyard on a visit to Joe's resting place, tall and lean Paddy Cole's thoughts wandered back to the great nights and fun days he had shared with his old pal.

On the first night he met Joe, Paddy was in the more successful outfit. The Capitol were then battling for the title of Number-One band with The Royal as The Drifters were just taking off. Later, when Brendan Bowyer and Tom Dunphy left The Royal, they persuaded Paddy to join their new group, The Big Eight, as their sax player and band leader. Brendan Bowyer and The Big Eight also featured female singing sensation Twink, and they split their schedule between a residency in Las Vegas and Irish tours.

Next, Paddy had his own band, The Paddy Cole Superstars. In the late 1970s and early eighties, Paddy's band often backed Joe around London when he was doing promotional appearances for new releases. 'Joe would come over to England, to promote some records without his band, and he'd want to play the Irish ballrooms, like The Gresham on Holloway Road or The Galtymore in Cricklewood,' Paddy recalls. 'A lot of bands were reluctant to have him on with them because they were afraid that he would steal their thunder. And he had arrangements written for the brass parts, which scared off a lot of the boys. But I did it with him. It would be only two or three songs.'

Paddy would announce: 'Ladies and gentlemen, as a special treat tonight we have one of Ireland's best known singers to sing a few songs for you. Would you put your hands together for Mr Joe Dolan.' And the place would go wild.

As he now reflects on Joe's guest appearances, Paddy says: 'It was hard work for him doing that kind of promotion, but that's how dedicated he was to keeping the show on the road whenever his career had taken a dip.'

Later in life, it was golf trips that drew the two entertainers together. They played in America, Spain and around Ireland with other entertainers, including Finbar Furey and Red Hurley. It was golf by day and entertainment by night during which they'd all do their party piece. 'It was unbelievable craic,' Paddy says.

In all their time together, Paddy only experienced one sour moment with his friend, Joe. It happened early one morning in the RTÉ TV studios, shortly after they had both arrived to rehearse for Joe's appearance on an afternoon show where he was to perform 'Good Looking Woman' with

Paddy's band backing him.

As Paddy tells it, Joe was very hungover when he turned up for the rehearsal that morning.

'Are you in bad shape?' Paddy asked.

'No, I'm alright,' Joe said brusquely, obviously in no mood to talk.

As Paddy began directing the band, Joe turned and put his hand up. 'Hold it,' he snapped. 'I'll give the feckin' tempo, okay! Don't be puttin' your own tempo on to me.'

Paddy nodded. 'That's okay, Joe, I prefer that because if it's wrong, then it's you that is wrong,' he responded.

Joe shot Paddy a look, but said nothing.

Later, after the rehearsal, he turned to Paddy. 'Are you okay?' he asked, clearly remorseful about his earlier outburst.

'Everything is grand, Joe,' Paddy smiled.

'Great,' Joe said, 'Now, when are we going to have that round of golf?'

They always had a tenner on their game of golf. 'It was never paid out or never collected,' Paddy reveals. 'And when we'd meet, Joe would ask, 'Who owns that tenner now?' Every time I met Joe it was big laughs and smiles and hugs. He was a disarming sort of a character who you loved to meet. And the wives all loved Joe; they all gravitated towards him. My wife, Helen, cried like a child the day he died.'

Today, Paddy hosts a top-rated Sunday morning radio show on the independent station, Dublin's Country Mix (106.8fm). 'Joe is still the most popular guy I play on the show. Every time I put on a Joe Dolan track the phones start hopping. And, as I sit there listening to him singing, I still find it hard to convince myself that Joe is gone.'

* * *

Brian Cowen has never forgotten his first encounter with Joe Dolan. It was early one morning in a leafy suburb on the southside of Dublin as the then gangly, young bespectacled student cycled furiously on his way to his law lectures at University College Dublin. On Zion road in Rathgar, young Brian noticed a distressed forty-something lady trying to start her car which had broken down in the middle of the road. He pulled on the brakes, stopped and got off his bike to help.

'Do you know anything about cars?' the flustered woman asked.

'Not a lot, but I'll give you a push and maybe that'll do the trick,' Brian suggested helpfully.

'As I started to push the little Fiat, a flash Saab car came from the opposite direction, suddenly slowed down and then stopped,' Brian recalls. 'The driver emerged from the Saab and as I turned to ask for his help, I did a double take. It was Joe Dolan in a white suit.'

'How'ya! Do you need a hand?' Joe asked.

'Eh … yeah … a shove might start this,' Brian said.

'Right,' said Joe, 'on a count of three …'

A minute later the student and the international singing star watched from the footpath as the Fiat and its female driver disappear off into the morning sunshine.

'Now, there's our good deed for the day,' Joe laughed.

Brian agreed. 'Where are you from?' Joe then asked, recognising the midland accent.

'Clara in Offaly,' Brian replied.

'Sure I know it well,' Joe said.

'What's your name?'

'Brian Cowen.'

'Great to meet you, Brian, and sure maybe we'll bump into each other another time.'

As he watched Joe's Saab roar off down the street, Brian Cowen shook his head in wonderment at what had happened. He had just met Joe Dolan for the first time. Joe Dolan was one of his favourite entertainers. Brian himself was noted for doing a great version of 'Make Me An Island.'

In the journey of life, Brian would go on to marry his wife, Mary, and become a father to daughters, Maedhbh and Sinead. 'As our children grew up, summer holidays were spent in Killarney with our extended family, where Joe was their entertainment at the Gleneagle Hotel,' Brian reveals. 'It was a great place to bring a whole family of different generations and we could all enjoy a memorable night out. There are few entertainers who have that sort of appeal. Whilst there are many people who can sing, there are very few who can entertain as well as he could. I often went to see him play in Tullamore and I met Joe on a number of occasions through the years. He was just a great man.'

*   *   *

In December, 2008, a year after his passing, Joe Dolan returned to his hometown of Mullingar. In a dramatic dawn scene watched by startled locals on their way to work one freezing cold Friday morning, the singer, wrapped in a protective coat, descended from the sky by crane from the back of a truck to take up a permanent position in the centre of the town.

Joe's nephews Adrian and Ray were standing in the small square as their uncle's statue was lowered on to its high-profile position. 'We're here this morning to keep an eye on Joe as he arrives back in town,' Ray told me. 'For years, Uncle Joe looked after us; now we're looking after him. Mind you, years ago when he'd be out partying we always made sure that he got home safely on those nights too.'

On the following Sunday afternoon, Brian Cowen, the law student and Joe fan who had gone on to become Taoiseach of Ireland, was then given the ultimate honour of unveiling the statue as 5,000 fans of the singer gathered for the historic occasion.

And it was Joe's music that once again whipped up a party atmosphere among the crowd as the singer performed his hits on a giant screen while his brother, Ben, nephews Adrian and Ray, niece Sandra and band members John McCafferty, Sean Kenny and Frankie McDonald played live on a big open-air stage.

Joe, who knew his value as an entertainer but carried it with humility, would have been proud of the honour that has been bestowed on him by the people of Westmeath and their local county council, whose chairman Joe Whelan told fans: 'Joe Dolan now holds a permanent place in his home town.

'Locals and visitors alike can now share a nod and a smile with Mullingar's most famous citizen as they pass him on the street.'

Joe would have been tickled pink to see his old pal Dustin the Turkey hovering around. 'The statue has more life than Joe had in him,' Dustin squawked. 'No, it's actually good and the funeral was a testament to the man with how many people turned up. I was there meself, I had to be … I wanted to make sure he was dead because he owed me money.'

*　*　*

It was two years after Joe's death that British pop superstar Robbie Williams heard the news when I met him in London. 'Of course I know Joe: he died two years ago? Oh Christ! I wasn't aware of that,' Robbie replied, visibly shocked, when I mentioned his passing.

Joe had been a presence in Robbie's young life when he was growing up. 'Robbie's mum, Jan, ran a guesthouse in Stoke-On-Trent and we always stayed there when we toured England,' Joe had told me years ago. 'Rob was just a little kid at the time. One night we called unexpectedly to the guesthouse and it was full. But because we were regulars, Jan insisted that we stay, so she got young Robbie up and out of his room and I got his bed. If I'd known he was going to become that famous I wouldn't have kicked him out of his bed that night. But that's showbusiness, you never know who is going to come along and do it. I went to see him in concert at

Lansdowne Road because I wanted to have a look at his live performance and there's no doubt that he has the magic. He had the audience in the palm of his hand from the off.'

Joe had a close connection with Robbie's father, Peter, who was a cabaret singer. Peter, who performed under the name of Peter Conway, often supported Joe on his UK tours.

'Joe stayed with me dad quite often and that pair were very good drinking buddies,' Robbie told me. 'I'm really shocked to hear that he has died. He's gone too soon, God bless him. Love to his family.'

CHAPTER 20

NO SHOW LIKE A JOE SHOW

Watching hundreds of fans filing into the TF Royal Theatre in Castlebar for *Joe Dolan: The Reunion Show* in February 2010, Pat Jennings, the owner of what was formerly the Royal Ballroom, remembers Joe as a role model in his young life and a close friend throughout his adult years: 'Joe was a big part of my childhood. I grew up around him and because I didn't have a father in my formative years, Joe was like a father figure to me. I got a lot of good advice from him about the business because you can't go to a school to learn what we do; there's no text book, it's the hard knocks of life.'

Pat's memories returned to his days as a skinny young schoolboy in short pants, standing patiently outside the Royal Ballroom in Castlebar, waiting for Joe Dolan with a bundle of comics tucked under his arm. It was 1968, and bored twelve-year-old Pat was watching for The Drifters' bandwagon to roll up to his family's ballroom, which was one of the biggest in the west of Ireland. He was waiting with growing excitement for some fresh reading which Joe Dolan was sure to provide. Young Pat and the then twenty-nine-year-old Joe always swapped their comics when the famous singer came to town.

Joe still acquired his comics from all kinds of sources, including Pat, whose mother, Mary B Jennings, was then running the Royal Ballroom, following the death of her husband, Pat Snr. As The Drifters arrived, Joe would hop out of the wagon with a big smile on his face, holding a dozen comics in his hand, including *The Dandy*, featuring Desperate Dan and Korky the Cat; and *The Beezer*. Then he would examine Pat's collection, stopping to flick through the latest edition of *Look and Learn*, which was one of his favourites. '*Look and Learn* was particularly interesting, as apart from comic strips it also had lots of articles covering everything from volcanoes to the Lough Ness monster,' Pat says.

Young Jennings would then race excitedly inside his home where he was soon engrossed in the fresh batch of stories and illustrations that came in the new collection from Joe. Growing up around a ballroom, Pat was also fascinated by the showbands who played in the venue and he yearned to be a part of the entertainment they created on stage. Mary B didn't allow her schoolboy son into the dances because he was too young, but Pat wasn't going to be deprived of such fun. 'Behind my mother's back I'd often sneak out of the house to do the lights for a band,' he says.

As Joe and The Drifters played on stage, Pat controlled the very basic lighting system. 'This involved switching on and off a few coloured bulbs from a series of normal domestic switches at the side of the stage,' he recalls. Joe would glance down and laugh at the sight of the excited kid flicking red, green, blue and white lights in the middle of his song, 'The House With The Whitewashed Gable', as the packed crowd danced around the floor. Eventually the switches would get too hot to handle because they hadn't been designed for this use; then Pat sat and watched the band playing while they cooled down. 'Afterwards, The Drifters often played indoor football in the ballroom against members of The Royal's security crew before everyone, apart from myself, retired to the bar till dawn the following day,' Pat reveals.

Pat's family booked out a dozen venues in the west of Ireland at the height of the showband years. At one point in their heyday, they were running four Saturday-night dances: the Starlight, Westport, Pontoon (the location for the BBC TV film, *The Ballroom of Romance*), The Beaten Path in Claremorris and Starland, Ballyhaunis. It brought young Pat into regular contact with Joe and helped him to maintain his friendship with the singer through the decades. In the 1980s, Pat often went on foreign golfing holidays with Joe and Ben, and several of their friends, including Jas Fagan, Damien Ryan, Paul Claffey, Paddy Cole and Ronan Collins.

'Joe remained the biggest attraction at the TF Royal Theatre right up to the end,' he says today. Pat had even booked his friend to play a Christmas party show at the Castlebar venue in December, 2007. Sadly, it was not to be. The next time patrons of the TF and other venues around the country would get the opportunity to enjoy the magic of a Joe show, the singer would be casting his spell over them as he performed in concert on a giant screen.

Joe Dolan: The Reunion Show, which has been created and produced by his nephew, Adrian, is now a critically-acclaimed tribute to the man in the white suit. It has been given the seal of approval by everyone, including Joe's old pal Pat Jennings. 'Adrian has treated his uncle Joe's memory with the respect the man deserved,' Pat says. 'It is a wonderful tribute by his family to Joe's life and times, but what makes it extra special is that it also has the man himself performing a full concert and all his big hits are there. The fans still have Joe and he will be there till kingdom come.'

The Reunion Show was first launched at the Gleneagle Hotel in Killarney on 11 July 2008, by Joe's long-time promoter and friend, James Cafferty.

James first met Joe in 1981 when one evening the singer, along with a party of friends that included Ben and Seamus Casey, walked through the door of his country pub, The Inn Place, which he was then running in

Charlestown, County Mayo. 'They were on a golfing weekend in the area and I was thrilled to meet Joe because I was a fan and had been to all the local dances where he played,' Cafferty recalls. 'I had the pub up for sale and I told Joe and the boys that I was hoping to get involved in the entertainment business in Dublin. They told me to give them a shout if I ever did.'

When James moved to Dublin, he hooked up with band manager and promoter Jim Hand and then realised his dream when the pair booked Joe for concerts at The Belgard in Tallaght. 'In those days Joe was concentrating on dances only,' Cafferty says. 'We put a small ad in the *Evening Herald* and the two shows were sold out in days. The third time he played The Belgard we had to put on nine shows in a row; and by 1983 we moved it to the Green Isle Hotel because it had a bigger ballroom.' In 1987, Cafferty chartered the first of the trains taking fans on the 'Showtime Express' from Dublin to Cork, where 2,500 people turned up, to see Joe perform at Neptune Stadium on Valentine's Weekend. He repeated the success in Galway.

The dapper businessman later staged Joe concerts in the Isle of Man; and in 1996 he launched a weekend music festival in Bundoran, County Donegal, starring the Mullingar superstar.

In 1996 after a show at the Mount Errigal Hotel in Letterkenny, County Donegal, Joe partied with James and their crew until 3am and then retired to bed.

At that moment a hulk of a man dressed in black stormed into the bar and pointed to the empty spot where Joe had been sitting.

'The man that was sitting on that seat is a Unionist and ye are all a shower of f***ing Unionists!' he roared.

Next, the irate man launched an unprovoked attacked on Cafferty. 'He proceeded to hit me and I fell to the ground,' James recalls. 'Then he did a Kung Fu on me and broke my ankle.' The melee sent empty glasses flying through the air as Jimmy Mullally, the keyboard player in the band, tackled the enraged assailant and the pair rolled around on the ground. Mullally eventually managed to restrain the attacker until the gardaí came. An ambulance was also called and arrived to take Cafferty to hospital. 'I didn't get much sympathy from the band and crew as I vividly remember their laughter when I was being wheeled out on a trolley. Needless to say, Joe laughed too when he heard about the drama,' James smiles at the memory. 'It later transpired that this gentleman's wife had been expressing her admiration and love for Joe and the husband flew into a jealous rage. He was subsequently charged and convicted.' The court hearing that day turned into a circus with ripples of laughter as Joe's drummer, Tony Newman, who was a witness but was then very deaf, kept giving wrong answers to questions posed by the legal people.'

James will never forget another incident in which he accidentally fell off a bar stool and banged his head, suffering concussion, while drinking with Joe and their gang after a Bundoran concert.

'We were based in a small hotel on the outskirts of Bundoran and, at the end of the festival, we stayed up drinking until the early hours,' James recalls. 'At some point, the owner of the hotel brought his dog inside the bar, to show him off to us, and I lost my balance as I stood up to have a look. Suddenly, the legs of the stool went from under me and I shot forward hitting my head off the bar.'

James passed out from the impact, but Joe and the lads assumed he'd had too much drink and left him 'sleeping', after they failed to rouse him by splashing cold water on his head.

Joe eventually went to bed and when the rest of the crew were retiring they tried to revive James again. It was now 8am.

'At this point, apparently, there was panic when someone announced that I was actually dead,' James reveals.

One of the lads then raced up to Joe, burst into the room and woke the singer with the shocking revelation:

'Joe, James is dead!'

'Oh, good Lord!'

Joe sobered up in an instant and rushed down to the bar in his underpants. At that point he was inconsolable as he stood over the 'corpse' of his dear friend.

Within minutes, Joe suffered a second shock when James opened his eyes and began mumbling.

'I woke up to find Joe standing over me crying,' James recalls today. 'I didn't know what was going on.'

Joe was now as white as a ghost and shaking with the fright. 'Jaysus, I need a brandy,' he said.

At noon that day, hotel residents passing through were bemused to see Cafferty and the famous singer sitting at the bar sipping brandy … with Joe still in his underpants.

Fun-loving Cafferty remained one of Joe's close friends and biggest fans right up to the end. Even after he became the singer's promoter, James would always sit in the audience, watching Joe perform. 'I looked forward to every one of his gigs and was in the audience enjoying them always. In my twenty-six years' association with Joe, I only missed one of his shows due to illness. Since Joe died, the buzz has gone out of the Irish entertainment business,' James says today.

* * *

The Reunion Show opens like a movie of Joe's life with recorded scenes of the legendary singer slipping behind the wheel of his Merc, easing it into gear and cruising along country roads on his way to a concert. He arrives at his destination and prepares for the show as he dons his famous white suit in a dressing room. Next, Joe is filmed strutting along a backstage corridor on his journey into the spotlight.

As the live band, which includes his brother, Ben, and nephews, Adrian and Ray, strikes up the intro to 'You're Such A Good Looking Woman' on the stage, the 'Man in White' suddenly bursts on to the big screen ... and we're transported back to the good old days when there was no show like a Joe show.

But, as the event unfolds, it becomes apparent that this is more than just a concert performance when it splits into segments and takes the audience on a truly memorable journey through Joe's life. Through a combination of still photography and video footage, fans are introduced to Joe's early years growing up in Mullingar while Ben narrates the story on stage as the live band provides the soundtrack. Here, through Ben's personal memories, we get a flavour of Joe as a kid. As the story continues we see Joe becoming a young adult and enjoying leisure pursuits like fishing, boating on the local lakes and duck shooting. The show follows Joe's steps to superstardom at home and abroad, with the video vaults being raided to produce some fantastic live performances of the singer through the decades. Presented as a celebration of Joe's life, the superbly crafted and tastefully executed tribute doesn't touch on Joe's death or funeral; instead, it leaves us with happy memories of a great entertainer.

Fans will still shed a tear, though, when they see it for the first time. Somehow Joe's big, warm personality comes to life in the room, and the audience soon forgets that this is a recording. The show begins to feel like every other great night the entertainer created when he was with us in concert venues. By the end, the audience are on their feet and women rush to the stage with flowers for the star. The spot where Joe stood is empty and they realise it has been an illusion; but for a couple of hours they believed that they had Joe back in their lives.

Joe's friend, Father Brian D'Arcy, was among the first of the singer's fans and friends to experience *The Reunion Show* in Killarney. 'I didn't think the show could be as good as it was. My instant reaction was that it made Joe so real, that it was lovely to be in his presence again,' Father Brian said. 'It was as close as humanly possible to experiencing a real Joe show. And when we saw Joe singing up close on the big screen, bringing us closer to him than ever before, I suddenly realised what a magnificent talent he was. And then I thought how few times I told him that when he was alive, and I felt sad about that.'

Ben gave RTÉ radio and TV personality Ronan Collins, one of Joe's personal friends and golfing buddies through the decades, the honour of MC-ing the tribute show to his brother. Ronan had idolised Joe in life and was known to carry off a very credible impersonation of the Mullingar singer.

Out on the golf courses, at home and abroad, in their happy times together, Joe and Ronan had shared many a laugh over yarns about the characters they both knew in showbusiness. When they first got to know each other, Ronan, who was reared in Dublin's Phibsboro, told Joe how he had grown up as a fan of the Irish showbands: 'From the time I was a kid, I had a fascination with the showbands. I went to school in St Vincent's, in Glasnevin and every day I passed a shop called Hurley's Sound Hire. That was the only place that did sound equipment and every band in the country seemed to be there. There were painted band wagons and fellas arriving in big cars, Triumph 2000s and Ford Consuls and Zephyrs. I saw all the groups and I was a bit in awe of them; I got talking to them and I got autographs and I was aware that they were having hit records.'

One of the big stars that Ronan recognised around the area was Dickie Rock of the Miami Showband. 'I never thought I'd one day end up becoming his drummer,' Ronan laughed as he chatted with Joe.

'Why did you choose the drums?' Joe asked.

'My uncle emigrated to Canada and left a drum kit behind,' Ronan explained. 'I started messing around with the kit and eventually I got the hang of it. Later, I played in several beat groups, including The Others. Then I got the offer to drum with Dickie's band. It was something I wanted to get out of my system.'

'Did you enjoy being a road hog?' Joe laughed.

'All the glamour I saw in it as a kid soon went out the window when I started on the road with Dickie, that's for sure,' Ronan admitted. 'As you well know, there's no glamour travelling for hours up and down the country in a van, even though I was in a top band and getting well paid. But I loved being on stage when we eventually got there.'

Joe agreed. 'Travelling is the only thing that kills me,' Joe said. 'But when I get there the journey is all forgotten and then when I go on stage, man, all hell breaks loose and it's "Let's go!" It's a great high when people start to react. They lift you up and you want to stay there forever. Every night I go on stage is a buzz for me.'

As they socialised together, Joe was curious as to why Ronan had remained tee-total all of his life. 'I just didn't like the taste of drink,' Ronan explained.

Joe laughed.

'Seriously, it's as simple as that,' Ronan added. 'There's no other psychological or philosophical reason for it.'

'At least you drive decent cars,' Joe joked.

'Yep, I have a weakness for cars,' Ronan acknowledged.

'I know another fella like that,' Joe laughed.

Today, Ronan Collins remembers Joe as a man who achieved greatness as a singer and entertainer in life, but never allowed his incredible success to distance him from ordinary folk. 'An awful lot of people, including myself, never fully grasped how big Joe was and that's really because he never flaunted it. He had no airs or graces despite his celebrity. Joe was just one of the guys and he liked it that way.'

* * *

Joe's manager, Seamus Casey, and PA Denis Mee, cried their eyes out as they sat and watched the rehearsals for *The Reunion Show* in the afternoon of its first night at the Gleneagle. Seeing Joe performing on the big screen brought back a million memories of great times with the man. There were laughs too as Seamus pointed out some of Joe's little stage mannerisms, like the way he gave his nose a tip with the mic to knock the drops of sweat off it.

Another of Joe's pals, comedian Syl Fox, gave everyone a belly laugh when he opened the show. One gag was at the expense of their old friend, Dickie Rock.

'Dickie Rock still has his Confirmation money,' Syl told the audience. 'In fact, Dickie is so mean, he only breathes in!' The crowd loved it.

Seamus Casey and Denis Mee got another laugh when they saw some of Joe's female fans producing their knickers during the performance. Joe would have loved it.

'The knickers job is fantastic,' Joe had told me. 'A lot of people that come to our shows actually buy knickers for the occasion. We see them taking them out of the boxes at the front of the stage. They are brand new — although we do get one or two soggy ones' he joked. 'There's also the occasional joker who'll throw up a pair of underpants; fellas don't like to be left out.'

And where did all those knickers that were showered on him end up when the show was over? For once, Joe didn't have an answer. 'You know, I've never thought about that one, and I haven't a clue. I don't take them with me anyway,' he laughed. 'I'll have to find out where they go. Maybe my road crew wears them. I'll have to check.'

He never did get back to me on that one.

Joe lives on through his music. He is the only Irish entertainer to have enjoyed Top 10 hits in five decades across two centuries. And EMI records have gathered together all his best recordings and big hits, to produce the ultimate package of Joe's music for his fans on a unique set of three CDs and one DVD called *Joe Dolan: The Platinum Collection*. It includes his remarkable performance of the classic carol, 'O Holy Night'.

Joe's nephew, Adrian, was forever luring his uncle down to their studios in Mullingar, to work on new recordings. 'Adrian is my producer; he has written hits for me, including "Ciara" (bizarrely the last song that Joe would sing live on stage); and he has kept my mind fresh and kept me fresh on new songs through the years. When he comes up with new ideas I'll try them,' Joe told me.

In the summer of 2007, Joe recorded several songs under the direction of Adrian. Neither of them were to know that it would be their last time working together in the studio. Among the tracks that Adrian had selected for Joe was 'O Holy Night'. 'It wasn't significant at the time,' Adrian says today. 'I had just chosen it because I thought Joe's voice really suited the song and it had never been recorded by him.'

Joe asked: 'Where are we going to use this?'

'I don't know. We'll put it aside and it might fit on an album down the line,' Adrian said.

Joe died four months later.

In 2008, a few months after Joe's passing, there was a strange occurrence when Adrian went back into the recording studio to begin work on an anthology of Joe's recordings for the EMI album. 'I went in, flicked a switch and suddenly the sound of Joe's voice filled the studio. He was sing-ing "O Holy Night",' Adrian recalls. 'It was as if Joe was actually singing it from beyond the grave.'

'O Holy Night' would go on to become the jewel in the crown of the EMI album after Adrian lovingly finished the track with backing vocals from Joe's niece, Maeve Dolan-Corroon, and the Mullingar Cathedral Choir. Adrian firmly believes that Joe guided him on this haunting track. 'Joe was on my shoulder. I felt his presence in the studio,' he says.

'O Holy Night' is now Joe's Christmas classic. 'Joe would have been delighted with that,' Adrian says. 'Joe was Christmas. He was always particularly happy then. It's amazing that it's the time of the year he was taken from us – and now Christmas will always be his anniversary.'

In the aftermath of his passing, Ben Dolan and all of Joe's clan have taken a leaf out of his book by moving on with their lives. 'Joe wouldn't want you to wallow in self-pity,' Ben reflects. 'When he went to a funeral he was the life and soul of the party. As they say, life goes on without me.'

His nephew Adrian agrees: 'Joe was the type of guy who would always look at the positive. He'd say if there was a setback, "Keep goin'", and he'd remain positive. Even when he was feeling down, Joe would put on a positive front.

'Joe never looked back. He didn't want to know about the past because, as he said, "The past is done and you can't change it." He lived in the present and looked to the future. I think that's why he related so much to young people because young people don't want to know about the past; they want to know what's ahead of them.

'That's the way Joe was in his mind; he always looked ahead and he was always a teenager at heart. Joe engaged with life and, while physically his body ran out of petrol, spiritually he's still going strong.'

Joe's niece and goddaughter Kathleen, or 'Goggeen' as he'd call her when he'd have a few drinks taken, admits she's still struggling to cope with the loss of the uncle she adored. 'People say the longer it goes, the easier it gets, but the first year you thought he was just gone away and you were expecting him to come back. And it's not any easier,' she reveals.

* * *

In Joe's favourite Mullingar hotel, the Greville Arms, general manager John Cochrane today greets the late, great singer's fans from every corner of Ireland and many from overseas.

There are two questions John and his staff are regularly asked: 'Where is

Dolan's pub?' and 'How do you get to Joe Dolan's grave?'

John was a Joe fan. 'Joe was a great ambassador for his home town,' he says. 'He was so fondly loved because he was accessible to everybody and he had a word for everyone.'

Ryanair's Michael O'Leary agrees. 'Joe was a brilliant ambassador for Mullingar, for Ireland, for Irish music and for the showband era, although I think it's unfair to characterise him as part of the showbands,' he says.

'I was too young to remember the showbands, but Joe was doing his thing in the eighties, the nineties and the start of this decade as well. He was like the Tom Jones of this world. He was one of these people who had enough talent to be able to transcend any kind of category that people tried to put him into. He was always reinventing himself, doing cover versions of the more up-to-date music and he did it brilliantly as well.

'He was able to take the piss out of himself with Dustin the Turkey and stuff like that. I don't think he ever took himself that seriously.

'But his shows were legendary and properly so. He was just brilliant, a great showman.

'These days pop stars are packaged to the nth degree and don't have a brain or a personality between them. I think the fact that Joe survived for so long is because he actually had a personality and he also had a life outside of showbusiness; a lot of it centred around playing golf.

'When I last met Joe a few years ago he was very complimentary about my own career, but the way Joe was, if I had been the petrol-pump attendant it would still have been, "Congratulations on your success." He was a really nice, genuine guy. I don't know anybody who had a bad word to say about him.

'Joe died at a relatively young age. They say that only the good die young. In Joe's case that was true.'

*   *   *

In his twilight years, Joe told me that he had no intention of ever retiring from the stage. It was his heaven on earth. 'I'd be happy to live out the rest of my days in showbiz,' Joe reflected. 'I don't believe in retiring. I know too many who did and, afterwards, they were only half the person they used to be. I have spent all my life on the road and I don't think I could live without it. But the one thing I never want to hear is someone leaving my gig saying, "He's not as good as he was." I don't want to hear that. I never want to hear that.'

And he never did.